COMPETITIVE RIDING

COMPETITIVE RIDING

Jane Holderness-Roddam

a Salamander book

Published by Salamander Books Limited
LONDON • NEW YORK

Author and Contributors

A Salamander Book

Published by Salamander Books Ltd
52 Bedford Row
London WC1R 4LR
England

© Salamander Books Ltd 1988

ISBN 0 86101 358 1

Distributed by Hodder and Stoughton Services,
PO Box 6, Mill Road, Dunton Green,
Sevenoaks, Kent TN13 2XX

All correspondence concerning the
content of this volume
should be addressed to Salamander Books Ltd.

Credits

Editor:
Jo Finnis

Designer:
Nigel Duffield

Diagrams:
Glenn Steward, John Martin and Artists Limited

Typesetting:
Poole Typesetting (Wessex) Limited

Color Reproduction:
Contemporary Lithoplates Limited

Printed in Italy

AUTHOR: **Jane Holderness-Roddam**

Jane won Badminton in 1968 and was the first British girl to compete in the Olympic Games' three-day event when she became a member of the Gold Medal Team at Mexico with Our Nobby. In 1976, Jane won Burghley, in 1977 a team Gold Medal at the European Championships and in 1978 she was a team member at the World Championships in Kentucky, all with Warrior. Warrior and Jane also doubled in the film *International Velvet*, starring Tatum O'Neal, and have done other film work.

Jane is a British Horse Society Steward, a member of the Horse Trials Committee and a dressage judge. She also judges and competes in show classes such as hunters, hacks, riding horse classes, as well as lecturing and instructing at home and abroad.

Jane trained as an SRN at the Middlesex Hospital in England, going to the Olympics in the middle of her training. She now writes articles and books on all equestrian subjects and runs a commercial farm and successful competition yard. Jane is married to Tim, a company director involved with travel and sugar. When time permits, she accompanies him on his extensive travels.

PHOTOGRAPHER: **Bob Langrish**

Bob has been photographing the equestrian world for 17 years and his photographs appear in more than 50 books. His pictures are also regularly reproduced in equestrian publications around the world, including *Chronicle of the Horse* (USA), *The Corinthian* (Canada), *Horse and Hound* (UK) and *Hoof & Horns* (Australia).

FOREWORD: **Bertalan de Nemethy**

Born in Hungary on February 24 1911, Bertalan de Nemethy came to the United States in 1952 and became a citizen in 1958. He coached the United States show jumping team for 25 years, from 1955 to 1980. His teaching, training and the subsequent outstanding performance of his pupils have exerted a profound influence not only on the success of the US team but on the overall standard of equitation in the United States and Europe.

The list of medallists at European, World and Olympic championships trained by Bertalan de Nemethy is simply staggering. From the 1950s and 60s, the list includes such highly-accomplished competitors as Hugh Wiley, Bill Steinkraus, George Maurice and Frank and Mary Chapot. More recently he has coached Melanie Smith, Katie Monahan and Michael Matz.

Designer of the Olympic show jumping course at Los Angeles in 1984, Bertalan de Nemethy, although officially in retirement, is still active in the show jumping world – training horses, designing courses and running clinics internationally. In short, he is the most widely-respected authority on show jumping in the world.

Bertalan de Nemethy lives with his wife, Emily, in New Jersey.

INTRODUCTION TO APPROACHING COMPETITIVE RIDING: **Richard Meade**

Richard has the unique distinction of winning three Olympic Gold Medals for Britain. At Mexico, he won a team Gold on CornishmanV and in Munich he won both the individual and team Gold on Lauriston. Richard was also the backbone of many teams at European and World Championships and in several CCI's, as well as being one of the few riders to have won both at Badminton and Burghley with The Poacher, Speculator and his own Barbary.

Now retired from competing, Richard lives with his wife, Angela, and three children in Wiltshire, England, and divides his time between various businesses and his work as a member of the Horse Trials Committee and field master to the Beaufort Hunt. He also instructs students at home when his busy life permits.

INTRODUCTION TO MANAGEMENT AND TRAINING TECHNIQUES: **Jennie Loriston-Clarke**

Jennie has been British National Dressage Champion ten times. She has represented Great Britain at the Olympic Games no less than four times (including the Alternative Olympics), riding Kadett at Munich in 1972 and Montreal in 1976, Dutch Courage at the Alternative Olympics in 1980 and Prince Consort in Los Angeles in 1984. In 1978, she won the Bronze Medal in the World Championships at Goodwood with Dutch Courage, came sixth in the European Championships in 1981 and won the Midland Bank Novice Championships at Locko Park in 1983 with Dutch Gold.

One of Britain's outstanding horsemasters, Jennie is holder of the British Horse Society Fellowship Certificate, appointed Chairman of the BHS Training and Examinations Committee in 1986. Jennie rides and trains horses and riders for all disciplines and regularly gives dressage displays astride, sidesaddle and in long reins. She is also the author of *The Complete Guide to Dressage*. Jennie is married to Anthony and lives in the New Forest where they run the highly successful Catherston Stud.

INTRODUCTION TO THE COMPETITIVE SCENE: **Virginia Leng**

Ginny is one of the world's outstanding women event riders, being a World and European Champion as well as the Bronze medallist at the Olympic Games in Los Angeles. Ginny won the Burghley three-day event on four occasions with three different horses, Night Cap, Priceless and Murphy Himself, and Badminton in 1985 on Priceless. She was second on Master Craftsman in Stockholm to former World Champion, Bruce Davidson, and third at Badminton '88 on the same horse.

Ginny has a unique record in one-day horse trials and in 1985, with Night Cap, won every one-day event in which she entered. Ginny lives near Badminton and when not competing does some photographic modelling and writing.

Contents

Foreword

I could not have been more pleased when I was asked to write a foreword to this book. It is not only that I know Jane Holderness-Roddam well, but throughout many conversations we have had together concerning the classic principles of the equestrian sport's disciplines, I have learnt her basic philosophy of riding and her approach to training horses for competition.

During the last decade, interest in equestrian sport has increased enormously, and the horse industry has expanded accordingly. More people would like to learn to ride, but the classical riding institutions are vanishing, and very few instructors remain capable of teaching the traditional techniques. Therefore, there are limited opportunities to learn and practise the sport properly and to get the right advice and guidance. Selecting the right books is one of the few ways still available for the rider to obtain a clear understanding of the basic principles and the classical theories. This will lead to an intelligent approach to the practice, and make progress and satisfaction in the competition easier.

Because riding is becoming more and more popular today, its literature is also expanding. Unfortunately, not every author of books on riding is really qualified to do the job. Even when they try to follow the established, classical principles in their writing, they seldom have the experience in training horses themselves from the start and preparing for competition step by step.

This book, *Competitive Riding*, is very different from most books on riding. Jane has trained many of her horses herself, from the beginning up to the highest level of international competition. She is not only able to explain the elementary training of the horse, but is also competent in advanced dressage as well as show jumping and eventing. Jane is one of the exceptions who can claim success in the competitions of all three disciplines.

How many times are we able to read about the mental and physical approach of the rider? About the importance of the rider's dedication, temperament and confidence? Even if riders try to become familiar with the principles of riding and in the proper style,

many of them are inclined to ignore their own physical fitness, not to mention the fitness of their horses. How many horses are ruined in competition because of their lack of sufficient physical conditioning, their riders only taking into consideration their horse's abilities and willingness?

From this book we can learn much more than how to sit on the horse and how to ride. It describes the relationship between human beings and animals, fine points of judgement and horsemanship.

Finally, we have a book teaching young riders the essentials of horsemanship, as well as reminding top competitors, which should be the priority interest and education for everybody involved in riding.

The careful study of this book will open many riders' eyes and will change the concept of their training and competitive riding for the better.

Bertalan de Nemethy

Introduction

To compete in any one of the three disciplines of dressage, show jumping or eventing at Olympic level is the ultimate competitive challenge. It is this competitive element that attracts an ever-increasing number of people worldwide to riding. To win is the realization of your greatest dreams after months and, in many cases, years of hard work and patience, good stable management and careful, thorough training for the type of competition for which you have prepared.

This book aims to present in some detail the general requirements for the sports and to tell you how to set about aiming for the top level competitions, focusing on both the mental and physical necessities for horse and rider.

The first section of the book opens with a history of equestrian sport in general. I have then assessed the basic essentials, such as equipment and training facilities, vital to each particular branch of equitation. Many a top rider has managed to succeed without any fancy or expensive facilities, and this is still possible with careful planning of a suitable programme of fitness and training for each discipline.

Finding the right horse is always the big question, since it is not only the horse but the partnership between it and the rider which is so vital. The two must work well together and this is strongly stressed throughout the book. I have offered main points on what to look for, plus hints on what is considered 'the ideal' for the different sports. However, only a superficial survey of the competitive scene reveals that the most unlikely animals in terms of size, shape or type have regularly gone to the top in all three disciplines.

The management and training of the horse is dealt with in the middle section of the book. This includes general stable care in specific relation to the competition horse. Feeding is also covered, with advice on the relative values of the different feeds available; the use of various types of bedding; the importance of worming, vaccination etc; plus helpful charts for use as reminders.

Fitness of the horse for the different events is discussed with suggested programmes, and general training techniques from novice to advanced level are presented. I have repeatedly stressed the importance of early slow work to prepare the horse for more strenuous work and the necessity of achieving the basic principles of free forward movement and straightness in all training. Without these, the horse will never fulfil its true potential.

The more advanced movements required for the dressage horse; grids and athletic exercises to help the jumper and event horse, as well as hints on riding a test and a show jumping course are all included. The methods used by some of the world's top trainers are explained and photographs demonstrate many helpful and interesting points to complement the text, together with some revealing action photographic sequences.

The competitive scene itself, relative to each sport, is the main focus of the third and final section, emphasizing what is to be expected at each level. There are hints and advice on how to plan your day and get the best out of it; a checklist of the correct clothes, tack and protection for you and your horse; what to aim for in relation to your horse's standard at the time and the special considerations of the 'big occasion'.

I have included practical advice on travelling and its effect on individual horses, as well as general tips on care at the show which can contribute to success on the day. Particular points in relation to the dressage, show jumping and eventing worlds are emphasized, and photographs – including sequences – show many of the top riders in action.

The tremendous atmosphere to be found at a competition can only really be experienced at first hand, and there is no substitute for the 'big moment'. Whether it is a novice dressage test or Grand Prix show jumping round, the competitive experience is unique to each rider. Concentration and the ability to perform at one's best on the day is crucial. Both horse and rider react in some way to the pressure: some rise to the occasion producing better performances than seen in training; others find they cannot attain the same degree of excellence as previously achieved. Some riders find they can perform brilliantly on one occasion but be disastrous on another. Confidence is one of the key essentials to success; consistency is another. Not only must a horse be ridden in a consistent manner at all times, but to be really great in whatever discipline, the partnership must be consistently placed top or thereabouts.

The overall aim of this book is not only to explain what is required to get to the top but to help encourage all those who really wish to get there and to give practical advice on how to do it. With the will power, dedication, a good partnership between horse and rider as well as that sometimes elusive bit of luck, it is to be hoped that many riders will achieve their ambitions. But that achievement will ultimately depend on the strength of your wish to succeed.

Good luck.

Jane Holderness-Roddam

Jane Holderness-Roddam

Approaching Competitive Riding

Competing gives both horse and rider a chance to prove themselves and find out their strengths and weaknesses. It builds character. Working at home without the deadline of a competition can make riders too careful and set in their ways. With competition riding, you have to just get on with the job. If you don't succeed, as long as you and your horse have not been overfaced, at least you know what to put right for the next time.

To achieve success, we have to set ourselves a goal, and one that we believe is achievable. At the age of 15, I set myself the goal of representing Great Britain in the Olympics. When, six years later, I watched the Games in Rome, I believed that it was all possible provided I had the right horse. I was lucky in that less than 18 months later, after a lot of searching, I came across a wonderful young horse. After ups and downs, which beset all competitors, I finally made the team to Tokyo. It is a very proud and special moment when you can hold your head high and know that you have achieved your goal in a competitive sport.

Richard Meade

A History
of the Sports

The horse has been used for a variety of different reasons over the centuries ranging from a pack animal, conveyor of man into battle, a long-term means of travelling overland and for sport in many different forms.

Prehistoric paintings all over the world depict man on horses hunting for food. The Syrians and Greeks learnt how to use the horse for every conceivable occasion. Classical Greek architecture illustrates how the horse contributed greatly to people's lives in the friezes that decorated their buildings. Xenophen's teachings on the riding and training of horses, written more than 23 centuries ago in Greece, remains an outstanding example of the basis of how to deal with horses.

The Egyptian tomb paintings give vivid pictures of how the horse was used, and the decorative scenes on early Chinese vases indicate that the Chinese were riding and driving horses at that time.

In many parts of the world the horse is still the mainstay to the life and livelihood of many families. The only means of travel in the more remote spots of the world is still by horse, and many a modern war could not have been fought without the use of horses, when even the most up to date machinery could not cope with the rough terrain encountered.

It may seem a relatively recent development that the horse has been considered primarily for sport, but hunting has taken place worldwide for centuries. Perhaps it was through this that man first realized what tremendous speed and jumping ability the horse possessed. Chariot races in Roman times were an exciting but dangerous sport, and races of speed and endurance have been recorded in various parts of the world in ancient times.

One of the first organized horse races in England is thought to have been held at Wetherby as far back as AD 210, and there

Left: *Equestrian sports of various kinds have been taking place for centuries throughout the world. This beautiful 16th century illustrated manuscript from Iran depicts polo players. The sport dates back to at least the 1st century AD in Persia.*

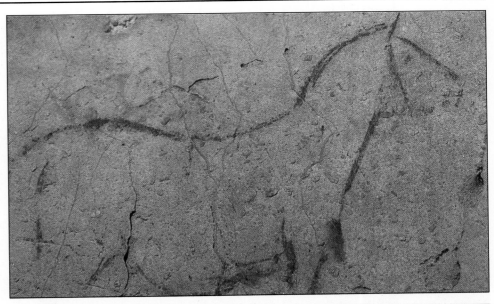

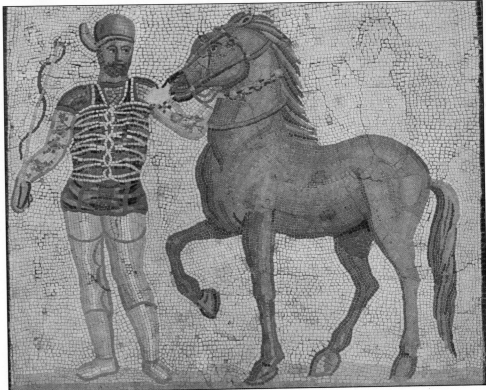

Top: *This cave painting of a horse was found at Puente Viesgo in Spain. It is the work of an artist of the Magdalenian Period dating back to approximately 15,000 BC. The extraordinary feature of this painting is the suggestion of a kind of primitive halter.*

Above: *A superb mossaic of a charioteer from Baccano dated 2nd to 3rd century AD. Chariot races were the main events of the Roman public games. The chariot teams were organized into four main factions, each distinguished by a different colour.*

Left: *Knights jousting, from a military Roll of Arms dated 1476, England. In the 14th century, jousting was still a highly formalized means of death, capture or ransom, but by the end of the 15th century it had become almost entirely a sport.*

is historic evidence that various equestrian contests took place in the north east of the country with Newmarket eventually becoming the 'Mecca' of the racing world, thanks to the enthusiasm and support of Charles II and his successors.

DRESSAGE

The word dressage is derived from the French verb 'dresser' which described the training and schooling of a riding horse. This is exactly what is understood by the word today, but perhaps it has become associated with the more advanced training of the horse on the flat.

The training of horses has fascinated man since the earliest times, but dressage became particularly fashionable in the 1700–1800s. Covered riding schools appeared and Europe became the centre of dressage and high school training, particularly Germany and Switzerland with their many great riding schools; Denmark and Russia also excel in dressage.

An Olympic sport since 1912, dressage is governed at the top level by the FEI (Federation Equestre Internationale) for international competitions. Each country adopts their own rules for national competitions, adapted from those of the FEI, and set their own dressage tests to be performed in one of the two recognized arenas: a small one measuring 20 × 40 metres (66 × 131 feet) or the larger size of 20 × 60 metres (66 × 197 feet). The various tests are designed to suit horses of all different levels of training from novice to advanced.

Types of Competition

The international tests start at an advanced level and progress to include all the movements required at Olympic standard for the ultimate competition – the Grand Prix test.

Dressage to music has recently been introduced at all levels and is proving tremendously popular with spectators and riders alike. Judged on similar lines to skating, there are two marks – one for technical merit and the other for interpretation of the music.

Top: A splendid print of Pelliers Riding School in Paris in 1836. It was considered inelegant for ladies to ride astride right up until the 20th century. The horse can be seen restrained between pillars and is being taught the kick back for one of the 'airs above the ground' movements.

Above: Switzerland's Granat and Christine Stuckleberger were one of the most highly successful combinations to be seen in the post war era. Seen here performing passage down the centre line, Granat's legendary and magnificent power can be clearly seen. His competitive record was exceptional.

Right: Britain's Blenheim Palace lends an impressive background to the competitions taking place in front of the house. There are two arenas catering for the enormous demand for dressage today. The rider on the left is warming up outside the arena.

Competitions are held for all age groups and standards, and every year there is a major international championship for juniors, young riders and seniors.

The Olympic Games are held every fourth year with the World Championships two years later, also held every fourth year. European and American Championships slot in-between every two years. Germany is undoubtedly the champion nation in the field of dressage, but Switzerland, Denmark and Russia have always produced good teams and Britain is now taking great strides to close the gap.

SHOW JUMPING

Jumping competitions have been taking place since the turn of the century, but it was not until after the Second World War that international championships took place.

It appears that the first organized class for show jumping took place in Paris in 1866. At that time, the riders disappeared, after an initial parade, to jump some fences outside; presumably these were more like cross-country jumps. This did not appeal much to the spectators who were left watching an empty arena. Since that time, fences were built within the arena.

Over the next 25 years, the sport developed as 'lepping' competitions, and in

Top: *France's world famous Cadre Noir show. The riders demonstrate their expertise at the canter half-pass during one of their stunning displays enjoyed by all spectators.*

Below: *Ontario and James Freyling in an early high-jump class in America reputedly clearing 2.10 metres (2.3 yards). Doubts arose about the levelness of the ground.*

1912 show jumping was included in the Olympic Games for the first time.

In 1921, eight countries got together to draw up some guidelines on rules for show jumping: Belgium, Denmark, France, Italy, Japan, Norway, Sweden and the United States of America. This group effectively standardized regulations on the sport – until that time each country had its own rules and these varied tremendously on how their penalty system was scored. This was the start of the FEI (Federation Equestre Internationale), now joined by all equestrian nations, which is the governing body of all international equestrian sport, including the equestrian events at the Olympic Games.

Types of Competition

As with other sports, the pattern of competition has been established around the Olympic Games for World, European and Pan-American Games, so that now there is a major championship every year and numerous special championships at all the leading equestrian shows worldwide. These competitions are held for juniors, young riders and seniors as well as for children on ponies. Points are given to the countries winning the team competitions held throughout the world, and the winners receive the coveted President's Cup at the end of the year.

The biggest shows in Europe are at Aachen, Rome, Hamburg, Dublin, Rotterdam, Hickstead and Madrid. Indoor shows at Wembley, Olympia and Birmingham in Britain; Paris and Amsterdam on the continent; the Toronto Royal Winter Fair and the Madison Square Gardens show in New York offer high-level competition with few weather problems. In fact, numerous shows are held indoors very successfully, which enables the show-jumping rider to compete all the year round if he or she so wishes.

Jumping Derbys, where the horse is expected to jump a much longer course of more natural fences, demand a special type of horse and clear rounds are relatively few. The Hickstead Derby, with its famous bank, and the Hamburg Derby are among the best known.

Quarantine regulations prevent many countries from freely moving their horses around the world, but they overcome this restriction by either mounting foreign riders on their own horses or by extending invitations to those countries which are able to avoid these regulations. Australia and South Africa stage large horse shows and the Dubai Horse Show is regularly visited by the world's top riders.

EVENTING

Horse trials originally started as a military sport for soldiers (in fact, eventing is still known as 'the Military' in Europe). It was considered an ideal way to test the stamina

Below: *Austria's Hugo Simon and Windzer are clearly demonstrating the concentration necessary when show jumping. The horse is using its forelegs, tucking them right up neatly to clear this upright with ease.*

Left: *Hickstead's famous Derby Bank poses no problems for Duncan Inglis. The rascal descends the 10-foot (3-metre) bank in perfect balance. Derby courses are long and incorporate a great variety of fences, requiring a very versatile horse.*

Below Left: *This entertaining print shows quite clearly that steeplechasing was much in evidence in the 1800's and midnight races were quite common. The event horse must be versatile and able to jump both cross-country and steeplechase fences clear.*

Above: *The cross-country phase of eventing is the most exciting part of the competition and the Trout Hatchery at the Burghley Horse Trials draws crowds every year. The spray created by the horse, if the fence is approached too fast, can cause problems.*

and versatility of the chargers. It was not until after the Second World War that civilians were permitted to enter.

Eventing has now become the fastest growing equestrian sport and international competitions are held in the Americas, Europe, Australia and New Zealand with the most famous of all held at Badminton in England. Started in 1948 by the late Duke of Beaufort after he saw the 1948 Olympic Games, Badminton is held in the Spring. Burghley, set in a beautiful park in Lincolnshire comes a close second in prestige and has hosted several European and World Championships to date.

Types of Competition

The world of eventing combines dressage and show jumping with a speed and endurance section which, at the top level, includes steeplechase, roads and tracks and the cross country course with the three phases being performed over three days: dressage on day 1; speed and endurance and cross country on day 2; the show jumping on the last day, the whole competition being called a three-day event. A condensed form of this competition, without the speed and endurance section, is used as the training ground for three-day events, in the form of a one-day event.

Eventing is a tough sport. Whereas pure show jumping and dressage are specialist sports, eventing is more for the all-round rider and horse. In most countries there are two seasons, spring and autumn, with the major three-day events coming later on in either season to give the horses time to build up to maximum fitness for the ultimate in eventing and every rider's ambition – to compete in a three-day event.

Because of the demands on skill and fitness involved in eventing, a horse is generally not expected to do more than two three-day events a year but it may compete in several one-day events, depending on the severity and standard of the competition itself. These events often act as qualifying rounds for the three-day event but in any case are designed for the different standards and experience of horses. The events are usually divided into a novice, intermediate and advanced grading. The Americans have a lower level called 'training', and a similar idea is at present under consideration in Britain to help encourage the young horse over smaller courses.

Requirements and Equipment

To perform successfully in any competition, it is essential that both horse and rider are mentally as well as physically fit to cope with the tough demands made on them. Obviously, the onus is always on the rider to ensure that the horse has been prepared and presented in the best possible way.

STARTING THE RIGHT WAY

There are numerous opportunities to develop competitive riding skills from a young age. Children are able to compete on ponies and horses in all types of competitions; from show jumping, dressage and horse trials to numerous other events like showing, hunter trials, tetrathlons and gymkhanas.

The Pony Club

As members of The Pony Club, children from an early age can attend riding rallies and camps all over the world. The care of the pony, attention to tack and an understanding of the basics of equestrian sport are instilled from the start, and with regular instruction the child learns to cope in company with the whole range of eventualities which such occasions create. These children, without their being conscious of it, are being prepared for a competitive career. Each is trying to outdo the other, whether it be racing through poles in a bending race or practising the movements of a dressage test in front of their instructor. The first instance provides the riders with the opportunity to increase their balance and steerage ability in a competitive atmosphere; in the latter

Left: *Competitive riding requires a large selection of tack, equipment and clothes. However, many a champion has got to the top with the bare minimum. The picture illustrates some of the necessary kit.*

Above: *The Pony Club has been the starting point for so many of the world's top riders. These competitive games, and the teaching of balance and general horse care, stand riders in good stead for future competitive work.*

Below: *Riders competing at Wembley for the finals of the Pony Club mounted games for the coveted Prince Philip Cup. The vital competitive skills of control, balance, speed and precision are clearly seen.*

exercise, they will be learning to perform in an isolated situation in front of someone in an 'assessment' role, a good rehearsal for competing on the day in a dressage competition.

Hunting

Many youngsters and adults enjoy hunting and for years this has been considered one of the very best ways of training both horses and riders. No amount of schooling can teach a horse better how to cope with uncertain terrain and weather conditions. In hunting, the horse has to learn to shorten and lengthen its stride (often quite suddenly), adapt to deep and wet going, jump off awkward turns and cope with all the other horses and riders in the field. The jumping experience will always be invaluable; since neither horse nor rider will know exactly what they may be taking on, they will learn to adapt to the unforeseen occasion, such as finding a wire fence or farm implement on the other side of an innocent-looking hedge. A good horse will learn to automatically stretch itself out over the fence to clear the hazard if possible, or generally brace itself ready for a short stride or awkward landing. In short, there is no better way of teaching the horse how to think and look after itself than engaging in a season's hunting.

From the rider's point of view, hunting soon helps to improve balance and an awareness of what is going on around. Confidence builds up between horse and rider as more fences are jumped and more situations coped with. Quite apart from the unique atmosphere of the hunt and the sheer thrill of galloping across often very beautiful

Left: *The Taunton Vale Foxhounds show the type of conditions often encountered on a day's hunting; a marvellous training ground for the horse and rider. Many top champion horses have learnt the basics in hunting.*

Below: *What hunting is all about – a superb jump over a big hedge and ditch with the rest of the field following. This is one of the best ways of teaching a horse to ride cross-country in varied conditions.*

countryside, one does become acutely aware of the power and agility of one of nature's most noble animals.

DRESSAGE

The term 'art' is perhaps more aptly applied to dressage than 'sport'. To produce your horse perfectly in balance and supple enough to perform the required movements accurately, smoothly and in rhythm is, in reality, an art. It requires great dedication and a large amount of patience. The real secret of riding dressage is for the rider to complement the horse rather than inhibit it in its performance of the movements. This is surprisingly difficult to achieve – hindrance of the horse can be caused by incorrect distribution of the rider's weight, too strong a hand or insufficient drive from the rider's seat and legs.

Presentation is of great importance in dressage. You need to produce a pleasing picture to the eye at all times – one of professional elegance. To achieve this, it helps to have a nice-looking horse, and the turnout should be immaculate. It is important, too, that the rider's clothes and the horse's tack are complementary.

The arena, whether large or small, should be used to its best advantage. Each movement should start or finish at exactly the marker indicated, since accuracy, especially in the higher tests, is judged and marked accordingly.

The Horse's Way of Going

The horse must go forward freely in all paces in a good rhythm without showing any signs of resistance. The latter include swishing of the tail, grinding the teeth, attempting and

sometimes actually managing to put the tongue over the bit, swinging of the quarters from side to side, and so on.

The paces should be loose and supple with no tightness through the horse's back, shoulders and ribs. The tail is a good indication of suppleness; it should swing evenly from side to side in the trot, following the movement of the horse. The horse's head should remain straight throughout the paces, with the neck arched, but it must not be allowed to dip so that the poll (top of the head) drops lower than the crest of the neck.

All paces must be worked at so that good marks are achieved throughout the test. It is very easy with a talented horse to ignore the basics but, while all might be well for a short time, there is nearly always a backlash when something has to be relearnt from the beginning again. The old saying, 'make haste slowly', really does apply to dressage training.

Always allow the horse to establish its own rhythm and then control it until you find a good speed and timing for that particular horse at its level of training. Remember that the young horse will tire easily, so it is better to do a little often than go on and on trying to achieve something better. Young muscles will take time to build up, and over-pressurizing the horse will result in head-shaking or stiffness as it tries to escape from the pain of tiring muscles. The build up to fitness must be a gradual process.

Paces and movements

The three basic paces, walk, trot and canter, are used in varying degrees in dressage depending on the level of training of the horse. The FEI, in its definition of paces and movements, describes exactly what is expected from each pace. The following is an extract from the FEI's text, reproduced here as a reminder of what is required in the art of dressage.

Above: *The walk is an important pace as it tells the judge a great deal about how the horse has been trained. A nice free walk on a long rein can be seen with the horse stretching forwards and downwards.*

Below: *Riders at Goodwood use the practice arena to warm up their horses and tidy up before competing. The judge's marks will very much depend on how this important time has been spent.*

Below: *This spotted horse is showing some nice lengthening at the trot in the arena. At novice level it is perfectly correct to wear tweed coats. The rider's legs can be clearly seen pushing the horse forward.*

Requirements and Equipment

1 The object of dressage is the harmonious development of the physique and ability of the horse. As a result it makes the horse calm, supple, loose and flexible, but also confident, attentive and keen, thus achieving perfect understanding with his rider.

2 The qualities are revealed by:
a) The freedom and regularity of the paces;
b) The harmony, lightness and ease of the movements;
c) The lightness of the forehand and the engagement of the hindquarters, originating in a lively impulsion;
d) The acceptance of the bridle, with submissiveness throughout and without any tenseness or resistance.

3 The horse thus gives the impression of doing of his own accord what is required of him. Confident and attentive, he submits generously to the control of his rider remaining absolutely straight in any movements on a straight line and bending accordingly on curved lines.

4 His walk is regular, free and unconstrained. His trot is free, supple, regular, sustained and active. His canter is united, light and cadenced. His quarters are never inactive or sluggish. They respond to the slightest indication of the rider and thereby give life and spirit to all the rest of his body.

5 By virtue of a lively impulsion and the suppleness of his joints, free from the paralysing effect of resistance, the horse obeys willingly and without hesitation and responds to the various aids calmly and with precision, displaying a natural and harmonious balance both physically and mentally.

6 In all his work, even at the halt, the horse must be 'on the bit'. A horse is said to be 'on the bit' when the hocks are correctly placed, the neck is more or less raised and arched according to the stage of training and the extension or collection of the pace, and he accepts the bridle with a light and soft contact and submissiveness throughout. The head should remain in a steady position throughout, as a rule slightly in front of the vertical with a supple poll as the highest point of the neck. Also, no resistance should be offered to the rider.

The Halt

1 At the halt, the horse should stand attentive, motionless and straight, with the weight evenly distributed over all four legs, being by pairs abreast with each other. The neck should be raised, the poll high and the head slightly in front of the vertical. The horse may quietly champ the bit, while maintaining a light contact with the rider's hand, and should be ready to move off at the slightest indication of the rider.

2 The halt is obtained by the displacement of the horse's weight on the quarters by a properly increased action of the seat and legs of the rider, driving the horse towards a

Above: *This rider has reason to look happy after saluting the judges at the end of a test. The halt is square and on the bit, so a good mark can be anticipated. The rider is correctly dressed and the horse well presented for advanced dressage work.*

Below: *The diagram illustrates the outlines of two of the four types of walk: left – the shorter and higher steps of the collected walk; right – the longer outline of the extended walk which is required while maintaining the contact.*

The Collected and Extended Walk

more and more restraining but allowing hand, causing an almost instantaneous but not abrupt halt at a previously fixed place.

The Walk

1 The walk is a marching pace in which the footfalls of the horse's feet follow one another in 'four-time', well marked and maintained in all work at the walk.

2 When the four beats cease to be distinctly marked, even and regular, the walk is disunited or broken.

3 It is at the pace of walk that the imperfections of dressage are most evident. This is also the reason why a horse should not be asked to walk 'on the bit' at the early stages of his training. A too precipitous collection will not only spoil the collected walk, but the medium and the extended walk as well.

4 The following walks are recognized: **collected walk**, **medium walk**, **extended walk** and **free walk**.
a) Collected walk The horse remaining 'on the bit' moves resolutely forward, with his neck raised and arched. The head approaches the vertical position, the light contact with the mouth being maintained. The hindlegs are engaged with good hock action. The pace should remain marching and vigorous, the feet being placed in regular sequence. Each step covers less ground and is higher than at the medium walk because all the joints bend more markedly. The hind feet touch the ground behind, or at least in, the footprints of the fore feet. In order not to become hurried or irregular, the collected walk is shorter than the medium walk, although showing greater activity.
b) Medium walk A free, regular and unconstrained walk of moderate extension. The horse, remaining 'on the bit', walks energetically but calmly, with even and determined steps, the hind feet touching the ground in front of the footprints of the fore feet. The rider maintains a light but steady contact with the mouth.
c) Extended walk The horse covers as much ground as possible, without haste and without losing the regularity of his steps, the hind feet touching the ground clearly in front of the footprints of the fore feet. The rider allows the horse to stretch out his head and

neck without, however, losing contact with the mouth.
d) Free walk The free walk is a pace of relaxation in which the horse is allowed complete freedom to lower and stretch out his head and neck.

The Trot

1 The trot is a pace of 'two-time' on alternate diagonal legs (near fore and off hind leg and vice versa) separated by a moment of suspension.

2 The trot, always with free, active and regular steps, should be moved into without hesitation.

3 The quality of the trot is judged by the general impression, the regularity as well as the elasticity of the steps – originating from a supple back and well engaged hind quarters – and by the ability to maintain the same rhythm and natural balance throughout.

4 The following trots are recognized: **collected trot, working trot, medium trot** and **extended trot.**
a) Collected trot The horse, remaining 'on the bit' moves forward with his neck raised and arched. The hocks, being well engaged, maintain an energetic impulsion, thus enabling the shoulders to move with greater ease in any direction. The horse's steps are shorter than in the other trots, but he is lighter and more mobile.
b) Working trot This is a pace between the collected and the medium trot, in which a horse, not yet trained and ready for collected

Above: *This young rider is pushing a good medium walk from her pony, even though some resistance in the mouth can be seen as she comes round the corner. The hands and arms are just a little stiff so that the whip is sticking up in the air too much.*

Below: *Three trots. On the left, the shortest collected trot, then the medium trot, with the real stretching demonstrated by a longer outline on the right in the extended trot. The working trot is the pace between collected and medium.*

The Collected, Medium and Extended Trot

movements, shows himself properly balanced and, remaining 'on the bit', goes forward with even elastic steps and good hock action. The expression 'good hock action' does not mean that collection is a required quality of working trot. It only underlines the importance of an impulsion originating from the activity of the hindquarters.

c) Medium trot This is a pace between the working and the extended trot, but more 'round' than the latter. The horse goes forward with free and moderately extended steps and an obvious impulsion from the hindquarters. The rider allows the horse, remaining 'on the bit', to carry his head a little more in front of the vertical than at the collected and the working trot, and allows him at the same time to lower his head and neck slightly. The steps should be as even as possible, and the whole movement balanced and unconstrained.

d) Extended trot The horse covers as much ground as possible. Maintaining the same rhythm, he lengthens his steps to the utmost as a result of great impulsion from the hindquarters. The rider allows the horse, remaining 'on the bit', to lower and extend his neck in order to prevent his action from becoming higher. The fore feet should touch the ground on the spot towards which they are pointing.

5 All trot-work is executed 'sitting', unless otherwise indicated in the test concerned.

The Canter

1 The canter is a pace of 'three-time', where, at canter to the right for instance, the footfalls follow one another as follows: left hind, left diagonal (simultaneously left fore and right hind), right fore, followed by a moment of suspension with all four feet in the air before the next stride begins.

Above left: *The impulsion and power is quite clear in this photograph, as this combination demonstrate the extended trot across the diagonal. The rider is allowing with his hands and sitting very straight.*

Left: *The extended canter across the diagonal shows the stretch of legs and the distance covered in just one stride. The rider is in perfect balance, riding forward and keeping a nice contact on the reins.*

The Canter Sequence

2 The canter, always with light, cadenced and regular strides, should be moved into without hesitation.

3 The quality of the canter is judged by the general impression, the regularity and lightness of the three-time pace – originating in the acceptance of the bridle with a supple poll and in the engagement of the hindquarters with an active hock action – and by the ability to maintain the same rhythm and a natural balance. The horse should remain straight on straight lines.

4 The following canters are recognized: **collected canter, working canter, medium canter** and **extended canter.**

a) Collected canter The horse, remaining 'on the bit', moves forward with his neck raised and arched. The collected canter is marked by the lightness of the forehand and the engagement of the hindquarters, ie is characterized by supple, free and mobile shoulders and very active quarters. The horse's strides are shorter than at the other canters, but he is lighter and more mobile.

b) Working canter This is a pace between the collected and the medium canter, in which a horse not yet trained and ready for collected movements, shows himself properly balanced and, remaining 'on the bit', goes forward with even, light and cadenced strides and good hock action. The expression 'good hock action' does not mean that collection is a required quality of working canter. It only underlines the importance of an impulsion originating from the activity of the hindquarters.

c) Medium canter This is a pace between the working and the extended canter. The horse goes forward with free, balanced and moderately extended strides and an obvious impulsion from the hindquarters. The rider allows the horse, remaining 'on the bit', to carry his head a little more in front of the vertical than at the collected and working canter, and allows him at the same time to lower his head and neck slightly. The strides should be long and as even as possible, and the whole movement should be balanced and unconstrained.

d) Extended canter The horse covers as much ground as possible. Maintaining the same rhythm, he lengthens his strides to the utmost, without losing any of his calmness and lightness, as a result of great impulsion

Top: *This collected canter is being rather spoilt by the rider getting too far forward as she approaches the corner of the arena. The horse is taking rather a large step behind and looks a little heavy in the hand.*

Above: *This medium canter is looking very tight and restricted as the horse tenses up at the faster pace. The rider is trying to sit as light as possible and soften the hands to encourage it to relax again.*

Left: *A series of illustrations showing the canter sequence as it passes through the three stages and moment of suspension. There are four kinds of canter recognized: collected, working, medium and advanced.*

from the hindquarters. The rider allows the horse, remaining 'on the bit', to lower and extend his head and neck; the top of his nose pointing more or less forward.

5 Counter-canter ('false canter') This is a movement when the rider, for instance on a circle to the left, deliberately makes his horse canter with the right canter lead (with the off-fore leading). The counter-canter is a suppling movement. The horse maintains his natural flexion at the poll to the outside of the circle, in other words is bent to the side of the leading leg. His conformation does not permit his spine to be bent to the line of the circle. The rider, avoiding any contortion causing contraction and disorder, should especially endeavour to limit the deviation of the quarters to the outside of the circle, and restrict his demands according to the degree of suppleness of the horse.

6 Simple change of leg at canter This is a change of leg where the horse is brought back into a walk and, after two or at the most three steps, is restarted into a canter with the other leg leading.

7 Flying change of leg or change of leg in the air This change of leg is executed in close connection with the suspension which follows each stride of the canter. Flying changes of leg can also be executed in series, for instance at every fourth, third, second or at every stride. The horse, even in the series, should remain light, calm and straight with a lively impulsion, maintaining the same rhythm and balance throughout.

In order not to restrict or restrain the lightness and fluency of the flying changes of leg in series, the degree of collection should be slightly less than otherwise at the collected canter.

The Rein-back

1 The rein-back is an equilateral, backwards movement in which the feet are raised and set down almost simultaneously by diagonal pairs, each fore foot being raised and set down an instant before the diagonal hind foot, so that on hard ground, as a rule, four separate beats are clearly audible. The feet should be well raised and the hind feet remain well in line.

2 At the preceding halt as well as during the rein-back the horse, although standing motionless and moving backwards respectively, remains 'on the bit', maintaining his desire to move forward.

3 Anticipation or precipitation of the movement, resistance to or evasion of the hand, deviation of the quarters from the straight line, spreading or inactive hind legs and dragging fore feet are serious faults.

4 If in a dressage test a trot or canter is required after a rein-back, the horse should move off immediately into this pace, without a halt or an intermediate step.

The Transitions

The changes of pace and speed should be clearly shown at the prescribed marker; they should be made quickly, yet must be smooth and not abrupt. The rhythm of a pace should be maintained up to the moment when the pace is changed or the horse halts. The horse should remain light in hand, calm and maintain a correct position.

The Half-halt

The half-halt is a hardly visible, almost simultaneous, co-ordinated action of the seat, the legs and the hand of the rider, with the object of increasing the attention and balance of the horse before the execution of several movements or transitions to lesser and higher paces. In shifting slightly more weight onto the horse's quarters, the engagement of the hind legs and the balance on the haunches are facilitated, for the benefit of the lightness of the forehand and the horse's balance as a whole.

Above: *The counter-canter is being demonstrated by this novice horse. While technically correct, the horse is too much on its forehand to gain good marks.*

Below: *These two pictures show the flying change of leg as the rider passes C on the short end of the arena; the horse changing from the inside canter to the outside. The*

rider can be seen to use her outside leg back behind the girth and to change the bend and her weight to enable the jump onto the other leg to take place.

Above: *The horse is reining back with the rider asking for the backward steps with the hand and using the leg to keep it on track and straight. The horse has come a little too much on its forehand to gain good marks from the judges.*

Below: *This rider can be seen using a half-halt to re-balance her horse. She has used her legs and restricted the forward movement to create extra balance, collection as well as attention before she reaches the next marker.*

The Changes of Direction

1 At changes of direction, the horse should adjust the bend of his body to the curvature of the line he follows, remaining supple and following the indications of the rider, without any resistance or change of pace, rhythm or speed.

2 When changing direction at right angles, for instance when *riding corners*, the horse should describe one quarter of a circle of approximately 6 metres (20 feet) diameter at collected and working paces, and at medium and extended paces one quarter of a circle of approximately 20 metres (66 feet) diameter.

3 When changing direction in form of *counter-change of hand,* the rider changes direction by moving obliquely either to the quarter line or the centre line or to the opposite long side of the arena, whence he returns on an oblique line to the line he was following when he started the movement.

4 At the counter-change of hand the rider should make his horse straight an instant before changing direction.

5 When, for instance at counter-change of hand at half-pass to either side of the centre line, the number of metres or strides to either

Top: *Concentration can be clearly seen as this young rider warms up before riding in a novice test at Goodwood's Junior Dressage Championships held annually.*

Above: *This well-turned out partnership at medium trot look poised to win at the championship in the Medium 30 test. A very pleasing picture with everything right.*

Below: *This large-size dressage arena has excellent herringbone-type drainage and is well-designed to cope with a heavy bout of rain without the surface deteriorating.*

Above: *An excellent example of a horse at a corner, bending well throughout its body showing the suppleness and training required from a top-level dressage horse.*

side is prescribed in the test, it must be strictly observed and the movement executed symmetrically.

The Tests

Dressage tests are written nationally for all basic levels. They begin at an elementary level for the young and inexperienced dressage horse. In these simple tests, the judges will expect to see the horse moving in a straight line, and this will be the first point to be noted as the horse makes its entry into the arena. Straightness is essential for the performance of all movements, but is not always easy to achieve if there are underlying problems. It is, therefore, very important to create a good impression at the very start of your test, since this will inevitably influence the judges' opinions throughout the rest of the test.

The tests become increasingly advanced at each successive level, with the six official FEI tests at the top of the scale. These are the Prix St Georges, Intermediares I and II, Grand Prix, Grand Prix Special and the Freestyle or KUR, which is often ridden to music and judged on technical merit, artistic impression and interpretation of the music to suit the horse's way of going.

Facilities and Equipment

For dressage, the prime requirement is a flat non-slip surface. The ideal is a full size (20 × 60 metres/66 × 197 feet) all weather

Herringbone Drainage System

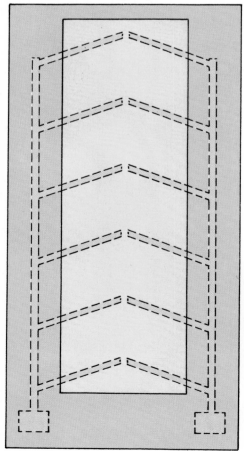

surface arena or something even larger. But if this is not possible, then any part of a field that is smooth with a reasonable cover of grass is perfectly adequate in good weather, especially for horses that have not yet reached advanced levels. If there is good drainage and you are lucky enough to live on sandy soil, you may get good use out of the ground with a little care and attention. Rollering and harrowing of the ground will make an enormous difference, and if the latter is done frequently, the ground should keep fresh.

Those that live on clay soil will not be so successful – it is seldom right for riding, either becoming too soft when it can be bottomless or too hard and rutted making it impossible for dressage. If these conditions exist, you need to give serious thought to the logistics of putting down some sort of arena,

indoor school or the cheaper option of finding one near enough to use that belongs to someone else!

Putting in a Training Arena

Consider carefully the following points, should you decide on putting in an arena.

The site is vital as, once the work is completed, it will not be possible to change. Drainage must be the first priority, an important point often ignored. The arena should be on well drained land with adequate drains inside and round the edge of the area. It makes sense if the arena is raised up and is slightly above ground level. Too often the mistake is made of digging down into the site thus creating a well in the ground, so that however much drainage there is the surface water will still tend to sit in the well.

The base should be carefully chosen. There are a lot of ideas on what is the best sort but some form of hard core and free-draining chalk is universally considered ideal. This must be packed down well and held in place either by the arena posts if there is to be fencing round the edge or by some other method.

Whether one uses a membrane (a layer of semi-permeable material) or not will depend very much on how the arena is drained, but if there is to be any jumping in the same arena these tend to be a short-lived asset and, if the drainage is properly done, should not be necessary. However, this does depend on the soil in some places and it may be essential in clay-type conditions.

Surfaces

The choice of surface is one of preference. There are so many to choose from that it is best to try out those that appeal to you and get the feel of them. Most arenas will take a few months to settle, so you need to know what the finished surface is like; and bear in mind that a new surface will often feel rather loose anyway.

Sand, various stonechips, woodchips, plastics and a variety of mixtures have all been tried and used, and many are very

Below: *In dressage competitions where a grass arena is used, the centre line is mown quite short, as illustrated here. Also, the 'X' marker should be clearly indicated on the centre line.*

Construction of Training Arenas

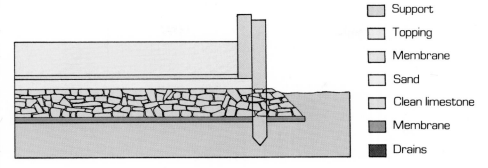

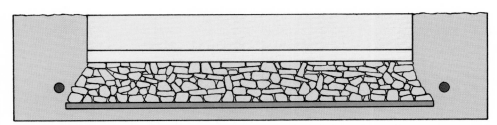

	Support
	Topping
	Membrane
	Sand
	Clean limestone
	Membrane
	Drains

Above: *Two section diagrams of an arena with different features. The top one is a raised arena with the various layers marked; the lower one shows the below-ground dug-down type, with drains.*

Below: *These riders can be seen riding in an arena using wood chips. The surfaces of all arenas need very careful consideration as does the choice of site, its drainage, type of base and amount of surface.*

Requirements and Equipment

The Dressage Arenas

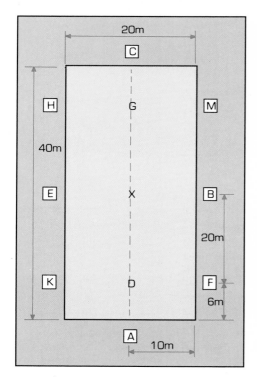

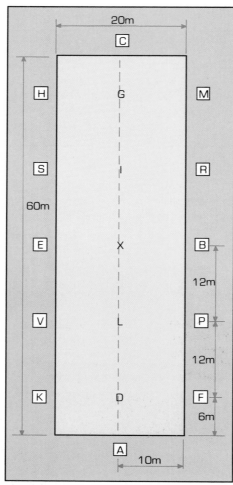

Below: *The Doctor Bristol bit, with double joints and a flat piece of metal in-between, is not allowed for dressage. Although it is similar in some ways to the permitted French Bridoon it is much more severe.*

The Doctor Bristol Bit

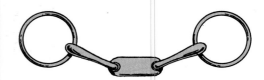

Cavesson Noseband

Above and right: *The small and large arena showing the markers and distances. Britain tends to use the small arena more than her European neighbours perhaps because there are insufficient competitions to meet the demand. The large arena is used for tests of Medium and above as well as for all FEI and other important national tests.*

good. Some are more successful if mixed with other ingredients, but as a general rule aim for something that is non-slippery, hard-wearing, free-draining but with a slight springiness that is neither too deep nor too shallow.

The horse should be tried on various surfaces particularly if it has sensitive feet. Some surfaces are quite abrasive and certain horses simply find these impossible to move on and so will tend to shorten their stride. Others may find a surface moves too much and so feel insecure, with much the same result. It is really worth checking these points with your horse first, rather than discover, when it is too late, that your horse does not agree with your choice of surface!

Arena Markers

The arenas, whether the small or large size, have the same basic markers round the edge and down the middle, but extra ones are added to the large one. For the small arena, A K E H C M B F are used clockwise round the edge starting with A at the entrance. Most people think up some silly sentence to remember the sequence, mine being 'All King Edward's Horses Cannot Manage Big Fences' which has nothing to do with dressage at all! The centre line markers, D X G, are simple enough to remember. For the large size arena, which is used for most tests

of medium standard or above, the four extra markers – R S V P – slot in with L and I down the centre.

For competition, the centre line should be mown and X clearly marked if grass is used. In sand arenas, the centre line is rolled regularly. Most international competitions at the top level are now held in sand arenas, since it is possible to maintain them to the same standard throughout the event. This is not possible with a grass arena if the weather deteriorates during the competition. All international championships, CD10's, have to be ridden in sand arenas.

Tack

Tack for dressage is especially important since, more than in any other form of riding, the horse must be seen to be performing at its best. The bit, therefore, plays an enormously vital role. Most horses go kindly in the ordinary loose-ringed or eggbut-jointed snaffle and, so long as they are fitted correctly and are of the right size and width for your horse, this type of bit is preferable. There are, however, several variations which are permitted in dressage competition, but always double-check that your choice is in accordance with the rule book. The most common bit **not** allowed is the double-jointed Dr Bristol snaffle, whereas the rather similar French bridoon snaffle is

Above: *The cavesson noseband is the one of choice, in which there is the least chance of interference. It is always used with a double bridle and should rest comfortably two inches below the cheek bones.*

Above: *This full-sized international arena has the required sand surface for FEI contests. It has been attractively laid with flowers, adding to the overall picture of this dressage meeting in progress.*

Below: *The French Bridoon or double-jointed snaffle is allowed in dressage contests. A fairly mild bit, it does not have the nut cracker action of other snaffle bits and so is preferred by some.*

French Bridoon

permitted. The choice of noseband may influence your choice of bit; in some cases it can affect the action of the bit by increasing the severity. A drop or flash as well as the cavesson noseband are allowed with snaffle bridles, but for pure dressage the grackle or crossover noseband is forbidden. It is, however, allowed in the dressage phase in eventing.

The double bridle can be used in tests above novice standard and is compulsory in advanced tests and all FEI tests. Make sure that your choice of curb bit and curb chain conforms to the rule book, and that they are the right shape and size for your horse's mouth; it is very important that the whole bridle fits comfortably. If the browband is too tight it can pinch the horse's ears and cause possible headshaking. Likewise, if it is too high because of the position of buckles and so on, this can also cause discomfort.

The dressage saddle is by far the most expensive piece of equipment, but it is well worth investing in a good one that is comfortable for you, is a good fit and sits square on the horse. There are so many to

Drop Noseband

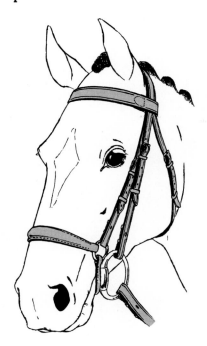

Above: *The drop noseband may be used with a snaffle only and can be useful for those horses who open their mouths or at times resist. It should fasten below the bit but must not restrict the breathing.*

Flash Noseband

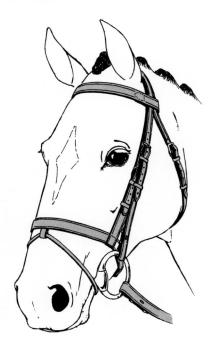

Above: *The flash is a combination of both cavesson and drop and may only be used on those horses wearing snaffle bridles. Both parts work together giving extra control and preventing the horse from opening its mouth.*

Grackle Noseband

Above: *The grackle noseband is not allowed in dressage competitions but is allowed in the dressage phase of horse trials. It has a similar action to the drop but prevents the horse crossing its jaw.*

Dressage Saddle

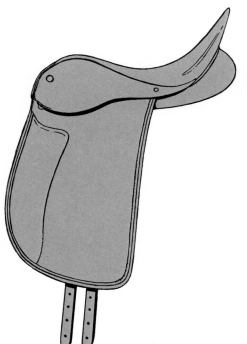

Dressage Whip

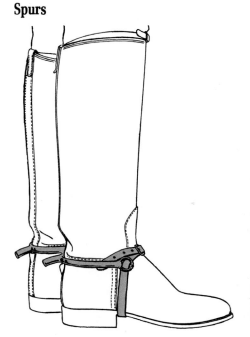

Spurs

Top: *The straight cut dressage saddle may have padding on the panel to help the leg to stay in the correct position.*

Middle: *The dressage whip, which can be of any length, is extremely useful for training and is allowed in some lower level tests.*

Above: *Spurs are compulsory in tests of Medium and above and all FEI tests. The points must face downwards.*

choose from, but it must be well-balanced and sit flat on the horse's spine so that the pressure is not concentrated on one spot, which can ultimately cause soreness. It must fit you the rider well, be comfortable and help you to sit in the correct position to perform well on the horse. Because of the straight cut, some dressage saddles tend to tip you forward too much, altering the true line of balance. The choice of girth is purely a matter of preference, but whatever is chosen must be comfortable for both horse and rider. Numnahs now seem to be used universally, but remember that the more distance placed between you and the horse, the less easy it is to communicate your intentions to the horse through the use of your body. Very often it is that subtle close contact which gives the extra bit of co-operation required to make the difference between just a good and an excellent performance.

The Aids

The dressage whip is an important aid and can be used in the arena at most levels, but check carefully as there are occasions when whips are not allowed, such as in finals or championship classes. Whips may be of any

length, although the longer ones are more useful, and it is best to have the stiffer variety in case the very flexible type bend too much and irritate the horse. It is correct always to wear spurs with hunting boots, and these serve as an important aid to the dressage rider.

Instruction

It is possible to work on your own and, if you are experienced, you should be able to school the horse up to a certain standard, but there is no substitute for 'the eye of the master'. You may think all feels fine and that you are riding correctly and the horse is going straight. In many cases this may be so, but one has to remember that dressage tests are performed in front of a judge and it is what that person sees that is going to decide your marks for each movement!

Regular instruction will be enormously helpful to both horse and rider, and while it is wrong to overdo this, it will ensure that you are progressing in the right direction.

If you already have an instructor who you find helpful to you and your horse, then you are obviously well set up for progression in 'the art'. But for those looking for help, it is worth first considering a couple of points. To get the best out of horse and rider, the instructor needs to understand the thinking and ability of both and then plan the best way to assist them. Get to know your instructor, explain what you and the horse are aiming for, and listen and learn from what he or she says.

The horse is a willing and generous creature by nature and should be treated as such. Be sure that your instructor is one that understands how to get the best out of you both by working you hard so that something

Below: *HRH Princess Michael of Kent and her trainer discuss her performance following a novice horse trial test on a young horse. As in all sports, regular instruction is invaluable.*

is achieved, and yet does not pressurize the horse into doing too much, physically, for too long a period. It is best to work at an exercise or movement little and often rather than do too much of the same thing at one time. Although the horse learns by repetition, it is very often best to do an exercise two or three times and then change to something else, coming back to the original one to perfect a technique. All work must be a gradual build-up and it is unwise to force a horse into a set position or movement when he has not physically developed the muscle and balance to be able to achieve this. Patience is a virtue few people possess, but it helps to remember that even the top professionals say it takes roughly four to six years to bring a horse through the ranks at novice level to being fully trained and capable of performing the movements required for the Grand Prix test. The movements required for the tests and how to train for and ride them will be covered in Sections Two and Three.

SHOW JUMPING

For show jumping, much the same accuracy and precision is required as in dressage. The approach to the fences and use of the arena is important if the vital clear round is to be achieved. Indeed it is the clear rounds that matter in the end so every fence needs studying in relation to the approach to it and what comes after. The rider needs to be quick-thinking and alert as the fences come up very quickly when you are actually on the course. The first essential is learning to listen for the bell to start; next comes learning the course and knowing what to do if you have a problem. The final lesson is to go through the finish and leave the arena mounted.

How many 'jump-offs' there are depends entirely on the rules governing that particular class, but generally they take place over a shortened but raised course. A clear round must be the first priority, but looking to see where and how to save time is the important factor. Often it is the economical rider who finishes ahead of the one who appears to be going at twice the speed.

There are different classes designed to suit almost every type of horse ranging from speed classes for the athletic, quick and wiry type of horse, to the Puissance for the specialist over big fences.

Show jumping is the ultimate in training for jumping. To be able to jump correctly, however, so that the horse approaches all its fences with confidence, in balance and under control, it must also be obedient and supple on the flat. Unless this is achieved, few horses will ever reach their true show-jumping potential.

The Competitions

Once a year, all nations affiliated to the FEI meet for a general assembly at which the rules and regulations controlling the equestrian sports are discussed and amended as necessary. Show jumping has by far the widest appeal through sheer weight of

Above: *The art of achieving a clear round is not easy and many near misses may occur before the elusive clears become regular occurences. Wearing your country's national flag is everyone's ambition.*

Below: *The final of the junior jumping at The Horse of the Year Show, Wembley is an exciting moment for young riders. The amazing agility of ponies means they often jump much bigger fences for their size than horses.*

numbers, and international competitions are arranged to cater for every standard throughout the different countries. Many of these have team competitions for coveted trophies which are contested annually. While the international calendar is set up around the four-year Olympic cycle, four-yearly World Championships and the bi-annual European Championships slot in-between, as well as the Pan American and Asian Games.

There are championships for juniors, young riders and seniors as well as for ponies and horses. New events and series of competitions are appearing regularly with points being collected at various qualifying competitions to compete in the finals. The most prestigious of these are the Nations Cup and World Cup for team and individual honours.

In Britain, the British Show Jumping Association controls the sport with a huge calendar of national and international shows held throughout the year. National competitions are conducted under BSJA rules, which are a slightly modified version of the FEI regulations. All international classes are judged under FEI rules. The types of competition are basically divided up into six main sections. The rules and regulations for these all vary slightly, but are based on a table system (see chart).

THE TABLE SYSTEM
Table A1:
If, after two jump-offs **not** against the clock, there is equality, prizes will be divided.
Table A2:
There are two jump-offs, the second one against the clock, the competitor with the fastest time and least faults being the winner.
Table A3:
The first jump-off is against the clock, and the fastest time with the least faults is the winner.
Table A4:
The first round is against the clock, the fastest round with the least faults being the winner.
Table A5 (speed):
Seconds are added to the time for each fence knocked down. The competitor with the shortest total time is the winner.

Above: *A stunning view of the jumping ring at Dinard showing the interesting bank and water ditch. The show jumper may be expected to jump ditches and banks* anywhere and it is very important that it has seen such fences before meeting them at a show for the first time. Cross-country or hunting is an excellent way of training.

Top: *Jumping indoors requires a nicely balanced horse capable of jumping well in a confined space. This big course tests a horse's ability to its utmost and requires skill and timing from both horse and rider.*

Above: *A good sized practise arena is necessary at a big show if there is to be room for everyone to practise and warm up before a class. Some shows have better facilities than others in this respect.*

The last section has its own special rules and includes classes such as Accumulators, Have a Gamble, Six Bar, etc.

The scoring system is now fairly universal and the details below are a general guide. The time allowed may have some effect on the result as this may prove quite difficult to achieve, especially in poor ground conditions. More detailed charts on scoring and timing are shown in Section Three.

THE SCORING SYSTEM

- ☐ A knockdown incurs 4 faults.
- ☐ A fall incurs 8 faults and a second fall elimination.
- ☐ A disobedience (refusal) incurs 3 faults for the first one, 6 for a second, and elimination for the third.
- ☐ Starting before the bell, failing to go through start and finish, omitting an obstacle, and jumping the wrong course all incur elimination.

The Competition Arena

This must be a suitable flat area on good non-slippery ground if possible. In Britain, arenas are usually on grass, but in other parts of the world they are often on sand, in which case regular raking of the take-off and landing areas is carried out to keep the arena in good condition. The minimum size recommended for a show jumping arena used in competition is 100 × 200 metres (109 × 219 yards).

Indoor arenas, used mostly during the winter months, require very special care with regard to the choice of surface. It is essential that the arena is a firm and secure one and is kept in the best possible condition otherwise horses will be liable to slip in these confined spaces.

The Practice Area

This is for warming up before competing and should not be used for general schooling. A minimum of two fences should be provided, one spread fence and an upright. All

Above: *International competitors warm up in the practise ring. The poles in front of the fence encourage the horse to choose a good take-off platform. A beautiful jump is being taken over the single rail.*

Below: *The start of it all. This promising combination are building up a partnership towards greater things. Grid work makes a horse think and work things out without relying on the rider the whole time.*

elements of the fence must be capable of being knocked down, and the fences must be jumped in one direction only. They should be flagged with red and white flags or have red and white supports. The red flag or support must always be passed on the rider's right-hand side, with the white on his or her left-hand side.

While the rules vary only slightly from country to country as to what may or may not be jumped in the practice ring, it is in the rider's best interests to read the rules carefully each year, noting any amendments which may have been made, thus ensuring that you do not commit an infringement. Stewards patrol these areas to ensure that rules are not abused.

Facilities and Equipment

The basic requirements for the show jumper are a good training area and a variety of jumping materials. Several poles and stands with jump cups make up the basics. Gates, planks, fillers of various kinds, a water jump, walls, etc, are an added bonus. If these can be brightly painted once a year, it is good for schooling young horses (and good for the jumps!) in getting them used to the many colours and shapes which they will encounter in competition.

Try and get into the habit of using your cups on the jump stands correctly. The points of the cups should be pushed through the stands away from the direction in which the horse is jumping so that, should there be

Types of Fences

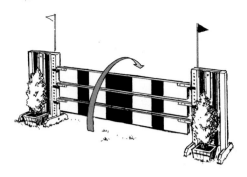

Left: *Planks are very upright, usually without a ground line, as in this example, and require great accuracy.*

Right: *Gates are nightmare fences for most riders. Being very upright, they present similar problems to the planks.*

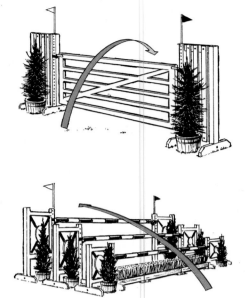

Above: *This fence is very inviting with a wall in front, but the rails could be thicker to make a really good fence.*

Above: *Stiles test obedience since they are usually quite narrow. This fence is improved by its inviting wings.*

Above: *Triple bars test height and spread. This fence would look less airy with brush under the second and third rails.*

a problem, the horse is less likely to injure itself on these. Also, be very careful not to leave cups lying around on the ground – they may be difficult to see, especially in a grass field, and should a horse tread on one, it could cause untold damage. Always keep the cups with the jump stands or in a container out of harm's way.

Jump Stands

There are numerous different types of jump stands available: lightweight or sturdy, wooden, metal or plastic, etc. It is really a matter of your own preference, but check them over carefully and do spare a thought as to whether they could possibly damage a horse if things go wrong. Are they well balanced? It is maddening if they fall over easily. Some are adjustable, which can be quite useful. There are also lightweight blocks designed specifically for jumping, which can be very useful for schooling.

Gates

Gates should be carefully checked over to ensure there are no protruding bolt ends which could seriously damage a horse's leg. These should be sheared off and filed down. Make sure that the gate is only jumped from the smooth side. Gates tend to be a rider's nightmare as they are so upright, and as the heights go up they can look airy and very flimsy in many cases. It is often the fence that causes the greatest number of faults in competitions.

Poles

Poles for jumping need to be sturdy and strong if they are to last and also serve as a

Above: *This oxer tests the horse's athletic ability over height and spread. The brush gives a slightly false ground line.*

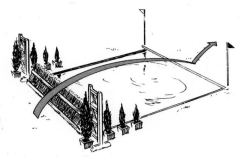

Above: *A water jump requires the horse to stretch out over the fence and the horse should be introduced early to this task.*

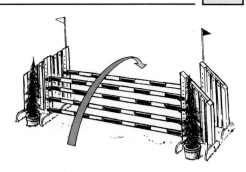

Above: *The true parallel is very square and requires great accuracy and ability when over 4 feet 6 inches (1.4 metres).*

Above: *Four vertical rails with no ground line require accurate jumping. The closer the poles, the more imposing it looks.*

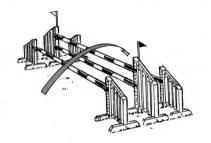

Above: *This hog's back, although airy, is straightforward to jump so long as the horse rounds its back well.*

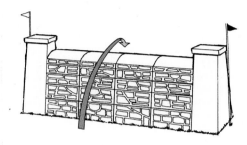

Above: *The wall is imposing and has a good ground line, but the top tends to fall easily. Traditionally used in Puissance.*

Left: *Horse and rider in perfect harmony over this big parallel. The rider must not in any way interfere with the horse's movement over the fence, but must stay in balance throughout the jump.*

Below: *The diagrams indicate how the width between two fences can influence the horse's stride. A shorter distance requires the horse to take a shorter and more collected stride in-between whereas a longer distance merits a longer stride or even two short ones.*

Jumping Strides

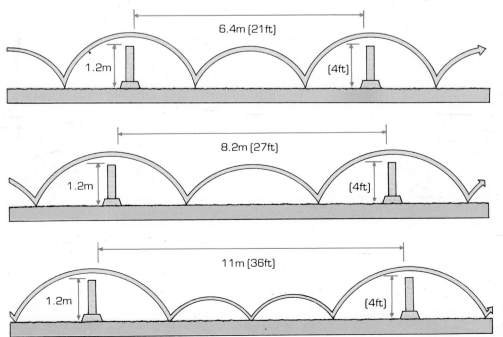

decent jump. Horses jump solid-looking obstacles so much better than flimsy ones and will respect a strong pole and jump it better. Most poles are 3.6 metres (12 feet) long but shorter ones of 3 metres (10 feet) may be used, and these are particularly useful indoors where space is limited, enabling you to fit in more fences.

The wider the fences, the less severe they look and good solid stands at either end complete an inviting picture. Styles are designed to test a horse's obedience – short poles are used for this type of fence. It is worth saving any broken poles and cutting them all to the same length for use in this type of fence.

Types of Fences

There are numerous types of fences with new variations appearing all the time, but these can roughly be divided into uprights, spreads and combinations.

Uprights are fences built vertical to the ground, with all parts placed one above the other. These include gates, planks, walls, straight post and rails, etc. Narrow fences such as those already mentioned – styles, small wicket gates, etc. – also come into this category and pose an extra test of obedience.

Spread fences require a horse to jump width as well as height. A spread fence should be built with never more than a single pole on the back upright. Such fences include parallels, hog backs, triple bars, double oxers, wall with rails behind, water ditches and open water jumps. Sloping or ascending rails make for a relatively easy fence, but the true parallel above 1.2 metres (4 feet) becomes quite an imposing fence, requiring accurate riding and the right degree of impulsion if the horse is to clear it with ease.

Combinations consist of two or more elements placed in front of one another, usually with a single or double non-jumping stride between each part. The fence is numbered as one.

The double consists of two fences, which may be of any design. In fairly novice competitions this may be an upright in and a

Requirements and Equipment

The Ground Line

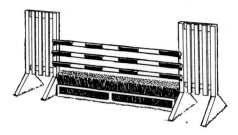

Left: *These two fences demonstrate how a good ground line, as in the right-hand fence, makes an obstacle look much more imposing and thus inviting. The spindly rails on the left would soon make the horse careless.*

Below: *A fairly straightforward course which can be easily erected at home. It gives one change of direction and encourages the horse to flow on without too many sharp turns, which is important in the early stages. Keep fences solid-looking.*

spread out, whereas in more advanced competitions it might be the other way round; it is more difficult to jump the upright having extended over the spread on the way in. The distance between the two elements will determine whether a very controlled approach is necessary or not. Two uprights on a short non-jumping stride would require this, but two parallels may need a much stronger attempt. A straightforward distance for one non-jumping stride in a double is 7.3 – 8 metres (24 – 26 feet). For two non-jumping strides 10 – 11 metres (33 – 36 feet) is good.

Trebles consist of three elements which again may include any type of fence or any combination of striding, such as one non-jumping stride between each or two non-jumping strides. It may well be one stride between the first element and two between the second and third, or vice versa.

The course builder needs to vary the distances according to what he or she is aiming to achieve. This tests the rider as well as the horse, and will also ensure that more than one type of horse's stride is catered for.

The Ground Line

This is the line at the bottom of the fence from which the horse judges its take-off point. In the lower level competitions or when training, this should be obvious and preferably slightly in front of the obstacle to help encourage the horse to take off at the right spot. A solid fence, such as a wall, has a definite ground line. However, if the front rails are higher off the ground with a hedge behind, this constitutes a false ground line and makes the horse's take-off point more difficult to judge as it will be looking at the bottom of the brush rather than the higher rail in front. Careful use of the ground line in schooling can be enormously helpful in teaching the horse to jump correctly by learning the correct take-off spot.

Courses at Home

It is important that your horse is confident about jumping a course of fences, especially if you are bringing on young horses, so it is helpful to have enough material to build at

Right: *A more advanced course with a fence on the short side of the arena and a figure of eight over bigger fences. The horse must be given the chance of jumping home courses before being confronted with a competition one which might undermine its confidence.*

A Simple Home Course

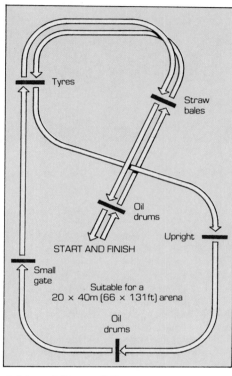

Suitable for a 20 × 40m (66 × 131ft) arena

A More Advanced Course

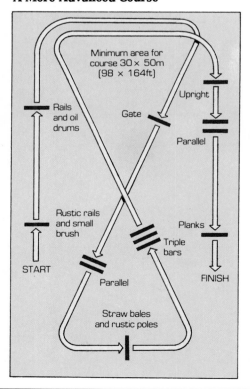

Minimum area for course 30 × 50m (98 × 164ft)

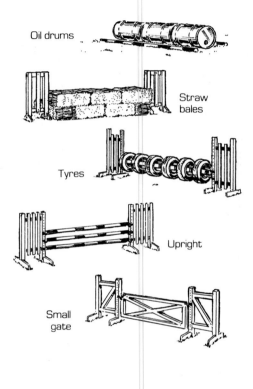

Oil drums

Straw bales

Tyres

Upright

Small gate

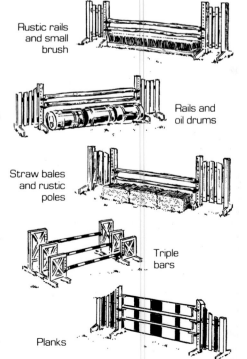

Rustic rails and small brush

Rails and oil drums

Straw bales and rustic poles

Triple bars

Planks

least six fences at home. Most of these you can design to jump in either direction but fillers make all the difference to a course. If you can accumulate as much filling material as possible, such as drums, planks, small fillers of all makes or shapes to put in front of or under the fences, so much the better. A horse will always jump a solid-looking obstacle so much better than the airy, flimsy type. When designing your course at home, think of making it flowing and inviting with no sharp turns, but include a double or treble if you have enough material, and at least two or three changes of direction.

Building a Competition Course

This is quite an art and needs careful planning. First you need to decide what it is you want to achieve and to what degree you want to test horse and rider. This should be carefully worked out and each fence should provide a definite problem for the rider. The first two fences are usually designed to be simple and to encourage confidence, and thereafter the course designer has many options depending on the type of class and standard of competition. In speed classes, the fences should not be high as it is the obedience at speed rather than the ability to jump that is being tested.

When building your own courses be sure to think of what you are trying to achieve. Check distances carefully (these are to be found in Section Three) to suit the size and type of fence, taking particular care in combinations. Make sure all fences are free-standing and the wings are placed to encourage a horse to jump centrally and to clarify the ends of the fence. Fill in any gaps carefully, make sure there is only a single rail at the back of any spread fence and that all cups are cleared well away from the jumping area.

Above: *The way this horse is raising its forearms rather than just tucking up its feet demonstrates the kind of ability required at top class level. There are many good show jumpers but few exceptional ones.*

Below: *A typical jumping whip. Under all show jumping rules, this must not exceed 30 inches (76 centimetres) in length. Care must be taken to ensure the stick does not injure the horse in any way.*

A Show Jumping Whip

Below: *Some horses catch themselves when jumping, causing quite severe bruising around the girth area. Protective pads can be fixed onto the girth to overcome this problem, such as worn by this horse.*

Below: *Open-fronted boots are favoured by jumpers as they protect vulnerable tendons, but do not clutter the front of the leg. The horse must respect the fences and will not do so if it is over protected.*

Open-fronted Boots

Tack

The equipment required by the horse for show jumping consists of a suitable, well-fitting jumping saddle to assist the rider in remaining in balance with his or her horse; a bridle that enables adequate control, the type depending entirely on what the rider feels is right for him or herself and the horse. The precision required for show jumping makes the choice of bit an important consideration and it is often necessary to experiment with bits, nosebands and martingales before the ideal combination for your horse is found.

Protection for the Horse

This is important as it is easy for a horse to strike into itself at any time. Open-fronted boots, which are extremely popular, protect the back of the tendons – the most vulnerable spot – without cluttering up the front of the leg. Over-reach or bell boots are used almost universally.

Some horses bruise themselves around the area just behind the girth. A protective pad can be fixed to the girth to prevent the hooves hitting this sensitive area as the

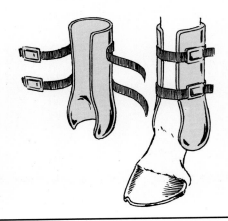

Above: *This rider clings on and sits tight as she survives a nasty twist in the air from her horse over this pallisade with a drop landing. Being able to stay on your horse whatever happens is a very important skill to acquire in eventing.*

Below: *The determination to get over the fence is what matters in eventing, as proven here, even though the pair have stood off quite considerably on take-off. Staying with the horse in the air is quite an art in itself, but must be perfected.*

horse springs into the air, snapping up its front legs. If large studs are used in front, this can add to the problem so it makes sense to use blunt rather than pointed studs with horses prone to this problem.

EVENTING

The same qualities are required for eventing as for dressage and show jumping but, as this is an all-round sport, the horse does not need to be as outstanding at each phase. It must, however, perform well enough in the dressage arena to have the benefit of a good start in the competition. The show jumping will be over a course ranging from 1.1 to 1.2 metres (3ft 6in to 4ft), depending on the standard of the event, so the horse need only be neat enough to go clear at that height.

The Event Horse

The extra essential qualities required for the event horse are boldness, agility, speed and stamina to cope with the cross-country phase; in a three-day event, the steeple-chase, roads and tracks as well.

While a lot can be learnt from schooling, if the horse is not bold enough and you know you have given it plenty of time to mature and to learn, then it may be that that particular horse is not cut out for eventing. It may be brilliant at something else, but the chances are the animal will always be too cautious to be a really successful eventer.

Many different types of horses may be able to event successfully at the lower levels, but at the top level your horse needs the quality to be able to cope with the opposition. A thoroughbred or at least a three-quarter TB, is the ideal combination and the horse should have attractive paces, be nimble and neat over fences and have the ability to gallop. Because of the toughness of this sport, its legs and feet become the most important part as they take the strain up and down the hills and over fairly frightening-looking obstacles. However brilliant the rest of the horse, if it has crooked or weak legs or feet, it is unlikely to stand up to the pressure of eventing for very long. Having said that, there have been, and I am sure will continue to be, the odd notable exception!

The Event Rider

He or she has to be a fairly exceptional person and, while we see several stars appear in show jumping and perhaps now more so in dressage, there are relatively few riders who really make it to the top of the sport of eventing and stay there.

The dressage phase, though relatively simple, can be a nightmare performance on a horse ready to run for its life round the gruelling cross-country section. Supremely fit, these horses often resemble time-bombs in the dressage arena. Many good show jumpers find the jumping phase rather small and tend to become careless, while it remains quite difficult to control a horse galloping at speed towards a combination fence on the cross-country when it is practically pulling your arms out. The rider therefore needs to be very fit, have extreme patience and nerves of steel in what is quite a competitive atmosphere.

The Competitions

The 'event' comprises three distinct tests: dressage, show jumping and cross-country. There are penalties for each test which are cumulative, the combination with the lowest score being the winner.

The one-day event is the training ground for the ultimate test to which every eventer hopes one day to aspire – a ride round a three-day event.

In one-day events the three different phases happen all on the same day, although at big events it is often necessary for some competitors to do their dressage a day earlier. The show jumping consists of a straightforward course varying from 1.1 to 1.2 metres (3ft 6in to 4ft) depending on the grade, and the cross-country consists of natural type fences varying from approximately 16 to 28 in number. The distance of the cross-country course varies from approximately 2 – 4 kilometres (1¼–2½ miles) depending on the grade of class.

Above right: *Good training should pay off and the water jump is always a good test of proper schooling. This horse is jumping in with a totally confident expression on its face. The rider is well positioned and in balance for landing.*

Right: *The ten-minute halt in the three-day event can be an anxious moment for the nervous competitor. David Green appears quite unworried as the vet checks over his horse before the start of the cross-country – the most arduous part of the event.*

Below: *A good start to the competition will be enormously beneficial since many riders are now very good at all three phases. The dressage is therefore even more important, as Lucinda Green has so often shown her fellow competitors.*

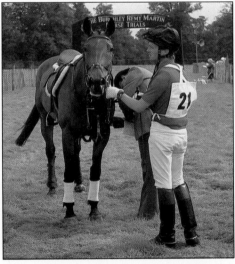

In the three-day event, the competition takes on new dimensions and is spread over three days with each phase taking place on a different day. Before the competition can start, each horse must pass a veterinary inspection which usually takes place in the afternoon before the event officially commences. There are two other inspections which take place, one on cross-country day and the final one before the show jumping phase takes place.

The Dressage Phase

The dressage phase consists of a single test with each movement marked by the judges from 0 to 10. Depending on the standard of the competition at a three-day event, there are between two and three judges whose good marks are added together and divided by the number of judges presiding. This average of good marks is then converted into penalty points and the total multiplied by 0.6 to give the correct influence of the dressage on the other phases (the ratio should be 6 for the dressage, 12 for cross-country and 3 for show jumping).

In a three-day event a 'multiplying factor' is used to reflect the severity of the course and its probable effect on the result of the whole competition. This factor, usually between 0.5 and 1.5 is decided by the Technical Delegate after his or her final inspection of the course and is announced before the start of the dressage phase so that this can also be applied to the dressage final scores.

While all this appears rather complicated, it is in fact only a problem for the scorers and the penalty mark for dressage is that which appears on the score board and to which future penalties, if any, are added as the competition progresses.

There are various rules relating to the dressage phase, which are the same as for pure dressage except that some variations in the type of bit or noseband are permitted. Errors are penalized as follows:

1st Error	—	2 marks
2nd Error	—	4 marks
3rd Error	—	8 marks
4th Error	—	Elimination

In international events, the FEI Three-Day Event Test may be used, which is that used in the Olympic Games. This is of a medium standard and consists of half-pass, counter-canter with changes of pace and degrees of collection. National tests may also be used to reflect the standard of competition and the FEI Junior and Young Rider Tests can also be used, confined to the younger riders or for adult events of a lower standard.

The FEI has now introduced a grading system by the use of stars to indicate the expected standard of the cross-country course on all Concours Complet Internationale (CCI) events. Three stars indicates a championship course with the Badminton and Burghley courses also falling into this category. Two stars denotes a course of medium severity, while one star is considered relatively straightforward.

In one-day events horses compete in classes graded from Novice, Intermediate

Above: *An interesting moment captured by the camera of this novice horse going strongly on its forehand in the test. The quarters will need to be brought well into play so that the hocks carry more weight.*

Below: *Galloping is an essential part of the eventer's life. A good galloper will cope much better with the demands of the sport. The steeplechase and cross-country times require fit, fast horses.*

(or Open Intermediate) to Advanced. In the USA, the equivalent classes are Training, Preliminary, Intermediate and Advanced. The levels are much the same internationally, although every country has a slight variation in its rules and regulations.

THE CROSS-COUNTRY PHASE

For one-day events the cross-country course is relatively short, depending on the class, and also varies in severity, getting more severe as the standard rises. Novice or training courses will consist of approximately 16 to 20 obstacles over about 2 to 2.4 kilometres (1¼ to 1½ miles). Intermediate or preliminary courses may have 20 to 26 fences and be up to 4 kilometres (2½ miles) long, while advanced courses are usually 4 to 4.4 kilometres (2½ to 2¾ miles) with approximately 24 to 28 fences.

SPEED AND ENDURANCE

The three-day event includes the extra phases A & C roads and tracks and B steeplechase along with the cross-country. This takes place on the second day, being called 'speed and endurance'. The length of these phases varies considerably. A & C generally speaking have a short phase A (the warm up phase), with a long phase C (the recovery phase) to give the horse plenty of time to return to normal after the speed required to complete phase B, the steeplechase phase.

Phase A may be somewhere between 1½ to 6 kilometres (just under 1 mile to 3¾ miles) with phase B usually somewhere between 1½ to 3 kilometres (just under 1 mile to 1¾ miles)

at a speed of 600 to 690 metres (656 to 754 yards) per minute.

Phase D, the cross-country phase, follows a compulsory 10-minute halt in which there is a veterinary inspection before the horse is allowed to continue in the competition. During this time the horse is refreshed and rested and the rider has a chance to consider his or her plan of attack round the most demanding phase of the competition. Phase D is usually run at between 540 to 570 metres (590 to 623 yards) per minute and may be between approximately 3 to 4 kilometres (1¾ to 2½ miles) long for a novice event; up to about 7 kilometres (4¼ miles) for a championship course.

Penalties are incurred for refusals or falls on the steeplechase and cross-country, as well as for exceeding the optimum time:

1st refusal run out or circle – 20 penalties
2nd refusal run out or circle – 40 penalties
3rd refusal run out or circle – Elimination
Fall of horse or rider – 60 penalties
2nd fall of horse or rider on
the cross-country – Elimination
All penalties are cumulative

In three-day events there is a penalty zone around each fence extending for approximately 10 metres in front of and to the side of the fence and 20 metres after the fence. Faults are only penalized if inside this area. Entering and leaving this zone without jumping the fence also incurs 20 penalties.

THE SHOW JUMPING PHASE

This consists of one round over a set of jumps which are between 1.1 and 1.2 metres (3ft 6in and 4ft) depending on the standard. The penalties for this phase are as follows:

Knocking down obstacles or
foot in water – 5 penalties
First refusal or disobedience – 10 penalties
Second refusal or
disobedience – 20 penalties

Left: *Steeplechase fences require bold riding but vary greatly in their design in different parts of the world. The rider should sit a little more upright and brace against the likelihood of a peck or fall.*

Third refusal or disobedience
in whole test   – Elimination
First fall of horse or rider   – 30 penalties
Second fall of horse or rider   – Elimination
Error of course not rectified or jumping
obstacles in wrong order   – Elimination

Exceeding the time allowed incurs one quarter of a time penalty for each second in excess of the time allowed, up to the time limit (twice time allowed) which involves elimination.

In a three-day event the show jumping takes place on the last day following a veterinary inspection to ensure the horse is fit to continue in the competition. In Britain it is usual for the show jumping to precede the cross-country in one-day events. This is not so throughout the equestrian world but does make it possible to accommmodate larger numbers.

Equipment and Facilities

The equipment required by the eventer can be considerable, but many a top rider has succeeded with very little. Tack suitable for each phase will depend very much on your horse as far as bridles, etc. are concerned and whether you require one all-purpose saddle to do all three phases, or a dressage and jumping saddle. Some riders even have a jumping saddle for each phase. Leg protection is important with bandages correctly put on; lightweight but protective brushing boots are essential.

A dressage arena is wonderful to have, but at least a decent flat training area is necessary for flat work as well as for jumping practice, plus plenty of stands with cups and poles for gymnastic jumping training. If you are lucky enough to have hills close by, this will help in your work to build fitness and save having to box the horses for some vital hill work during your training programme. The close availability of cross-country fences is helpful and, if you are thinking of riding in a three-day event, some steeplechase fences will come in handy. Many racing trainers will be happy to allow you to practise once or twice over their fences and will perhaps give valuable advice at the same time.

If you live in a quiet/rural area, you are lucky to have safe roads and probably good hacking country in which to fitten and train your horse, but this ideal situation seldom arises and one simply has to make do with what is easily available. Once your horse is fit, a suitable site for a few gallops and fast work becomes essential.

Before embarking on eventing as your chosen sport, it is worth considering carefully the above points to ensure you have at least some facilities readily available or can take yourself and your horse off to train somewhere more suitable, since proper training and preparation is vital to success in this sport.

Above: *The show jumping phase is really designed to test the horse's training and ability following the rigours of the cross-country phase. A neat jumper is vital if this phase is not going to let you down.*

Below: *Any combination fence requires extra care, especially over the first elements. This horse has screwed over the jump and will need all the help possible from the rider to rebalance before the next fence.*

Left: *The take-off is especially important since it will affect the whole jump if it is unbalanced. Riders must take care not to unbalance the horse by getting their weight too far back or forwards.*

The Mental Approach

The rider's attitude to sport will ultimately govern the success or failure of the chosen project. Nothing worth doing comes easily and succeeding in any sport can be disheartening in the extreme at times, just trying to get to the first rung of the ladder, let alone anywhere higher up.

THE WINNING QUALITIES

There are certain 'psychological' qualities in both horse and rider that play a vital role in success in competition. Do not underestimate their importance; recognize and nurture them.

Dedication

This is probably the prime quality required. Without dedication it is easy to be side-tracked or to give up when things go wrong. With all equestrian sport, it is necessary to get the balance right between you and your horse and what can and cannot be attempted or achieved at certain times. There is also a considerable time element which must be appreciated if you are to bring on a young horse and aim to succeed and get to the top.

The professionals expect a good horse to take time and are prepared to wait and let this happen, despite the fact there is no guarantee at the end that the potential super star will ever reach the pinnacle expected of it. Accidents, training set-backs, temperament, physical limitations or simply horse and rider never quite producing the form together that is hoped for, will all crop up at times.

The amateur may easily accentuate any or all of these problems by expecting too much too soon or, alternatively, will not know how and when to push his or her horse that little bit more to find out what talent actually exists in the animal.

Temperament

The temperament of both horse and rider and how they cope together is one of the major aspects in all equestrian sport and many a brilliant horse has been wasted by being mishandled by the rider.

In all sports there are endless stories of consistently successful riders getting on with horses with which other riders have failed. This outlines the merits of the true horseman

Above right: *A dramatic moment captured on camera as the rider tries desperately hard to remain seated. She has dropped the rein which has given the horse complete freedom, but with a sloped landing there is no hope.*

Right: *The helpless feeling of heading for disaster; the horse having taken off early and failed to make the spread, screws in the air. Event riding is not a sport for the faint-hearted horse or rider.*

Left: *To win at top level requires a very controlled, well-disciplined as well as highly motivated rider. The very highly specialized form of training for dressage takes years of hard work to perfect.*

The Mental Approach

or woman. It is no good making a horse adapt to you. It may and will work occasionally but the real horseman should be able to assess his or her horse and the attitude necessary to coax the best from it. They must know when to soothe and quieten and when to drive ahead and at all times ride in a consistent manner if a true partnership is to be achieved.

The horse will gain confidence with a rider who consistently rides and reacts with that horse in the same way. It will learn to trust you and feel confident, whether you are riding Grand Prix dressage or jumping in your first ever competition. Be consistent always and you are at least half way towards starting to build that all important 'rapport' with your horse.

The Will to Learn

This plays another vital role. If you do not possess this, you might just as well not bother to continue. No-one ever knows everything and you can pick up so much on a day-to-day basis and learn so much from each different horse.

Unfortunately some people cannot take criticism and so miss out all along the line as they fail to take this wonderful opportunity of learning from other people's observations. So often it is something very minor which is blocking progress and preventing a breakthrough, and even a casual remark from an

Above: One of those frustrating moments as the horse decides to say no. If this does happen you have to question what and why things went wrong. It is important to sort the problem out as soon as possible. Be sure not to overface a young horse.

Below: Horse and rider are listening as a certain fence is explained by the trainer. It is very important to understand fully at the beginning what is required and then go out and jump the course positively and in a steady, consistent rhythm.

onlooker should be given thought and assessed as to if and how this might be put to good use. The most successful riders are the ones that listen and learn all the time and never take for granted that they know it all. If you are lucky enough to watch the champions at work, you will see them spending hours and weeks with their horses patiently building up muscle and confidence and having regular help from trainers wherever the need arises.

Problems will arise at any time, and how you cope in certain situations, particularly with difficult horses, is something that may affect the whole future of a particular animal. Making a mistake at such a time may mean the end of months of hard work, so the ability to correctly assess the situation quickly and act immediately can be vital.

Confidence

Confidence between horse and rider is ultimately what is going to win competitions. Sometimes a horse will be the one to give the rider the necessary degree of this to take on even the biggest fences, while other riders are able to give a young or inexperienced horse just the right instructions to gain in confidence over a course of fences that may be considerably larger than they have previously encountered. On such occasions it is possible to see the horse improve quite considerably from the beginning to the end of that round. It is then up to the rider to build on what has been achieved without expecting too much on future occasions until this new-found confidence has been consolidated by further training.

Confidence is built through consistent riding on the part of the rider and it cannot be stressed strongly enough that the rider must give the **same** instruction to the horse each time a certain response is required.

In this way the horse does not get confused by conflicting instructions. It knows exactly what is expected of it if it has been well prepared and will give of its best. For this reason it is so much better for the competition horse only to be schooled by the same rider who will compete on it. Everyone inevitably rides a little differently and may ask for a reaction in a slightly different way. So while someone else may quite happily exercise the horse, go out for hacks etc., it is best to stick to one rider for the actual schooling, at least until the horse is fully competent at whatever it is expected to do, be this dressage or jumping.

Above: *Final instructions and a dust up as this rider prepares to leave the practice arena and go in to do her test. Concentration, dedication and acceptance of constructive criticism all play their part towards making a successful dressage rider.*

Below: *An unfortunate landing off the big bank at Hickstead. Fortunately horse and rider recovered to complete the course without further incident. Fitness and fast reaction to such an occurrence has saved a lot of riders hitting the ground.*

Left: *A beautiful sequence of world champion Virginia Leng riding the comparatively novice horse, Master Craftsman, at Stockholm over an imposing combination of steps. The horse was placed second in this big event. Throughout the different stages of the obstacle the rider is perfectly positioned to encourage the horse forward, so that it gains in confidence with each stride. An inexperienced rider might have failed to maintain the forward momentum resulting in the horse having to struggle at the top. This could well result in undermining confidence in one go.*

The Physical Approach

The fitness of the horse will be discussed later in the book, but the rider's fitness is very important from the start. No-one can ride well if they are the wrong shape through being overweight.

Getting yourself fit for riding is very important if you are to be correctly balanced on the horse and able to assist it in all that is expected. A healthy, balanced diet with the correct degree of protein, carbohydrates and energy-giving foods is essential to ensure that you, as the rider, are in a basically fit state to ride and control one of nature's fastest and most powerful creatures. While physical strength is rarely necessary to control the horse, it is essential to be fit enough to ensure you can get the best from your horse through the use of your body if you wish to compete on equal terms with other competitors. Excess fat will be no help at all, so priority number one is to get to the right weight so that you can then concentrate on being fit enough and strong enough through riding, walking and running to give your horse all the help it requires.

While diet is one factor essential to personal fitness, muscle tone is equally important, since you will not get the best from your horse or yourself if you are not fit enough to cope with the physical demands of your chosen sport.

Left: *The fitness of the rider is essential in all competitive riding but particularly so for eventing, where the rider can help the horse over the last few fences when it may be getting tired.*

Everyday riding is by far the best way of building up fitness, but certain exercises will increase balance and strength, and generally help tone up those muscles particularly pertinent to riding a horse.

EXERCISES WITHOUT THE HORSE

These are good in themselves for general fitness but care must be taken not to overdo these by building up the wrong muscles. Walking is always healthy, and jogging will help with breathing and increase of lung capacity which becomes increasingly important when galloping for eventing. (This may also strengthen calf muscles, which is less important.) Relaxation when jogging is vital if stiffness of the shoulders is not to develop, so be sure when you go for a run that you breathe well, sink your shoulders and really allow your body to swing in time to a good, rhythmical pace.

Arm exercises can be done on and off the horse and will be described as for being mounted further on, but an additional exercise for added strength, particularly important for controlling strong horses, is press-ups. Start gradually and be sure to keep your back straight and really push yourself up on the arms. Most women will probably find two or three quite an effort to

Below: *There is no substitute for riding, and the more time spent working horses the better and fitter you will become. Working with shorter stirrups is a very good way of toning up the important thigh muscles.*

Above: *A daily run is excellent to clear your own wind and improve your lung capacity. Fitness is essential if you want to win and give your horse the best chance, especially for cross-country riding.*

start with, but with regular practice can quite soon be doing between 10 and 20. While seldom having to resort to this exercise myself, I did come across one horse who was definitely too strong despite endless experiments with different bits. Refusing to accept everyone's advice that he was a man's horse, I worked myself up to doing 25 press-ups a day and then had the satisfaction of winning several events with a horse that had previously been considered a 'nut case'. Once I could hold him between my hand and leg he settled and concentrated, whereas without that control he dashed blindly into everything, which did have its worrying moments!

For jumping one rides fairly short and it is essential that the thigh muscles are strong enough to keep you in balance throughout a jumping round or during the steeplechase and cross-country phases of eventing. An extra exercise which may help consists of the jockey's favourite of sitting against the wall without a chair. Place your feet about 30 centimetres (1 foot) out from the wall, lean back against the latter and slide down until you are in an upright sitting position. Remain there for as long as you feel able. Then slide up again. One minute may be all you can manage to start with, but it will not take long to improve with practice and you will certainly realize how lacking in tone your muscles are when you try this.

Another good exercise is bicycling without the saddle (or at least stay out of the saddle which may be safer!). This strengthens the thighs and knees as well as using the ankles, and has the added advantage of making you breathe deeply as well.

Swimming is perhaps one of the best forms of exercise as all parts of the body come into play, including good use of the lungs. The crawl, breaststroke, backstroke and butterfly all exercise arms, legs and back and short

Top: *The jockey's sitting position is very good for strengthening the thighs and for general fitness, so necessary when shorter stirrups are required.*

Below: *Practising the sitting trot on the lunge or just on one's own helps to improve the rider's seat and position in the saddle. It is best done in slow trot or canter.*

Above: *An excellent lower back exercise to strengthen the back. Rest the hips on some form of pillow or rolled blanket and swing legs up in the air in a steady rhythm.*

periods underwater will help lung capacity as well.

The back is one of the prime factors in riding and how you sit on a horse, and your position in the saddle very much depends on the strength and suppleness found there. Some people are naturally strong throughout the spine and find it easy to relax into the movement of the horse beneath them. Others find this difficult, either because of a previous injury or general stiffness which has accumulated through incorrect posture.

Stretching up and then bending over to touch the toes, gradually sinking the body downwards in easy movements, is a good exercise. Swinging the arms from side to side when down in one, two, three, four and up motion will help. Lying on your back, bending up the knees and then lifting them straight in the air is another useful exercise. Bicycling movements, stretching them out to the side and forwards and back will all help with the back and loosening of the hips. Lying on a pillow placed just under the pelvis with your head resting on your hands and lifting the legs in a one-two-three then relax motion is wonderful for strengthening the lower back. This can also be done with the legs stretched apart.

With all exercises, it is very important that they are done properly. To strengthen oneself and tone up the body, it is necessary that oxygen is reaching the muscles. Therefore correct breathing throughout the exercises is essential. Far too often people hold their breath when doing something taxing, and this is particularly so with riders, thus losing the benefit of whatever exercise is being practised. Keep up a regular breathing pattern throughout the exercise. Often it is possible to use a breathe in-two three-out two-three pattern as you go through a sequence.

Remember also that the point of all exercises is to increase muscle tone through contraction followed by relaxation. You must therefore do your exercises to a pattern that allows for this. Most exercises are best done in a sequence, e.g. the back exercise lying on the floor – breathe in – raise the legs one-two-three times, breathe out and relax – then repeat. No exercise should be overdone but gradually built up over a period of time. It is always better to do a little and often to start with, on a regular basis, and once you have reached a satisfactory peak you can keep yourself in trim by twice-weekly sessions. Ideally, daily exercises throughout your life should ensure you keep supple and young and many who suffer from arthritis will say this is the only way to keep rusty joints in good shape. So a bit of daily self-discipline, started when one is young and healthy, should become a habit that will be beneficial right into old age.

If you find it difficult to make yourself do exercises alone, join a club or class where these are done; aerobics, health clubs, fitness classes etc, are now in evidence everywhere so there is no excuse for those who are perhaps unable to ride enough to get fit through riding alone or who need that extra help to be in top physical shape for competition.

EXERCISES ON THE HORSE

These are undoubtedly the best way to improve one's balance, position and suppleness. Riding on the lunge with an experienced trainer in command and on a steady horse will work wonders. In many establishments the rider is only allowed on the lunge until the trainer is satisfied that a sufficient degree of balance and sympathy exist between horse and rider, both on the flat and over fences. This is a feature of continental riders who are drilled much more on the lunge than their British, American or Australian counterparts. The firm, deep seat which results from such work on the lunge is the envy of many. But it is interesting to note that, while most of the continental breeds are more placid and so take this stronger form of riding in their stride and in fact require a very positive approach to training, the English thoroughbred, more highly-favoured outside Europe, often cannot take such strong and positive riding. It requires a softer, lighter way of riding. This may be the reason that the different styles of training have evolved to cope with these variations in temperament.

Riding on the Lunge without Stirrups

Acquiring a good firm seat is the basis for all good riding and riding on the lunge without stirrups will encourage the rider to concentrate on sitting square in the saddle, softening the back into the movement of the horse and acquiring a long but effective leg position. First attempted at the walk until the rider is in the correct position, most work on the lunge to improve the seat can be done on a well-trained and placid horse at a steady sitting trot.

Starting from the head and working downwards, the following exercises should be

For the Shoulders

For the Head and Neck

Below: *Folding the arms behind the back to tighten the shoulders. Pull the shoulders back three times, relax and repeat. This can be done off the horse as well.*

Above: *Head and neck exercises can be done on or off the horse but must be done very slowly and only with a stationary horse. A stiff rider may benefit, and learn to relax.*

done with the horse stationary or at the walk only, except where stated otherwise. To avoid the possibility of an accident, it is very important that the instructor keeps the horse under control at all times.

For head and neck to improve stiffness and tension and loosen the neck there are two common exercises which are very beneficial:
1 Turning the head slowly to the left and then to the right as far as possible.
2 Rolling the head forward onto the chest, round and backwards as far as it will go, continuing in a circular movement first in one direction, then in the other.

For the shoulders
1 Lifting up the shoulders and then relaxing them downwards as far as they will go, with the arms hanging loosely at the sides. Continue this three or four times, then relax.
2 With low shoulders, draw the shoulders backwards without hollowing the back and count three then relax. Repeat four to six times, then relax.
3 Fold arms behind back and tighten shoulders backwards three times, then relax. Repeat four to six times.

The Physical Approach

For the Arms

Above: *Exercises on the lunge should only be done with a suitably quiet horse. They are excellent for improving position.*

Below: *Energetic arm exercises should be done with the horse stationary. Circular movements can be done on the move.*

Bottom: *Exercises such as these are designed to loosen back and waist. The handler should hold the horse so that it remains still.*

For the arms, elbows and wrists to improve the posture and looseness of the arms and supple the elbows and wrists.

1 Swing one arm backwards in a slow, circular movement keeping the body and leg still and straight. Repeat six times then relax and change to the other arm. Both arms may then be swung slowly backwards, relax, then slowly forwards, relax, then back again. Be careful not to poke the head forward.

2 Raise both hands onto shoulders then raise upwards, back to shoulder, forwards, back to shoulder, sideways, back to shoulder. Repeat three times, then relax.

3 With hands out sideways away from the body, rotate the wrists and forearm out and round in a circular movement three or four times, then relax. Repeat three or four times.

For the waist and back to loosen and supple the body and help with balance.

1 Lean forwards bending from the waist towards the neck, come upright, lean back as far as possible and come upright. Repeat three or four times being sure to breathe

properly throughout. Take care that the leg position remains constant.

2 Lean forward and touch the toes and come upright again. Repeat on both sides three or four times.

3 Raise right arm above the head then lean forward and touch left toe, return to upright position, then relax. Raise left arm and touch right toe, upright and relax. Continue alternate arms, three or four times both sides.

4 With arms outstretched, swing body three times to the right and relax. Repeat three or four times both ways.

For the knee, leg and ankle to increase independence and suppleness of the joints.

1 Swing legs forwards and backwards slowly six times, then relax. Repeat six times.

2 Draw legs up and hold ankles with hands, pull upwards firmly three times, then relax. Repeat three times.

3 Take lower legs away from the horse and rotate feet inwards in a circular manner, then relax. Repeat the exercise this time rotating the feet in an outwards direction, then relax again.

For the Arms and Elbows

For the Waist and Back

Right: *Another good exercise for suppling both waist and back. Repeat with alternate arms three or four times on both sides.*

For balance a sitting trot on the lunge without stirrups or reins will help enormously. The handler should watch your position constantly and ask the horse to do frequent transitions from walk to trot and canter for experienced riders. Making sure you remain in balance with the movement of the horse throughout is the important factor. If you feel you are losing balance backwards, then incline the weight of your body a little further forwards until you can find your own centre of balance.

Exercises off the Lunge

These should be done with care to ensure that the horse does not get frightened at any time. Sitting without stirrups, being sure to always sink down into the saddle rather than tense up and draw upwards out of it, is always good practice as the exercise helps to stretch the legs down for the longer leg position required in dressage. Many of the single arm exercises featured here can be practised whilst controlling the horse with the other arm.

Shorter stirrups for jumping, trotting and cantering in the jumping position, whilst holding the reins away from the horse's neck and balancing only from your leg and knee, is excellent for increasing security and balance in the saddle. It is essential to keep the heel well down to develop a strong leg position.

Riding with short stirrups up and out of the saddle at the canter is good for strengthening thigh and back muscles and fairly long periods in this position will be extremely beneficial to the event rider preparing for a three-day event.

While all the above exercises will be of considerable help, particularly to those who are not as 'riding fit' as they might be, there is no substitute for general riding and schooling on an everyday basis. The top competition riders will be riding for hours on end. This means that they are in peak condition throughout the year and have a single-minded dedication to succeed, sometimes riding for up to 10 hours a day, in varied weather conditions and often on a wide variety of horses.

For the Knee and Leg

For the Waist and Back

Above: *Swinging the arms will help to loosen shoulders, and in this case the waist as well. Shoulders must be kept low.*

Below: *Little purpose is being achieved here since the rider's leg is drawing forward and up. The rein could be dangerous left loose.*

Above: *Swinging the leg forward and back loosens the knee and hip joints, but must only be done with the horse stationary.*

For the Knee and Leg

Above: *Drawing the ankles up and holding them helps to stretch the thigh muscles and loosen the knees. Do not overdo the stretch.*

For the Waist and Back

The Right Horse

Finding the right horse to do the job you have in mind can be a desperately disheartening pastime. One can search for years for the superstar to take you to the top, and looking back over the lists of champion horses and riders there are numerous names that have reached the top with one good horse but comparatively few have succeeded with two or more.

Sometimes it is the least likely animal that turns out to be the best and one has to be prepared to accept that, for most equestrian sports, the picture of the ideal dressage horse, show jumper or eventer seldom actually exists in reality. Many a world champion horse has had defects which would put anyone off buying them for one reason or another. So what is it that makes these horses succeed?

TEMPERAMENT

Over the years I have studied many top horses quite carefully and the one single factor that seems to always come to the fore is the character of each horse. Its temperamental make-up seems to me to be the one thing that stands out above all to make that horse 'special'. When talking to riders as to why they acquired a certain horse, so often the reply is that despite the faults there was 'just that something about him' which appealed to them.

What that 'something' is can be terribly hard to define but there is no doubt that when you look at a horse it is either the way it looks at you, holds its head or its general bearing that will strike you as being 'something different'. I must stress at this point that everybody has different ideas on what they like and while a less experienced rider may need guidance the professionals will see a horse with that 'something' and buy it on that quality alone, so long as it also possesses the necessary basic movement or jumping ability.

Conformation

The 'ideal horse' we have already decided does not often exist, but conformation is something that all riders will be looking at. A well balanced horse with good limbs and feet, sloping shoulders, strong back and quarters, a well set on neck and head with a generous eye is a good start.

Above right: Temperament is particularly important for dressage, and especially in the case of the eventer – it has to be supremely fit for the speed and endurance, but must be tension-free in the dressage.

Right: The cross-country is designed to test the horse's jumping ability as well as its agility, suppleness and boldness. The horse's conformation plays an important part in coping with today's demanding courses.

Left: Rachel Hunt and Friday Fox have an excellent record in horse trials, graduating together through junior to senior ranks. Despite her strange markings and diminutive size, the horse has that special quality.

The Right Horse

Limbs and Feet

These take a lot of strain in jumping, so any weakness here is not a good omen. Although the dressage horse is basically working on good flat ground all the time, the very nature of its training means it also takes considerable strain in its hocks. The show jumper also requires strength at this point as it springs off the ground. Hock weakness may cause problems as the training gets more strenuous. While it is not ideal, many good event horses have suffered no ill-effects from having curbs, but of course they do not require as much power from the hocks as in the other two disciplines.

Strong Quarters

These become the engine of the horse and strength over the back and loin area are particularly important for the dressage and jumping horse where such concentrated effort is required. The whole back should be wide, strong and level or slightly sloping on either side of the spine. Short backs are favoured by the dressage riders but reduce the capacity for speed, so the slightly rangier type is favoured by eventers. Horses with roached backs are seldom suitable for competitive work having a rather stilted action. Too long a back is liable to weakness.

It is very important to view the horse from behind to ensure the quarters are even and that the horse is equally developed down both sides to the hocks. The hocks and fetlock joints should be straight without turning out or in, causing strain and possible eventual injury, and the whole should look strong and in balance.

Ribs and Chest

The former should be well sprung and give a roundness to the body, and the withers should be well-defined with a good sloping shoulder so essential for free-flowing movement. The chest should be deep through the girth allowing plenty of room for heart and lungs. Shallow horses seldom seem thrifty, probably because there is insufficient room for really effective lung action. There should be plenty of room between the forelegs for strong pectoral muscles. This also ensures that the horse has 'a leg at each corner', which often goes with a sure-footed animal and one less likely to knock itself. A narrow chested horse with 'both legs coming out of the same hole' is undesirable as it is more difficult to balance and prone to injury.

Head and Neck

The head may vary widely depending on the type and breed of horse but should never be out of balance with the rest of the horse. The ears vary but supposedly large ones tend to indicate a generosity of character and 'lopped' ears are also a sign of a good horse. However, it is how they react which is more important and may give a useful guide to the temperament of the horse. Watch if they flicker back and forth in nervousness, have a bold forward look, are mostly back in boredom, tight back in aggressiveness. Ears can be quite a useful indication of the character of the horse along with the eye. The latter should be bold and generous looking with a pleasing general appearance. The face should be broad and, while its shape is not so important, a workmanlike appearance is preferred by jumpers and eventers. A narrow face is undesirable as it indicates lack of sufficient room for nasal tubes and the nostril should be wide and flaring to allow for adequate air intake. Pinched nostrils are undesirable for all competition horses.

The shape of the neck varies but should rise up from the withers and set off the head well. Its length and strength should be in balance with the rest of the body and it should be lightly crested. Stallions may have quite considerable crests. Ewe necks are quite unsuitable for competition work as they interfere with proper flexion so vital for balance and control, and low set on necks are not favoured. For dressage it is particularly important for the horse to have a well set on head and neck if training is not to be seriously hampered through inadequate conformation.

The Overall Picture

The whole horse should be looked at after studying each aspect carefully, to ensure that there is an overall picture of strength and compactness and that the whole presents a pleasing outlook. Narrow, weedy,

Right: *Running the horse up in hand is a very important part of an overall assessment. Straightness and good movement are key qualities, particularly when choosing a dressage or event horse.*

Desirable Conformation Points

Well-shaped neck

Well-shaped withers

Kind, intelligent eye

Workmanlike outlook

Sloping shoulder

Plenty of heart and lung room

Good bone

Strong, well-shaped feet

leggy, long-backed or necked animals will not make the robust competition horse required. Likewise the heavy, stuffy, straight-shouldered type will lack the quality to be able to perform at top levels.

Movement

Having studied the horse standing still, one then needs to assess how it moves. See the horse walk away and towards you and notice how straight it moves. Then see it trotting and look again at the straightness. This straightness is very important for the competition horse in all disciplines. For dressage in particular, straightness is essential as is regular, rhythmic movement with a certain degree of elevation. If this is there naturally, you are starting with an added advantage which no amount of training will ever quite attain.

The show jumper needs good movement ideally, but straightness above all else to prevent unnecessary injury, as does the eventer for the same reason. An attractive mover with some elevation to the trot is certainly a bonus nowadays when the dressage phase is playing such an important part in the sport.

Jumping Ability

This is an obvious essential for the show jumper and eventer. When trying out a horse it is often difficult to assess exactly what it is capable of, but the essentials to look for are bravery, technique and ability. How much of this can be assessed with a young or very green horse is hard to say, but if you like the horse, your own intuition may be the best thing to rely on.

See the horse over a small fence and watch its attitude. See it over an upright, which can be gradually raised. Then see it over a parallel and watch its technique: is it careful, how does it use its forearms, how does it use its head and neck over the fence and, if it is athletic, does the horse seem to enjoy it? If it makes a mistake how does it react to the fence the next time?

The Partnership

If you still like the horse by this time, try it yourself and see if it gives a good feel generally. Does it feel the right size for you, is it strong or does it need to be pushed; does it seem the right sort of horse for you as a person? Will your temperament suit it and vice versa? A timid rider on a timid horse seldom spells success, but many a timid rider put on a very confident and often rather overbold horse will settle into being the perfect partnership. Dominant riders are best not put on the temperamental types, which usually go best for the non-interfering type of rider. An uncertain horse is most suited to the strong rider who will often bring out the very best in that animal.

Below: *The technique used by this athletic horse would be the envy of many. Bringing the forearm up to clear the fence is an important point to notice when assessing the show jumper's competition prospects.*

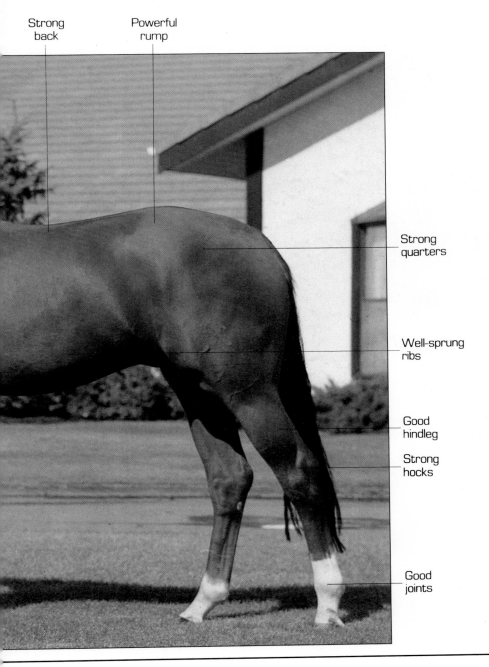

Strong back

Powerful rump

Strong quarters

Well-sprung ribs

Good hindleg

Strong hocks

Good joints

Above: HM The Queen's great eventer, Columbus, ridden by Captain Mark Phillips, won Badminton and was in the lead at the World Championships when a damaged hock muscle virtually ended his career.

Left: Ferdi Eilberg, British team trainer, shows how the heavier built horses can excel at dressage where their temperament and impressive regular movement can really impress the judges to get top marks.

Below: The agility of the smaller horses can often make up for the lack of size if they possess the necessary courage. The diminutive Tutin is one of many small horses which have excelled in show jumping.

Above: *Eventing has also produced several small champions, one of the most attractive being New Zealand's Charisma, Olympic gold medallist in 1984, ridden by Mark Todd who certainly makes it appear very small!*

Right: *Ireland has produced a lot of good horses of all shapes and sizes which have done particularly well in the jumping and eventing fields. Here, Rockbarton and Gerry Mullins show great style in the jump-off.*

Below: *The lighter, more quality horse is generally favoured in America, for show jumping in particular where they have a very impressive record, regularly winning medals and a great run in the World Cup.*

Above: *The fitness of this horse is clearly demonstrated making it appear lighter in build than is in fact the case. Good bone, straight movement and abundant courage is required from the eventer.*

Right: *For dressage, movement, suppleness and a good, receptive temperament are so necessary if you are to succeed and reach the top levels. Careful training and a gradual build up help achieve the rest.*

Management and Training Techniques

Training is the most important part of all horsemanship. Without it, the rider becomes tired and unbalanced. The unprepared horse's muscles tire very quickly and give way. The horse becomes unbalanced and strains a tendon.

The horseman must pay great attention to detail in the stable. Study what is normal in your own horse. If there is any change, you must decide the severity of the symptoms and act accordingly. Do not ignore anything.

A proven star horse can only perform as he is ridden. Without correct, balanced riding, sympathy and understanding, a horse quickly loses confidence in his rider and will become upset and unhappy. The same applies to dressage. If the rider is out of balance with the horse and has an incorrect seat, the horse tenses his back against the pain inflicted by the bad rider, and this in turn makes him even more difficult to sit on. A good horseman never stops learning, and it is this quest for knowledge which is so important to the well-being of the horse and the success of the rider.

Jennie Loriston-Clarke

General Management

Whilst this book does not intend to go too deeply into the general care of horses, there are certain basic factors which are pertinent to the well-being of the competition horse. The following chapter gives practical advice on all the relevant aspects of producing a horse ready to perform in peak condition.

To understand the horse's basic needs, you must remember that it is a herbivorous creature, and would be roaming and eating at will if left to nature. The horse's stomach is relatively small and its system was designed to cope with often eating rather basic herbage. Through man's domestication, the stabled horse has had to adapt to being confined for most of the day as well as learning to cope with often quite concentrated feed. The horse has taken to this change remarkably well both physically and mentally but horsemastership plays a very big part towards competitive success.

THE STABLE

This must be roomy, warm without draughts, safe and secure. The horse needs enough room to be able to move about and roll, with 3 × 3.7 metres (10 × 12 feet) being the minimum size necessary for the average 16.1 hh horse. The larger the better from the horse's point of view, 3.7 × 3.7 metres (12 × 12 feet) to 4.3 × 4.3 metres (14 × 14 feet) or larger providing a very spacious stable. Warmth is important, so the box should not be draughty nor face into very exposed areas, but must have adequate ventilation.

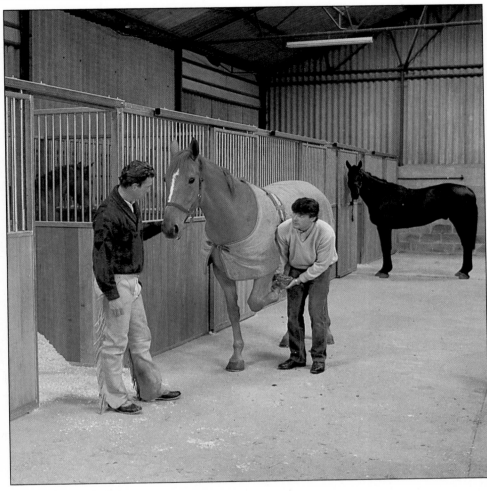

Left: These stables have been painted and decorated to enhance their otherwise somewhat basic appearance with great effect. A little careful thought can help tremendously in making the most of your stable-yard and creating a good impression.

Above: The indoor-barn type stabling is becoming more and more popular. It is very easy to work in, especially where weather conditions prove rather unpredictable. The boxes shown have been assembled inside an existing agricultural building.

Below: This line of stables has been put up at the back of a large barn. The over-hang of the roof keeps the horses and grooms dry. The two taps in weather-proof boxes save a lot of carrying to and fro. Tie-up rings are an added bonus for general care.

Bedding

Straw, shavings, sawdust, peat, tan or paper are all popular. Paper is ideal for horses prone to respiratory problems; straw is the warmest and most attractive. Deep litter or the continental system involves a generous base with only the droppings being picked up with fresh straw sprinkled on top. This is very warm and labour-saving.

All these types of bedding are good so long as they are kept as dry and as clean as possible. Allowing a bed to get wet is not only poor horsemanship but can have a seriously detrimental effect on the feet and general well-being of the horse. For this reason, good drainage should be a priority when designing stables and will make an enormous difference to the daily mucking out chores. Bedding should be banked at the sides to prevent injury.

Security

This is essential, so a good strong stable with adequate bolts is a crucial item, with a bottom flip-over catch as a sensible precaution. Many horses try and often manage to open their doors, so do be alert to this possibility. There are various designs on the market which are supposed to prevent such happenings but some horses are very persistent and remarkably adept at opening their stable doors, often at extremely inconvenient times!

Safety

The importance of safety cannot be overstated. Any protruding nails or sharp edges must be removed or smoothed over. Remember, some horses love to roll frequently and will manage to get themselves cast if there is anything likely to hinder them. Also, if the box is on the small side, this can often be a contributory factor. In many stables, the sides of the box are rubberized or may have horizontal grooves from 0.5 to 1 metre (18 inches to 3 feet) enabling the horse to get a grip and so push itself up or away from the wall, thus allowing it the space to get up again. Horses prone to getting cast should have plenty of bedding. An anti-cast roller with a hoop may help to prevent the horse rolling right over and getting itself trapped.

Any fittings in the box should be up high out of the way. A tie ring for securing the horse, and for a haynet, if used, is the one essential fitting required. If automatic watering devices are used, be sure these are high enough and well protected. Fixed mangers should be smooth and preferably across a corner with any gap underneath filled in.

Electrical fittings should never be inside the box or near where the horse can chew at them. They should be well covered and all flex should be safely threaded through tubing to ensure that no loose or exposed wires can ever be tampered with. Electrocution and electrically-caused fires are hazards which should never arise if care and forethought go into the planning of stables, and subsequent maintenance is properly

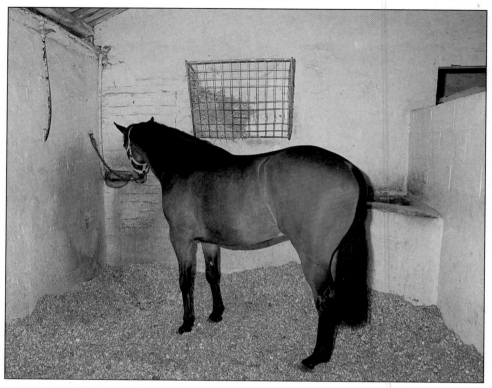

Above: *This horse is tied up on a chain; a rope can be easily chewed. The stable has a bed of shavings, a nicely-rounded, built-in manger and an automatic water bowl. The water pipe on the left-hand wall could be chewed or bent by the horse.*

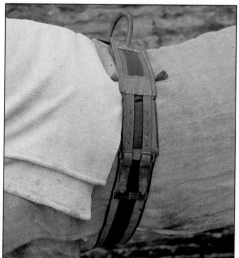

Left: *The hooped, anti-cast roller is useful in helping to prevent horses getting cast, especially those that like to roll. In theory, it prevents the animal rolling right over and getting stuck. However, some horses still manage to get themselves cast!*

Below: *This horse is being strapped with a strapping pad to increase circulation and tone in the long muscles of the neck, shoulders and quarters. The full effect of contraction and relaxation is only achieved if a slow, even rhythm is maintained.*

carried out. It is barely necessary to state how distressing and usually fatal such accidents can be.

Fire is, of course, always a tremendous worry as so many of the traditional stables are made of wood. But with obvious precautions, such as safe electrics as just mentioned and forbidding smoking in the stable area, the risk will be reduced to the minimum. Fire-fighting equipment should always be at hand, however, and a sensible fire drill worked out so that everyone knows exactly how to react should the unexpected happen. A word here about horses' reactions to fire is worth bearing in mind. All animals are terrified of fire and the horse is no exception. They tend to become rooted to the spot and may be extremely difficult to move or become disorientated and rush back towards it if there is no obvious way of escape.

GENERAL CARE

Having discussed the stable and safety aspects of management, we can now return to caring for the horse. There will always be room for improvement in your general care routine.

Grooming

Regular grooming is required to keep your horse's coat in top condition. It also acts as a massage to the skin helping to increase its elasticity and tone.

Strapping with a wisp acts as a massage to strengthen and harden the muscles. It should be used on the hard, flat muscles along the neck and quarters. The wisp should be used slightly dampened and brought down with a vigorous 'bang' onto the muscles in the direction of the coat. The secret is to do it slowly enough to let the muscles contract as the wisp hits the body and then allow time for relaxation before repeating: in the form of, for example, *one* (bang), *and* (wait for relaxation), *two* (bang), *and* (wait), etc. Done this way, it will help to develop the muscles. All wisping should be done gradually

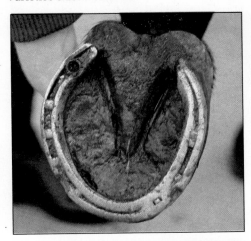

Below: *Proper care of the feet is vital to the success of all competition horses. The shoe must be made to fit the horse, rather than the reverse, and should be of a suitable weight and shape for the work.*

Middle: *Studs are extremely useful to help the horse to get a good grip. These different sized studs and the tools to fit them are typical of those found in the UK, but many varieties exist worldwide.*

Below: *These four, well turned-out horses demonstrate just a few of the many different types of rugs, rollers and fastenings available on the market today. They each have various useful attributes to recommend them.*

starting with about 10 bangs on each side and building up steadily to a hundred bangs. All competition horses will benefit by this process, particularly on the quarters which is really where the power is needed when grooming daily.

Feet and Shoes

The use of the hoof pick before and after exercise goes without saying, but it is important to inspect the feet and shoes carefully, not only to make sure that the condition of the foot is healthy but also to check that the correct angle of the foot is maintained through proper and regular shoeing.

The farrier plays a major part towards the competition horse's soundness and success, and close liaison with him is well worthwhile. Study your horse's action together and work out if there are any adjustments to the type, weight or setting of the shoe which might be of benefit to your horse in its particular role. The ground conditions can make quite a difference to some horses and seasonal changes might be advisable. Horses that brush, tend to slip, dish, swing a leg, etc can all be helped quite considerably by your farrier over a period of time if you work together on spotting and correcting such problems.

The choice of shoes and the type of studs used vary from country to country, as does the positioning of the studs. Some people prefer one stud, others two in each foot. There are theories for and against these differing practices, but finally your choice must be determined by what works for you and your horse.

The size and shape of the studs used varies according to the ground, but generally speaking large studs are used in soft ground and smaller, sharper ones on the hard going. There are numerous different styles to choose from but safety plays a big part. Therefore, choose ones that you think will assist the horse but not damage it in any way should it fall, since some stud designs are rather too sharp.

Rugs

Keeping the horse warm is essential if it is not to use up all its energy stores; a cold horse is never a happy one. In hot climates, it becomes more a matter of keeping the animal cool and ensuring there is plenty to drink to compensate for the dehydrating effects of over-heating.

In more temperate climates and in very cold weather, rugs are necessary for providing extra warmth for the stabled horse as well as for those horses that have been clipped recently or lack sufficient coat and are turned out.

The main types of rug consist of day and night rugs of different materials as well as blankets, all designed to keep the horse warm. New Zealand rugs are warm and waterproof and are meant solely for horses out at grass. They are designed to be non-slip with leg straps and special fastenings to keep them in place. Summer sheets protect the horse from dust and flies, or act as an under-sheet to protect rugs and blankets from natural grease. Anti-sweat rugs are useful for the wet horse, allowing air to circulate a little even if rugs are placed on top. They are also good put on under other rugs for warmth or for horses likely to break out after strenuous work.

The fitting of rugs is terribly important as far too often one sees horses with sore withers, shoulders and rub marks elsewhere. This should be preventable if the rug fits properly. It may be necessary to sew some sheepskin on to the rug to protect withers and shoulders. But with the many varieties of lightweight rug now on the market, this sort of pressure problem is hopefully confined only to some of the heavier kinds of rug. Some rugs are shaped to fit a certain size of horse; care must be taken to ensure that they are in fact the right shape for your horse otherwise they will pull in all the wrong places. When choosing it is worth remembering that you will probably need a rug at least 3in (7.6cm) longer than the traditional type. These lightweight rugs usually come with adjustable cross-over straps or with leg straps which make the use of rollers unnecessary.

Above: *These horses and riders are well protected against the elements wearing water-proof sheets and kneecaps while they are doing the early slow work at the start of their fitness programme.*

Below: *This horse has been given a type of blanket clip. This clip is very useful for horses that go out in the field a lot, or for those not involved in very hard work during the winter.*

Rollers, if not correctly padded, can cause pressure on the spine and it is obviously to the horse's advantage if they can be dispensed with. However, sometimes extra blankets are required under a rug and the roller is really the only way to secure these. A good wither pad should help to prevent any pressure problems arising.

New Zealand rugs are a boon for those horse owners who want to turn their horses out in the cold weather, and there is no doubt that all horses enjoy a few hours out in the field. It relaxes them and gives them a break from routine work as well as acting as a reward after some intensive schooling. There are now a variety of hoods – pullover, stretch types or tie-on ones – which reduce the problems of horses coming in from the field plastered with mud, a situation not appreciated by staff coping with a busy yard. By putting a hood on with the New Zealand, your horse can enjoy its spell in the field without being the cause of a major clean-up session afterwards.

Clipping

This is essential for horses in serious competition work if they possess thick coats. Horses in hot climates tend to have very fine coats anyway and may be all right for most of the year. The main reasons for clipping are to enable a horse to do more work without

getting too hot, and to prevent loss of condition through excessive sweating. While it is obviously easier to look after a clipped horse, it also dries quicker and thus reduces the risk of chills from a long wet coat which can take some time to dry.

Generally horses are clipped once their winter coat has appeared and are then reclipped as necessary. Do not clip too close to when the summer coat is going to come through. How often one needs to clip depends entirely on the horse and the work it is doing. It is worth thinking of your long-term plan of training and competition work so that your horse has its maximum coat during its easy months if the weather is likely to be cold. The competition horse will inevitably have periods of strenuous training or the competitions themselves, and during these times the less extra coat and heavy sweating it does the better, particularly in hot weather.

Most competition horses are given either a full or hunter clip. Visually for the dressage horse the full clip may be better, but for jumpers and eventers the extra protection given by not clipping the legs is an advantage, particularly for the latter. Leaving a saddle patch gives just a little extra protection to the back for the dressage and event horse. For horses having to do hours of slow work during the winter months to harden up legs and tendons, such as the

Above: *A groom's best friends, these hoods and weatherproof rugs not only keep the horse warm and dry but also stop it getting too dirty. Turning out whenever possible is very relaxing for the competition horse.*

Below: *Teeth care is very important, not only for effective mastication, but to ensure the bit and bridle cause no discomfort from sharp hooks on the teeth, affecting the horse's way of going.*

eventer, a blanket or racing clip can be used or a paddock sheet worn to keep the horse's back warm during the important preliminary build-up to peak fitness.

Vaccinations and Inoculations

These are particularly important for the competition horse who comes up against large numbers of horses from not only a national competition world but also the international scene. Because of this, the risk of various bugs and diseases from different parts of the world is an added problem and while many horses may have built up a natural immunity to the local varieties, they may be very badly affected by an alien variety unless they have been adequately protected.

All horses need tetanus protection and most countries now insist on equine flu vaccinations. Be sure you are quite clear on how and when these have to be given; two preliminary doses are required, followed by a third approximately six months later with yearly boosters thereafter. For international competition horses requiring an FEI passport, these particulars must be recorded, stamped and conform exactly to the FEI requirements.

While different countries obviously need different requirements, such as Coggins test against infectious equine anaemia, which is usual in the USA and required by all horses when entering most foreign countries. It is always worth checking with your veterinarian whether it would be prudent to take precautions of one sort or another when competing regularly, especially if you are involved in the international scene. It must always be better to be safe than sorry and your horse will certainly appreciate simple methods of prevention rather than cure.

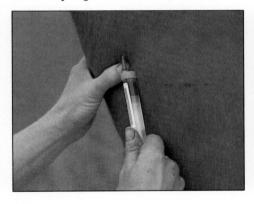

Above: *Blood is being taken from this horse for analysis. All horses require a rigid programme of vaccination against the various diseases. These must be recorded in passports or on official certificates.*

Below: *This chart can be used as a reminder for vaccination, worming and teeth care. In-between the broad spectrum wormers, other types should be used to give a regular eight-week cycle of worming.*

Teeth Care

This, along with worming, is vital not just for the horse's general health, but also because the sharp edges can affect its way of going, causing soreness and ulceration in the mouth. Teeth should be rasped (floated) twice a year and any rough edges smoothed

Worming, Vaccination and Teeth Care

MONTH	WORMING	TEETH	FLU/VACS/ETC
January		Rasp	Vaccinate
March	Broad Spectrum		
May			
July	Broad Spectrum	Check	Check
September			
November	Broad Spectrum		

off by the horse dentist or veterinarian. If a horse is seen to have difficulty with eating or chewing or tends to drop a lot of food out of its mouth, it is worth getting its teeth checked. If the horse is very unhappy in its mouth when schooling, it may well mean that there are some rough edges causing discomfort, or there may be wolf teeth present which will need removing.

Worming

An important part of the horse care routine, worming should be carried out on a regular six to eight-week cycle. A regime of worming should be discussed with the veterinarian if necessary but must be religously carried out. All horses have worms to a certain degree and the belief that stabled horses do not have worms is both ignorant and naive. Depending on the country and time of year, worms are generally at their most active during the spring and summer and an extra strong broad spectrum dose at the beginning of the spring and end of the summer is considered a wise precaution. Check that whatever brand of wormer used is effective against all the general types of worm, including red worm and bots which are two of the most debilitating worms found in horses.

If your horse looks dull and stary in its coat or has a slight pot-bellied appearance, your first concern should be to check that it has not got a heavy worm infestation. No horse will compete successfully unless it is in top condition, and a wormy one will not only be off-colour but the effects of a large infestation may cause anaurisms and severe internal damage leading to all sorts of problems later on.

First Aid

Be sure to have your first aid cupboard well stocked up with poultices, antiseptic solutions and sprays, wound powder, dry non-stick dressings, a thermometer, antiseptic creams, salt for cleansing wounds and plenty of cotton wool, gamgee, bandages and a good pair of scissors. Inevitably cuts and bruises may happen at any time, but immediate treatment and care will ensure that problems do not worsen and are given the best possible chance to improve. Have your veterinarian's telephone number placed in a prominent position so that everyone knows how to contact him or her immediately, should the need arise.

FEEDING

Feeding is a specialized subject and there are many different ideas on what and how to feed horses. What is very important for the competition horse is that it is obtaining enough of the *right* food, minerals and trace elements to produce consistent performance with the minimum of effort.

Right: *This contented and healthy-looking horse is enjoying its feed in a corner manger. These should be removable for easy cleaning and care taken to ensure no rough edges develop as they get older and worn.*

First Aid for Home Use

Thermometer
Antiseptic Solution
Bowl
Cotton wool
Poultices
Kaolin/plastic/paper
Bandages – gamgee
Non-stick dressings
Wound powder
Wound spray
Colic drench
Cough electuary
Scissors
Vet's number in prominent place

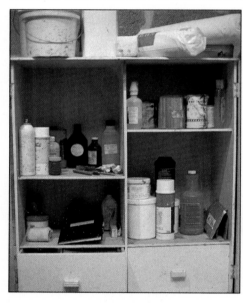

Top: *A simple list of items which should be available in your first aid cupboard. There are many additional items which individual stables may use regularly.*

Above: *This first aid cupboard is stocked with quite a variety of different potions to treat the everyday-type of injury or ailment. Check regularly to see what needs replenishing so that you never run out.*

First, let us consider the basic principles of feeding. Food and water are essential for survival. They are necessary for the growth and development of the horse and to supply the energy for that horse to work.

Water

A horse cannot survive for long without water, and so this has to be the number one priority. Water should be freely available at all times and be clear and fresh. Depending on how water is available for the horse, water containers must be kept clean. Buckets can be placed on the floor in the corner of a box away from hay and mangers, or hung up for the horse that likes to play and knock them over. Automatic drinking bowls need to be checked each day and are labour-saving, but they have the disadvantage of preventing the horse from taking a full drink and the groom from knowing how much water is being taken, which can sometimes be an indication of illness.

Water should not be given before strenuous work and, depending on the weather conditions, is best removed between two to four hours before work. A stomach full of water or a big feed will press on the diaphragm and may interfere with breathing and cause discomfort leading to colic.

If the horse has had its water restricted, be careful that it does not gorge itself when it is made available. Offer small drinks of a quarter to a half a bucket at a time every 10 minutes or so until it is fully satisfied. Do not give icy cold water to a hot horse; always just take the chill off.

Remember that water makes up approximately fifty per cent of the adult horse's body. It is a means of nutrition as well as excretion, and aids digestion and circulation as well as maintain correct body temperatures. A horse drinks between 27–54 litres (6–12 gallons) of water a day obviously requiring more in hot weather. While running water or fresh rain water is best and leaves the coat looking soft and glossy, this is rarely available. Moderately hard water contains lime and magnesium as well as salts and is more refreshing than soft water. Very hard water affects horses in a similar way to humans, leaving them with a harsh coat and skin which can be corrected when softer water is used.

Some horses can be affected by a change in the water, such as when away competing, and this may present a problem. If just away for a day or two, it is possible to take a large churn of home water with you, but on longer trips this is obviously not practical. If this fairly rare problem does ever present itself, it may be worth varying your horse's water once a day sometimes giving rain water and sometimes tap water, if this is practical. Take a large container of home water and mix it with the strange water for a couple of days so that there is a more gradual change-over. Never forget, though, that water is essential to all life and therefore must be given careful consideration should you ever come up against a problem such as a metabolic disorder, a dehydration problem or dry, pinched skin conditions.

The Main Constituents

Food requirements vary tremendously according to age, the type of horse, the work being done, the weather and, if turned out, the condition of the land as a source of sustenance.

To mature and be capable of work, the horse requires the following in its daily diet.

Proteins which are vital for the maintenance and build up of body tissues. Any excess of protein gets stored in the body and used as energy. Proteins are absorbed into the body in the form of amino acids of which there are 23 known varieties. Out of these, 10 are considered essential for a horse's diet. Not all protein, however, has these 'essentials' which adds to the complications of feeding the competition horse. Animal proteins tend to have higher values than plant proteins, which are responsible for most of the traditional diet fed to horses such as hay and oats.

The important factor, however, is to feed a balanced diet giving enough protein to complement the energy content derived from carbohydrates. The competition horse requires only a slight increase in protein to make up for the extra work it does as it gets fitter, to complement the energy it receives from its carbohydrate intake. Feeding high levels of protein is pointless and expensive as the excess is not used but broken down and used as alternative energy.

Carbohydrates are the horse's main means of heat and energy and include sugar, starch and fibre. The basic form is sugar which, when broken down in the digestive process, is absorbed through the small intestines as glucose. This is stored as glycogen and fat and is used as required by the muscles during exercise.

Starch is the major source of energy and is found in plants, roots and cereals. It makes up an important part of the diet.

Fibre or roughage comes from the cellulose part of plants and is an important source of energy in the grass-fed horse. Fibre is essential in giving the horse's system the bulk it requires to aid and stimulate the digestive process. The main source of fibre is hay or grass in whatever form.

Fats are a highly concentrated food source which provide warmth and energy as well as insulation. Nowadays, fats are being seriously considered as a more useful source of energy and less likely to cause problems such as laminitis and azoturia often associated with an excess of carbohydrate. Fats and oils in the diet are reflected in the skin and those horses on a higher intake of fats have wonderful glossy coats. It is best not to overfeed fat in hot weather as it can affect natural evaporation of heat due to the efficient insulation produced. Overfat horses are put at a definite disadvantage in the heat and efforts to reduce this should be taken. An overfat horse is never really fit.

Proteins, carbohydrates and fats, along with water, make up the main constituents of

Top: *There are so many different types of food being fed around the world depending on local availability, but those shown here are fairly common everywhere. Whatever is fed must be of good quality and fresh.*

Above: *Grass is the horse's natural food and every opportunity should be taken to give it as much as possible. If the horse cannot be turned out, hand grazing for half an hour a day is very beneficial.*

the horse's diet. But these are useless unless certain minerals, vitamins and trace elements are included to ensure that proper utilization and biological processes take place.

Minerals

These include calcium, phosphorous, magnesium, sodium, manganese, iodine, copper, iron, zinc, chlorine, cobalt and selenium and are all essential for correct metabolism. A deficiency in any one can affect the horse and its performance in a variety of ways.

It is incredibly difficult sometimes to pinpoint the systems of mineral deficiency. The horse may look well and be generally in good health, but will just not perform quite as it should despite careful check-ups on all the usual problem areas. In such cases it is worth having blood tests taken to see if there is a lack of an obscure element in the diet and then compensate for this by feeding a suitable, corrective supplement.

Certain areas of the country will be high in some minerals and low in others and this will inevitably be reflected in the food grown. Modern farming methods mean that sprays and chemicals are used widely on animal fodder which often alters or affects its feeding value, and the intensive methods used eventually deplete the soil of certain minerals.

The most usual deficiencies tend to be calcium, phosphorous, magnesium and sodium chloride. The latter, being common salt, is likely to follow heavy sweating and can be corrected by prompt use of electrolytes. Common trace element deficiencies include selenium, zinc, manganese and iodine.

The vital roles played by individual nutrients in keeping horses in good condition are outlined below.

Calcium and phosphorous are both essential for sound bone structure and are involved in other important body functions. The correct ratio of calcium to phosphorous is essential to the metabolism of both nutrients. If the intake of phosphorous is greater than that of calcium, the absorption of calcium may be reduced resulting in calcium deficiencies. The calcium phosphorous ratio in the diet should not be less than 1:1. Ratios of up to 6:1 are not detrimental to mature horses so long as the phosphorous intake is adequate.

Signs of deficiency or excess include poor mineralization and bone deposition in the developing foal, crooked and enlarged joints or weakening of the bones and shifting lameness, especially connected with the hocks. Excess phosphorous with low calcium levels is common with high-grain diets and can result in osteofibrosis symptomized by enlarged head and jaw in severe cases.

Magnesium The mature horse requires at least 8–13 mg of dietary magnesium per 1 kg (2.2 lb) of body weight per day purely for maintenance alone, and this is vital for proper bone and tooth development. Deficiency can cause serious problems with

A Typical Compound Feed

Barley meal
Wheat meal
Maize meal and maize germ meal
Oatmeal
Dry extruded whole soybean meal
Calcium Carbonate
Sodium Chloride
DI Calcium Phosphate
Magnesium Oxide
Sodium Sulphate
Sodium Bicarbonate
Sulphur
Potassium Sulphate
Magnesium Sulphate
Manganese Sulphate
Zinc Sulphate
Copper Sulphate
Iron Sulphate
Potassium Iodate
Cobaltous Sulphate
Choline Chloride
Sodium Selenite
Niacin
Vitamin A supplement
Vitamin D3 supplement
Vitamin E supplement
Thiamin
Vitamin B1 supplement
Riboflavin
Vitamin B2 supplement
Folacin
Vitamin B1 2 supplement

the developing foal. Horses which are involved in heavy work or endurance competitions may benefit from a higher intake of magnesium.

Sodium and potassium help control the fluid balance in the body and are important for blood formation and digestion. Deficiency can show as tiredness, dry skin and a pinched look around the nostrils with large hollows above the eye. In hot weather or if the horse is sweating profusely and in heavy work, 28.35 g (1 oz) of extra salt should be given in the diet daily.

Iron and copper are essential for the formation of haemoglobin which is responsible for the oxygen content in the blood.

Left: *A typical analysis of ingredients which are to be found in compound feed, including vitamins and trace elements. These are necessary for the proper utilization of the foods during digestion.*

Above right: *Three buckets of typical feed: bran, oats and nuts. Good quality food and a thorough understanding of its value and how it can affect the horse are essential to successful stable management.*

Right: *Sugarbeet pulp nuts should be soaked in water overnight before being fed as a high-energy food. Many horses have died of colic from unsoaked sugarbeet. Note the difference in volume soaked and unsoaked.*

Below: *Feeding time requires some thought and each horse must be fed according to the work being done taking age, size and temperament into account. All food should be stored in vermin-proof containers.*

Copper is needed for the formation of a wide variety of blood tissues and for the utilization of iron. Some fetlock swellings have been attributed to the lack of copper. Good levels are important for growing foals and breeding stock which develop and mature early. Deficiency symptoms include anaemia and impaired reproductive performance. Poor bone formation is also attributed to copper deficiency. White or non-pigmented patches appearing on the face and body may also be related.

Manganese and zinc help activate the enzymes which break up food during digestion and contribute towards maintaining the health and condition of the skin and coat. The availability of manganese in the soil is greatly influenced by the pH level, high pH levels often being low in manganese.

Iodine is an essential part of the hormone thyroxin which is responsible for governing the rate of the body's metabolism.

Selenium is thought to help prevent cell damage and has been useful in preventing azoturia. Recent research has shown that by increasing the level of selenium in the diet of racehorses they have produced improved racing performance, reduced respirations

and a better general condition. This may be due to better oxygen utilization. Some nutritionalists recommend selenium and vitamin E as supplements for the high-performance horse.

The pH factor can play a part in the levels found in certain pastures with a Ph of 6.8 being the recommended normal. Recent research has shown that a slightly lower level of 6.5 may increase copper availability without affecting other factors. A high pH can cause all sorts of aggravations. Acid soils usually have low calcium levels resulting in an imbalance of the important calcium to phosphorus ratio.

Vitamins

These are essential for the normal metabolism of the body functions. Vitamins occur naturally in freshly-grown foods. The most important of these are detailed in the following text.

Vitamin A is found in fresh plants; the carrotene is converted into vitamin A. The stabled horse tends to lack this, so care should be taken to ensure adequate green fodder is available if poor feet, reduced resistance to infection and nervousness are not to result.

Vitamin B is a complex vitamin and is necessary to maintain the blood in good order. It is not stored in the body but can be greatly affected by lack of other essential nutrients.

Vitamin C is essential to maintain good health and is supplied by the bacteria in the gut from fresh foods.

Vitamin D is produced by the horse with the aid of sunlight and for this reason a supplement may be necessary if the horse is kept indoors all winter, even though adequate supplies are found in good quality hay.

Vitamin E is found in fresh foods and is essential for stamina and high performance. It reduces nervousness (and may help in' cases of azoturia) along with selenium, which is necessary to produce the enzyme used by the vitamin.

Vitamin K is essential for normal blood clotting and is present in green food as well as being made by bacteria in the digestive tract.

Types of Feed

Oats are the most important and traditionally used diet for the horse. They must be of good quality, plump, dust-free and with a clean, slightly sweet smell. They should be fed slightly bruised to break the husk, which is extremely tough. Bruising should be done not more than a month before being consumed if the food value is not to deteriorate. It is worth ensuring that your corn merchant does this on the premises, or installing your own machine so that you know that this is a freshly performed process. Some people boil oats and this increases digestibility and is particularly useful for horses in poor condition and warming in very cold weather.

Oats make up for most of the horse's concentrate requirements but do have a poor calcium to phosphorous ratio and are known to be low in methionine and lysine, important amino acids.

Barley is more fattening than oats and has a higher energy content. It should be full, clean and rounder than oats. Barley must not be fed whole but may be rolled, which tends to make it rather crumbly and dusty; boiled, which is highly palatable; or micronized, which is becoming the most popular method. In this instance, the barley is put through a heat-treating process. Barley is considered less 'heating' than oats and more suitable for the excitable horse and, although difficult to explain why, many horses appear to be more amenable on barley rather than oats. Like oats, barley also has a poor calcium to phosphorous ratio.

Bran used to be fed in much higher quantities but the discovery that it inhibits calcium absorption has meant that it is now much less popular. Bran has a low energy content and consists of the inner husk of the wheat grain. Only good quality bran should be used which should be good broad flakes, pinkish in colour and have a sweet smell. Bran acts as a filler and a hot bran mash is a useful way of feeding the sick or resting horse, since it has a low energy content. Fed in this form, the bran mash has a slightly laxative effect but when fed dry it can be an effective 'binder'.

Chaff or chop is fed as roughage and is a useful addition to the feed. It also helps prevent the greedy horse eating too fast. Usually made in a cutter, hay and sometimes a small quantity of straw are mixed together to produce chop. This is often blended with molasses to give added value and to increase its palatability.

Maize along with oats and barley is a high-energy cereal and is usually fed flaked or micronized. Thought to be quite heating and possibly the cause of small, flat lumps appearing under a horse's skin, it is perhaps less popular than it was.

Peas and beans are high in protein as well as energy content and are a popular addition to the increasingly used coarse mixes. They are fed either split, crushed or micronized and are highly palatable.

Linseed comes from the flax plant. The seed should be flat, small and shiny. It has a high protein and fat content and is excellent for keeping the coat glossy. Linseed is fed boiled and needs careful preparation as it is essential that the seeds split and the jelly-like liquid is produced. It is fed either hot or cold with a bran mash or normal feed. The linseed should be soaked well for at least eight hours and then brought to the boil and simmered for an hour or until the seeds have split.

Sugar-beet pulp is a highly digestable fibre with high energy content and is extremely palatable. It is essential that it is well soaked overnight. Roughly two-thirds to one scoop will require a whole bucket of water as it swells dramatically.

It is vital to store sugarbeet pulp securely in case a horse gets loose or into the feed area since, if eaten in its dry form, it could have disastrous consequences for the horse. With its high calcium to phosphorus ratio it can help to right the imbalance caused by some cereals such as bran.

Compound feeds are those which have been specially prepared to produce a balanced ration and come in the form of cubes (nuts) and coarse mixes.

Cubes come in quite a variety designed either as a 'complete' feed to be fed alone – these contain the forage and concentrates necessary for the horse's diet – or in a concentrated form to be fed with hay or other normal roughage. Some are designed purely for their protein content for use with other cereals and come in a variety of percentages ranging from the horse and pony nuts of about 9–11 per cent up to the stud and racing cubes containing between 22 and 26 per cent.

A Typical Coarse Mix

Oil 3.1 %
Protein 10.8%
Fibre 10.0%
Ash 8.0%
Vitamin A 8000 iu/kg
Vitamin D3 1000 iu/kg
Vitamin E
alpha tocopherol 15 iu/kg
Copper 12 mg/kg
(Cupric Sulphate added)

The coarse or sweet mixes are designed to be fed alone with hay. They consist of a variety of oats, barley, cubes, peas, beans etc and are very palatable. Although there are different grades suitable for horses in different types of work, the high-performance horse may require more energy and protein so more individual feeding is usual.

Hay

Bulk must make up a proportion of the horse's diet and while a horse in light work may eat up to approximately 70 per cent bulk food such as grass or hay, the high-performance horse will be requiring as little as 25–30 per cent bulk, the remainder of its diet being made up of concentrates. Hay is the traditional method of conserving grass for feeding to the stabled horse. It must be remembered, however, that hay will only be as good as the original grass from which it was made. Therefore, it is worth checking your land to ensure it contains essential nutrients if making your own hay so that you can judge what extra supplements may be required in your horse's diet. Hay-making is a specialist art and while there is relatively little difference in the energy content of good and not so good hay it is the protein content that can vary dramatically. How the hay is made and when it is cut will determine the protein content.

There are three main types of hay: meadow, seeds and lucerne (alfalfa).

Meadow hay is soft and made from permanent pasture and usually has a fairly low protein content.

Seeds hay, made from rye grass-based mixtures, is a coarser and harder hay crop with a higher protein value. Because of the harder stems, it is vital that a good drying spell of weather allows the stems to really dry out before baling as natural drying, if properly done, produces much better value hay than that done artificially in a barn. This is probably best for the competition horse.

Lucerne hay is made from a legume and has a particularly high protein value and should be used in small amounts. This is used mostly to supplement other hay or partial grass diets.

Silage and Haylage

In their various forms, these are becoming increasingly popular and because of the way they are made tend to have a higher feeding value than hay.

Left: *The power and strength of the horse can be clearly seen during this canter uphill demonstrating the need for proper care and feeding so that it can perform whatever is required with ease. The glossy coat and rounded muscle on this animal are indications of good stable management.*

Below left: *Analysis tags are to be found on most bags of horse feed and should be studied to ensure that you are feeding the right amount for the work required. The protein content is an influential factor.*

Right: *Some horses require soaked hay to relieve respiratory problems. This method is simple and effective in most cases, but proper soaking overnight may be necessary for those with a serious dust allergy.*

Below: *The difference between the quantity of hay and haylage can be clearly seen. The vacuum-packed haylage should be fed in small quantities and used straight from its plastic bag to preserve moisture content.*

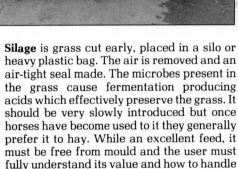

Silage is grass cut early, placed in a silo or heavy plastic bag. The air is removed and an air-tight seal made. The microbes present in the grass cause fermentation producing acids which effectively preserve the grass. It should be very slowly introduced but once horses have become used to it they generally prefer it to hay. While an excellent feed, it must be free from mould and the user must fully understand its value and how to handle it before embarking on this type of forage.

Haylage is vacuum-packed hay which, because it is sealed immediately it is made, loses only the bare minimum of nutrients. Because of this, only small amounts should be fed.

There are various different types available and, because of its slightly damp consistency, haylage is widely used with horses which have a tendency to cough or have a dust allergy. With all vacuum-packed products or those in plastic bags, it is essential that the cover is not punctured since the contents quickly deteriorate and ferment.

How and When to Feed

Feeding horses is a great art and is a subject in itself, but some of the important points to remember are mentioned below.

The horse, in its natural state, is a roaming herbivore and as such would pick at vegetation continually throughout the day since it was designed to have some food in its stomach all the time. Horses are also creatures of habit and seem to respond better if a regular routine can be established whenever possible. It makes sense, therefore, to try and stick to a regular feeding time, feeding little and often.

Hay in whatever form can be fed throughout the day and night, the amount depending very much on the horse's condition, state of fitness and the type of work it is doing. The fitter the horse, the less bulk it will require. The horse will need, instead, a high-energy diet.

However, the competition horse often has a rather hectic life, and because of this it is not always possible to stick to a routine if it is often away travelling to and from events. On such occasions it is best to give rather smaller feeds but maintain the balance of necessary nutrients essential to keep it in top condition. Adequate, clean water must always be available except when the horse is just about to be involved in strenuous exercise.

Be sure that only top quality feed and hay is given; it is detrimental and pointless to feed your horse on anything other than the very best. Ensure all mangers and water buckets are kept scrupulously clean and never leave any unfinished feed in the manger to be finished up with the next feed. This will only put the horse off its rations even more. The best way is to either miss one feed altogether or give a late feed when your horse may be quieter and more relaxed. Shy eaters will often eat well at night but touch little during the day. Leading out in hand for some grass will often be successful with horses of this kind.

Generally speaking, the management of the competition horse is very much a matter of common sense and a true understanding of the horse's character and its basic needs. The horse needs regular exercise and a time of quietness for relaxation. It needs proper feeding to ensure it is in peak condition and proper care through grooming and regular care of its feet. It requires a warm and airy stable kept clean and fresh, and above all it needs to be happy and contented. The horse that is well produced, quietly handled and ridden and treated as an individual rather than a machine will reward you with its very best at whatever is within its capabilities. If you produce your horse properly, you are at least 50 per cent on the way to success; the other half lies in correct fitness and training for the role required.

Fitness and Basic Training

Fitness is a state of health in which the horse is able to carry out reasonable demands by the rider with the least amount of physical stress. How this is achieved depends on the horse's state of general health, its feeding and the way in which it has been prepared for the demands expected of it.

No horse can be brought to the point of fitness if it is not in good physical condition generally, and this has already been discussed in the previous chapter. A regular worming programme, attention to teeth, proper food in relation to the work being done, a good environment, as well as vaccination precautions, are all vital to the horse if it is to be in the right physical state to start a steady build-up to peak competition fitness.

Whatever type of work the horse is eventually expected to do, the early stages are the same. A gradual and slow build-up of fitness to harden and tone muscles, tendons and ligaments is the secret of success. If this is done in a sensible and responsible way, the risk of injury caused by weakness is minimized.

Fitness work should start in ample time before you aim to compete seriously. It is wise to allow a couple of extra weeks in case of minor injuries. Exactly how long to allow will depend on the length of time the horse has been off work, the time of year and the type of competition for which you are training.

Fitness work can be divided roughly into three stages, the first being the initial slow work designed to harden legs and start the horse off correctly, so important to later success. The second stage consists of building up fitness once the slow work is over and the third is the final sharpening-up process to ensure the horse is at its peak for competition.

STAGE ONE

This begins with the walking process. Start by walking the horse between approximately a half and three-quarters of an hour on the first few days until it is out for approximately two hours by the end of the second week. This walking period may need to continue for longer with horses that have

been off work for more than two to three months, varying from four up to eight weeks for the horse having suffered some form of tendon injury previously. The importance of this slow period cannot be over emphasized. While for the first few days the horse may not be held up together too much, it must be encouraged to really use itself thereafter and not be allowed to just slop along. It must be encouraged to carry itself and walk out properly so that all its muscles are brought into play. If it is possible to use some hills, this will be enormously beneficial. It is the long gentle inclines which are so useful for fittening a horse. As it gets fitter, steeper hills can be used, but do not strain the horse

on these until it is ready for them. Encourage your horse to stretch forward and downwards in-between periods of gathering it together so that it develops its muscles correctly. Keeping the horse in one position all the time will create tension and stiffness. As with all fitness work, it is the degree of effort followed by periods of relaxation which has proved the most effective method of building up muscle. As the horse gets more toned up, more work time and less relaxation time can be employed. Monotony can be relieved by the introduction of simple suppling exercises and shortening and lengthening of the stride, asking for half-halts and a little shoulder-in, renvers or

Left: *Schooling over natural fences such as this log is the best way of training the horse for cross-country. Take every opportunity to jump over ditches and logs and go through water to build up confidence and experience from an early age.*

Above right: *Harvey Smith and his two sons school their horses out on the Yorkshire moors. The hills are invaluable in helping to create that vital basic fitness which is essential before real training can begin, and will ultimately determine success.*

Right: *The start to any fitness work must begin with walking on a firm, even surface to harden and strengthen the tendons and ligaments of the legs. A period of walking before and after any strenuous work is beneficial in loosening and relaxing.*

travers (see page 93). All these can be incorporated into your daily fitness regime at the walk.

Depending on the area available for riding, this slow work is best carried out on the roads or firm, even tracks. This will ensure that the horse's legs are not put under any strain from unsuitable ground until they are sufficiently hardened up. Obviously in this urban age, many roads are not suitable, with too much traffic making it dangerous for riding, so those that live in rural areas have a great advantage. If it is not possible to give the horse this early road work, more time should be given to compensate for this and the horse must be walked and trotted for short periods after the first week in large circles in both directions. Deep and heavy going must be avoided at all times, particularly during this important first stage of fitness work.

Once the walking-only period is completed, the horse should then start to do walk and trot. Begin with a half-hour walking then five minutes trotting followed by more walking. Gradually introduce more and more periods of trot being sure that this is only done quite slowly. Fast trotting will only jar the horse's legs, but a slow balanced pace will help to increase elasticity in the tendons and ligaments which in turn will allow greater flexion of the joints. Slow trotting is invaluable for building up muscle and again simple suppling exercises can be carried out such as lengthening and shortening the stride a little, half-halts and a little shoulder-in. All this will increase balance and lightness and encourage the horse to carry itself well. Remember to continue your periods of relaxation allowing the horse to stretch forward and down at times, although as the horse gets fitter these will not need to be so frequent. The rider's legs must be used correctly throughout this time to ensure the horse does not start to lean on the hand but, through the leg, is using itself from behind, thus steadily increasing the strength in its back and quarters.

Above: *Hill work is excellent for strengthening and building up muscle during the fitness programme but care must be taken not to overdo this in the early stages. Hindlegs are seen in action here.*

STAGE TWO

This second stage can commence once the initial walk and trot period has been carried out. Periods of schooling on the flat should be introduced, starting with just 15 minutes two or three times in the first week along with a period out on road work. As time goes on the road work need not take up so much time but more emphasis should be placed on flat work. It is far better for the horse if the road work is carried out first, since this ensures that the circulation to muscles and legs, which may have been standing in a stable for up to 22 hours, is really working well before any serious schooling commences. Whatever way you work your horse, 10 minutes at the walk first to loosen the horse up should be a firm rule throughout the training

Below: *Slow cantering is very beneficial not only for schooling and creating better balance but also for improving lung capacity, so important to the event horse which must perform over long courses.*

Below: *An eight-week chart suitable for dressage or show jumping horses which have had less than a six-week break from work. Work will be based on the standard the horse is aiming at.*

A Fitness Programme for Dressage or Show Jumping Horses

WEEK	STAGE ONE	STAGE TWO	STAGE THREE
1	Road work – walking 1 hr		
2	Road work – walk & trot 1 hr		
3	Road work – walk & trot **or**	Schooling $\frac{1}{2}$ hr or hack	
4	Road work – walk 10 mins	Loosening up – Schooling – Walking out	
5		Loosening up – Schooling – Walking out	Loosen up – Schooling $\frac{3}{4}$–1 hr
6		Loosening up – Schooling and relaxation	Loosen up – Schooling $\frac{3}{4}$–1 hr and relaxation
8			Competitions

Above: *It is not too difficult to make some very effective training fences at home, such as this simple trakhena type. The rails could be moved before or after the ditch to create different problems.*

Above: *Pacing poles (seen on the left) can be very useful if used correctly. This one, however, is too far from the fence and has encouraged the horse to flatten rather than bascule over the jump.*

programme and this also applies at a competition. Not only does the horse need this period to loosen it up physically but it also allows it to associate its work periods with a relaxed manner and to be calm. People who tack their horses up and immediately start to work them expecting instant suppleness and obedience are ruining all subsequent training. The horse will be tense mentally and physically, its muscles will not develop in the right way, it will be prone to strains and stiffness and will seldom be relaxed in its work because there will be no general routine in its programme. It is particularly noticable at a competition how different riders start off working their horses. Those who walk off allowing their horses to stretch down and relax into their surroundings are rewarded with mental calmness and supple, loose paces whereas, those that force their mount into a set outline and immediately start circling and working their horse are invariably seen with resistant, tense paces and the frustrations of the occasion are plainly apparent.

STAGE THREE

The third stage is really the sharpening up or final preparation for the big day. What this should consist of depends to some extent on the sport involved and the experience of your horse. For the dressage horse, it may just be a couple of warm-up competitions to settle it so that it is at its best for your bigger contests. The show jumper, likewise, may need a couple of outings to set it up and concentrate its mind on what is expected.

The eventer is the horse which perhaps requires a more serious approach to this stage, since this is the time for fast work to clear the lungs and to make the finishing touches towards peak fitness. Whether interval training is used or not, the horse will require some three or four sessions of fast work before going to its first event. A cross-country school may well count towards this, but how many sessions and how long, as well as how fast, will depend so much on the type of horse, the standard at which it is working and your future programme for it. A novice horse expecting to compete round a 2.4 kilometre (1½ mile) course does not, for instance, require the same sort of fast work as the advanced eventer about to do a 4 kilometre (2½ mile) cross-country course and the three-day event!

Below: *This chart could be used as a guide for the jumper which has come up after a lay-off or is preparing for the first season's jumping. Again, the work very much depends on the standard of the horse.*

A Fitness Programme for Show Jumpers

WEEK	STAGE ONE	STAGE TWO	STAGE THREE
1	Road work – walking 1 hr		
2	Road work – walk & trot 1 hr		
3	Road work – walk & trot 1 hr		
4	Hack out **or**	Schooling on flat	
5	Hack out **or**	Flat work + jump schooling × 2	
6	Hack out **or**	Flat + jump schooling × 3 or 4	Small show
8	Hack	Schooling and jumping 1 or 2	Show
12	Hack	Schooling and jumping 1 or 2	Show

Fitness and Basic Training

The charts for both interval-trained horses and those doing traditional workouts are designed to serve only as a possible guide for those aiming towards a novice one-day or a big three-day event. Each horse will require a special programme designed to bring it to its peak in the best possible way for that individual horse.

Factors which must always be taken into account when planning your final fitness work include the age, type and temperament of the horse you are working. At all levels the degree of fitness required should ensure that the horse is fully prepared for the event so that it is able to compete with the minimum amount of stress.

Your horse's physical state, and whether special care needs to be taken because of leg

A Fitness Programme for Eventers

WEEK	STAGE ONE	STAGE TWO	STAGE THREE
1	Road work – walking $\frac{3}{4}$–$1\frac{1}{4}$ hr		
2	Road work – walking 1–$1\frac{1}{2}$ hr		
3	Road work – walk & slow trot $1\frac{1}{2}$ hr		
4	Road work – walk & slow trot $1\frac{1}{2}$ hr		
5	Road work – walk & slow trot 1 hr	$\frac{1}{2}$ hr schooling on larger circles + hack	
6	Road work – walk & slow trot 1–$1\frac{1}{2}$ hr	Up to $\frac{3}{4}$ hr schooling and pole work + grids × 1	
7	Road work $\frac{1}{2}$ hr	Schooling – Slow cantering – Grids × 2 + hacks	Commence interval training
8	Road work $\frac{1}{2}$ hr or hack	Schooling – Commence interval training	Long slow cantering
9	Road work $\frac{1}{2}$ hr	Cantering	Cantering with short sharp gallop × 2
10	Road work $\frac{1}{2}$ hr	Schooling – Cantering – Grid work	
11	Road work – walking $\frac{1}{2}$ hr	Quiet week – 1 canter – flat work	Schooling – 1-day event – Slow cantering
12	Road work – walking $\frac{1}{2}$hr	Quiet – slow canters interspersed with other work	1-day event – Fast work as necessary – Walk and quiet work for 2 days after
14	Road work – walking $\frac{1}{2}$ hr		1-day event – Fast work – Easy for 2-3 days after
16	Road work – walking $\frac{1}{2}$ hr		3-day event
17–18	$\frac{1}{2}$–$\frac{3}{4}$ hr walking	Hack and/or turning out	Let down period

Left: *Stage Three successfully reached: a square, balanced halt is just what the judges are looking for. First impressions are so important and a good entry and halt is an excellent way to start any test.*

Right: *Schooling over cross-country fences is an important part of the event horse's training. Water fences come in a variety of designs and the horse must be confident at jumping into, in, over and out of them.*

Below: *Schooling the show jumper at home to be neat and accurate requires months of patience but parallels encourage the horse to round well over the fence. This one has its front legs neatly tucked up although it has 'stood off' some way from the fence.*

Left: *This chart takes the eventer through from week one to after a three-day event but could easily break after week ten for horses only aiming for one-day events. The charts are only a suggested guide and each horse must be treated as an individual.*

problems or previous lameness worries, should always be taken into account when planning the programme. Galloping must be treated with caution since it is speed that has proved to be the main reason for lameness in the eventer. While this is one of the best ways of clearing the horse's wind and generally fitting it for the sport, it need only be done in moderation with most animals and alternative methods such as swimming and the careful use of hills can be equally good and less demanding on the legs.

Whatever methods are used there are many roads that lead to success. But the one vital factor is fitness for whatever is required, and every horseman is responsible for ensuring that the horse receives the very best preparation and is at its peak for the big event, whether it is dressage, show jumping or eventing.

SCHOOLING ON THE FLAT

For whatever type of competition, schooling on the flat will begin with the same general principles. Looseness and suppleness of pace must be the aim to ensure that the horse is able to carry out the rider's wishes with ease. Obedience can only be fully obtained if the horse is given the correct aids from the rider for that particular movement and for this reason consistency by the rider is essential. In all work the rider must ride the horse forward with the leg into an 'allowing' or 'restraining' hand. This forward movement is so vital to all work and too often it is this basic principle which is at fault. The rider must be aware at all times that this forward movement is being maintained in all paces, and must be sure that the hand does not become too strong and restrictive forcing

the horse to lose the forward impulsion and so start to develop the many faults associated with this: overbending, head coming too low, croup high, hocks not engaged but trailing out behind and loss of rhythm and cadence.

All schooling must be progressive and have a sense of purpose. The horse must be continuously schooled to develop its muscles and balance for higher aims, and all paces must be evenly worked on in both directions.

The move off is the first lesson to be learnt by the horse in its initial training. This must be immediate and easy and leads on to transitions from one pace to another.

Transitions

The way these are performed is essential to all future work and is the basis of all training. Whether jumping or dressage, it is the ease with which the horse can increase or decrease its pace and the way in which it does so that will govern its way of going. Changes of pace must be worked at and perfected early in the horse's career and these must be smooth and even without resistance. Practise going from walk to trot and trot to canter as well as the downward transitions. Maintain an even and balanced position so that the horse carries itself and does not 'fall' into a canter or out of the trot. The transitions must be ridden forward even when coming back from canter to trot or walk with the rider pushing the horse up in front with his or her legs so that it carries itself and learns to bring its hindlegs more and more underneath to carry more weight.

Transitions may be progressive to start with, but as the horse becomes more advanced they should be direct, such as going immediately from halt to trot or canter. The advanced dressage horse must also be able to go directly into piaffe and passage with ease and suppleness or into the flying changes, but whatever the stage of training the horse must be obedient, listen to the rider and be ready and able to carry out his or her demands immediately without tension, anticipation or resistance.

No transition will be easy if the horse is not properly prepared by the rider beforehand. It is therefore very important that the rider indicates his or her intentions and gives the necessary aids to enable the horse to carry out the required change of pace. Generally a slight rebalancing is required in the form of a half-halt to create a little more energy which is then released into an upward transition or restricted into a downward transition, remembering particularly in this latter type to maintain the forward movement through the rider's legs.

Changes of Direction

These should be practised frequently being sure to maintain an even rhythm. The rider's body must remain upright and balanced with no collapsing of the inside hip thus throwing the weight to the outside. There are numerous ways of changing direction: across the diagonal, via half-circles, changing through the circle, figures of eight, loops off and onto the track, and serpentines, to name just a few. All these exercises in changing direction will help to supple and balance the horse as well as improve its muscle development and mental awareness.

Right: *Circling over poles or round and through them is an excellent way of loosening and suppling the horse for all work on the flat. There are numerous variations in what can be done over poles.*

Below: *An excellent demonstration of riding straight across the diagonal by Dane Rawlins, who is preparing his horse for the turn onto the track. Accuracy plays a big part in riding a dressage test.*

Below: *A fine example of the medium trot circle in the FEI three-day event test by Kim Walnes on the Grey Goose at Luhmühlen. A difficult movement for the eventer, requiring great impulsion and balance.*

Right: *The much rounder outline of the collected trot performed by David Hunt at Goodwood. Higher, more active steps are required for this pace which is asked for in the more advanced tests.*

Transitions and changes of direction are two basic exercises which every horse has to master. But before progressing much further a certain degree of collection is necessary. As the work gets more demanding the degree of collection will become more essential.

Collection

This is achieved by driving the horse forward with the seat and legs into a sensitive but restraining hand. This creates extra energy which can be released into greater activity generated through the quarters. The hocks become more actively engaged under the horse and so enable it to be lighter in front. The quarters are lowered and the neck will come up as greater engagement is achieved. Great care must be taken to ensure the rider's hand does not become too strong and inhibit the forward movement as this could result in all sorts of problems. If the horse is held back in the hand, overbending, shortened steps and loss of rhythm inevitably follow, along with other resistances which quickly develop if free forward movement is not maintained.

Straightness

This is one of the most important aspects of schooling and without this little can be achieved correctly. It is one of the most common basic problems and may well be caused by the fact that we start off leading horses from the left side from their earliest

Left: *This horse is being schooled in an outdoor menage and is appearing rather strong in the left hand and too far in off the track. The rider is trying to push the horse over while maintaining straightness.*

training, since more often than not there tends to be a left-sided stiffness. The horse is stiff on the left rein and tends to swing its quarters in to the right and push its near shoulder out to the left. Because of these evasions, it is inevitable that the horse will tend to become stiff in its back and hocks, which may eventually lead it to being unlevel.

It is essential to work on straightening the horse from the start but this must always be in a forward way. Aids which usually work in loosening up a horse that is stiff to the left are a firm forward driving seat and taking and releasing the contact rein on the left.

The right rein should remain in a supporting role with both legs maintaining the forward movement by creating a little extra energy. Working the horse on the circle towards the stiff side will require patience and suppleness from the rider. Maintain the outside contact with the right rein which will usually mean the horse will be looking slightly to the outside as it stiffens on the left. Maintain forward movement and keep the horse moving until it gradually gets tired of keeping its head and neck tense, accepts the supporting hand and softens on the stiff rein. As the horse relaxes it will lower its head and soften through the neck and back. The rider

Schooling Exercises

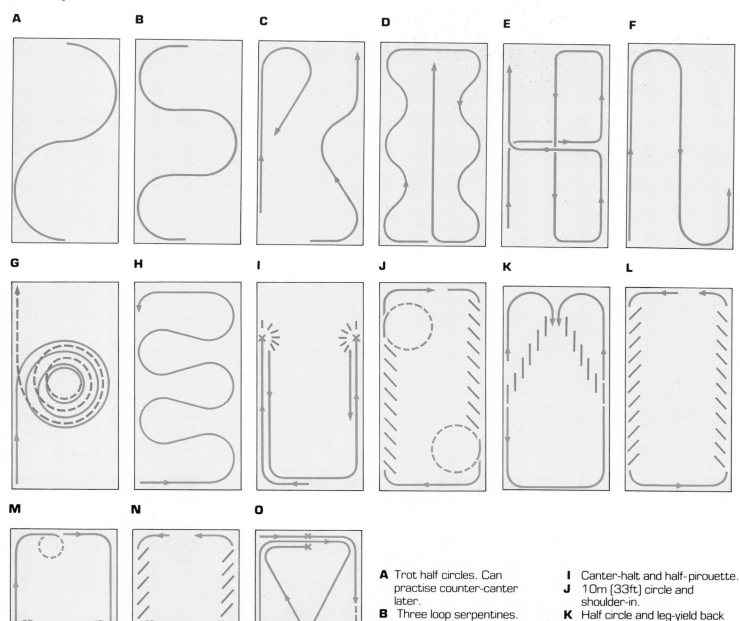

A Trot half circles. Can practise counter-canter later.
B Three loop serpentines.
C Loops and turns back onto the track.
D Loops, turns and straightness.
E Turns and corners.
F Turns and straightness.
G Spiralling in and out of circle in trot or canter.
H Tighter loops on serpentine.

I Canter-halt and half-pirouette.
J 10m (33ft) circle and shoulder-in.
K Half circle and leg-yield back to track.
L Transitions to trot and canter from walk (3m/10ft circles).
M Travers to shoulder-in to travers.
N Travers and renvers.
O Halts and rein-backs with medium and working trot.

Left: *Training horses on long reins is one of the best methods of teaching it to go forward and accept the driving aids and the bit. This Lipizzaner is giving a demonstration without the training roller.*

must reward it with a slight give and retaking of the reins but keep moving the horse forward. Once the horse has accepted this way of going, it can be ridden forward in a straight line.

The rider must feel an even contact from the horse's mouth and should see only one set of footprints on the track. As the rider looks up the neck to the ears, it should look straight and he or she should not feel that any part of his or her body is being pushed away from the centre of the horse. As straightness is developed, flexion in the joints will be improved and this in turn will lead to looseness and a better rhythm.

Developing Balance

This must be an ongoing process if the horse is to perform at its best. The young horse carries most of its weight on the forehand and has a much longer, lower outline. As the horse develops in its work this outline comes more together and the centre of gravity is pushed further back as the hind legs become more active. The neck is raised, the quarters are lowered and the hind legs come well under the body making the steps more active and rhythmical.

This shortening of the frame of the horse is developed over a period of months and years as the muscles in the quarters and back take time to build up. A gradual programme is necessary to firstly get the horse fit and then work at improving its balance through dressage work and using hills, pole and cavaletti work, show jumping, long reining and cross-country riding. All will help the horse to find its own balance which can then be built on by the rider to achieve more cadenced even paces with softer and longer steps which can be shortened with ease and no loss of rhythm by the rider.

The horse must be ridden with strong leg aids to achieve this and under no circumstances must it be pulled back into a position through the hand.

Below: *This rider is creating extra impulsion by closing her legs and re-balancing the horse by the half-halt, immediately getting higher more active steps. This is one of the most widely used and useful training movements.*

The half-halt is one of the most useful methods of achieving balance and should be used throughout the horse's training. It is used to rebalance the horse, prepare for the next movement and to keep the horse's attention. The half-halt is achieved by the rider pushing the horse forward into a restraining hand. The rider must not lean back, as this could restrict forward movement, but rebalance the horse momentarily and achieve a shorter outline allowing the horse to go forward again. Care must be taken that the contact is not lost at this point, since this will only lose the collection and balance gained through the half-halt. Repeated half-halts prepare the horse for the halt and help it to pay attention to the rider.

The halt and move off are among the easiest ways to check the training of the horse since a horse that does not do this correctly after a reasonable period of time has not been brought on satisfactorily. For a correct halt, the horse must be straight with the weight evenly distributed on all four legs which should be straight. The horse should be on the bit with the head raised and giving at the

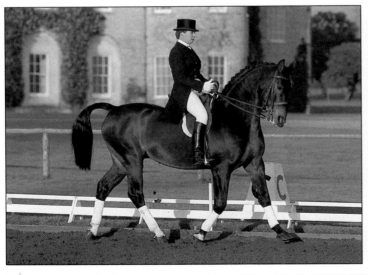

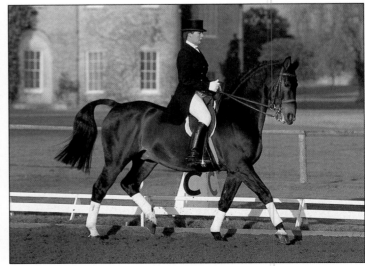

Above: Lunging over fences is an excellent way of introducing the horse to jumping. It also adds variety to the training as well as helping towards creating better balance and confidence in the young horse.

Above: Riding a correctly-shaped circle is as important as making the horse go straight. This rider has too much bend and is collapsing and tilting his body to the side, thus losing the correct curve.

Below: This neatly turned out horse and rider has come to an almost square halt and both look expectantly towards their arena at Goodwood, awaiting their turn at the dressage championships for novice horses.

poll. The movement into the halt should be soft and supple with no abruptness. This can only be achieved if the horse is sufficiently contained between the rider's seat and legs. After the halt, the horse must stand quite still and the rider will ease the reins slightly without losing contact and keep the legs softly against the horse's sides. At no point should the horse step back – a fault sometimes seen if the rider has not eased the rein early enough – nor move forward until the rider indicates.

Depending on the standard of test, the horse must move off immediately it receives the aids from the rider. It can only do this if it is listening to the rider and awaiting his or her instructions. A bracing of the rider's back and stronger use of the leg will enable the horse to move straight forward into canter or trot. In tests of novice standard, progressive transitions are allowed but from medium standard upwards these should be direct with the very first step going straight into the pace required. The move off must not be abrupt but purposeful and straight.

Turns and Circles

These are required in dressage of all levels as well as in the show-jumping arena and are essential to the horse's everyday training. The horse must first be moving forward in a straight line before it is possible to position it correctly for the circles. Early training on the lunge will have helped tremendously to teach the horse to work on the circle and to increase its balance. With the weight of the rider, however, it is not always so easy for the horse to remain in balance unless it is even and supple on both reins and the rider sits correctly with no uneven distribution of weight. The horse's body must follow the curve of the circle and in principle the rider's hips should be square to the horse's quarters. The pressure required from the leg, hand and seat bones will keep the horse on the line of the circle. The inside rein must indicate the direction of the circle while the outside one keeps it straight on the line and prevents too much neck bend. The outside leg is used a little further back behind the girth to maintain the bend and prevent the quarters from swinging out, and the horse is driven forward with both legs and seat bones.

To ride turns and corners the horse must be prepared for the bend as for the circle and then ridden forward through the turn. It must not shorten its stride nor stiffen against the rider but remain soft and supple to produce an even rhythm throughout.

Lateral Work

This is one of the best methods of producing suppleness and can be started as soon as the horse is going forward straight and in balance. Some people prefer long reining to start with and this has long been a popular method in Europe and is becoming increasingly so in Britain. It has the advantage of teaching the horse the basics without the added weight of the rider and, with the instructor driving the horse forward from behind, teaches the horse to go forward into the movement from the start.

Turns on the forehand Horses that have been taken out on hacks will undoubtedly have had a slight introduction to lateral work in the form of a turn on the forehand, the principle of which is used when opening gates. This exercise when carried out in an arena helps to supple the horse and increase its obedience to the leg aids. The horse is

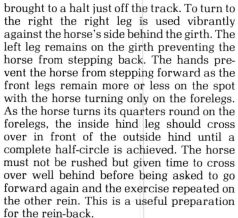

Above: *The rider is concentrating hard on completing her circle in the arena. Perhaps a slightly lighter outside hand could have allowed the head and neck to remain on the line of the circle to gain better marks.*

Below: *This horse is being ridden well into the corner of the arena showing balance and suppleness. The rider is controlling the impulsion with sympathetic hands but has slightly collapsed her left hip.*

brought to a halt just off the track. To turn to the right the right leg is used vibrantly against the horse's side behind the girth. The left leg remains on the girth preventing the horse from stepping back. The hands prevent the horse from stepping forward as the front legs remain more or less on the spot with the horse turning only on the forelegs. As the horse turns its quarters round on the forelegs, the inside hind leg should cross over in front of the outside hind until a complete half-circle is achieved. The horse must not be rushed but given time to cross over well behind before being asked to go forward again and the exercise repeated on the other rein. This is a useful preparation for the rein-back.

Leg yielding is the start of lateral work and can be practised from early in the horse's training as there is little necessity for collection. It is quite simply asking the horse to move forwards and sideways away from the rider's leg with the horse's head bent slightly away from the direction it is going. A half-halt should be used to prepare the horse. To leg yield from the right use the right leg firmly behind the girth with the left leg on the girth maintaining the forward movement. Ask for a slight yielding with the right rein and control the shoulders with the left rein. At all times the forward movement must be maintained, and be careful that too much flexion is not employed resulting in the horse putting all its weight onto the outside shoulder.

The shoulder-in is an extremely useful suppling movement which encourages the horse to become more engaged and lighter in the forehand. The horse must be collected together to be able to perform this lateral movement correctly on three tracks. Prepare the horse with a half-halt and for shoulder-in to the right, ease the horse's shoulders in from the track by using the inside leg and hand and control the degree of angle with the outside hand. The outside leg used just

Above: *This young rider is demonstrating many of the early faults seen with horses ridden onto the forehand: stiff arms, ineffective legs and tilting body. The horse is not using its hocks at all.*

Below: *Straightness is a very important aspect to master. The horse is cantering with quarters to the inside, probably caused by lack of engagement of hind quarters and too strong an outside leg.*

Right: *This rider is asking for the rein-back having first lightened his seat. The horse is responding and using its hocks well as it steps backwards with an obvious ease and lightness.*

behind the girth will prevent the quarters swinging out off the track. Avoid asking for too much angle. It is a three-track movement only, and by asking for too much you lose the purpose of the exercise which is to activate the inside hind leg so that improved collection is possible as well as suppleness. The rider must keep the horse moving forward but sit very still so as not to unbalance the horse. The shoulder-in can be performed on the straight, when it is best started just after a corner or on the circle for greater effort. It can be performed in walk, trot and canter and is an extremely useful preparatory movement before starting half-pass, which will be discussed in the next chapter along with the more advanced movements.

Counter canter is a useful movement to improve balance, suppleness and obedience. The horse must be collected to perform this correctly and the rider must be consistent,

quiet and remain in balance with the horse throughout. Any sudden change of the rider's weight will unbalance the horse and encourage it to change legs. To prepare for counter canter, balance the horse with a few short half-halts then ride it forward. The counter canter can be practised in many different ways but is best started by doing loops off the track and then returning, all the time maintaining an even feel on the inside rein, which will become the outside one in counter canter. The angle of the loops can be increased as the horse gets more confident, until it is able to do serpentines of three or more loops depending on the size of the arena. Other methods of using counter canter can be to do a small half-circle in true canter and on returning to the track in counter canter continue round the arena or on a circle. Be careful to keep the horse in balance by maintaining the feel on what becomes the outside rein in counter canter. Any problems encountered are nearly always caused by the horse not being collected together enough or not prepared before the movement. Problems are also caused by the rider swinging the body and unbalancing the horse.

The simple change is another useful balancing exercise that increases awareness and is a useful preparation for the flying change. This exercise of canter, walk two or three strides, then canter on the other leg should be perfected as the horse progresses in its training. Used in many tests up to medium level, it is always performed through walk unless stated otherwise, which is sometimes confusing when simple changes are done through trot when schooling. To prepare for the simple change, a series of half-halts will ensure that the horse is listening and is sufficiently balanced to perform smoothly this downward followed by an upward transition. A half-halt brings the horse back to walk and the rider must relax herself and the horse to show a few definite walk strides and change her position to be ready to strike

off on the other leg in canter. In the early training, several walk steps should be made and at all times the rider must keep the horse going forward and take care not to allow it to fall onto its forehand.

The rein-back will benefit the horse's suppleness and obedience as well as help with collection. The horse must step backwards, picking-up alternate diagonal pairs of legs rather than dragging them, and remain in a straight line. To prepare for the rein-back, the horse must first be brought back to a square halt. The rider should not sit deep in the saddle but lighten his or her weight off the saddle and ask for forward movement, but restrict the horse with the hands. When the horse feels it cannot move forwards, it will step backwards. This should be encouraged and the horse rewarded, then moved forward again. As the horse learns what is required more steps can be asked for, but to start with be satisfied with just one or two. Common faults include too strong a hand 'pulling' the horse back, leaning forward, leaning back and sitting too heavy, a bad halt making it difficult for the horse to move and lack of straightness. The rein-back is useful for schooling dressage horses and jumpers, and is sometimes used to reprimand a horse that gets too strong in the hand and does not listen to the rider.

The turn on the haunches creates collection. It is a good strengthening exercise and teaches the horse to be light and handy. At the walk, the horse's forehand is turned step-by-step around the arc of a small circle made by the hind legs. These must not pivot but take even and regular steps. The horse should be flexed in the direction of the turn and guided forwards and sideways round onto the track facing in the opposite direction.

All of the above exercises should be practised and perfected during this second stage of fitness in-between hacks out on the road. A gradual build-up of work should be aimed at with straightness, rhythm and impulsion as well as collection being practised. Once the above has been worked on for three to four weeks, depending on the horse's fitness, jumping should be incorporated into the weekly programme. Pole work may already have been used during schooling on the flat. This helps to increase rhythm, balance and suppleness as well as making a change for the horse. It is an excellent way of quietening the rather over excitable horse which can be twisted and turned over, round and through them.

Left: *The turn on the haunches or half-pirouette at the walk is being well demonstrated showing balance, a good bend and suppleness throughout. The overall picture is good, only spoilt by the rider looking down – a common fault in the dressage arena. Suppling exercises such as this are excellent for balancing the horse and should be started early on in training and worked on regularly throughout.*

Poles and Cavalletti

The use of poles on the ground is an excellent method of teaching the horse to establish a rhythm and encouraging the horse to look down, which helps to strengthen the back muscles. Poles also have a relaxing effect and are used widely by dressage and jumping trainers alike for this reason, and also as a change from the normal routine.

In Europe the use of cavalletti is much wider than in Britain. They may be used at three different heights and are particularly helpful in teaching horse and rider to remain in balance with one another at the different paces. A horse that can remain relaxed and balanced over cavalletti at all three heights in trot and canter is ready to move on to more advanced jump training. The rider that can use his or her hands correctly and keep his or her weight light and stay in time with the horse's movement can feel confident that a good rapport has been built up with that horse and can remain in balance throughout. It is very important that the horse is allowed to lower its head over poles, particularly with the higher cavalletti, so that the horse can use itself properly with a good swing in the back. This will not be possible if the horse's head is held up, which creates tension and prevents the horse being able to 'come through' correctly from behind, thus defeating the whole object of the exercise.

Unfortunately, in Britain cavalletti have become unpopular because of various accidents where the cavalletti have rolled. But these mishaps have been mostly caused by children becoming rather too exuberent,

Above: *Pole work can be invaluable in training horses for flatwork and jumping. This pony is using the poles well but would benefit more if it lowered its head and neck to increase suppleness. Poles must be placed to suit the animal's stride.*

Below: *The next stage using cavalletti and small jumps seems wonderful to this child but many trainers, especially in Europe and the States, spend months schooling over cavalletti. They can be set at three heights, depending on the work required.*

Fitness and Basic Training

children becoming rather too exuberant, especially during Pony Club camps where, because of the inevitable variation in the size of the ponies in a class, their use is often unsuitable. Young children are seldom experienced enough to understand the dangers which may arise from using cavalletti, but experienced riders universally recognize their use.

Leading dressage trainers have found cavalletti useful in helping to prepare the horse for passage (see Advanced Dressage Training), as the exaggerated movement over the poles helps to strengthen muscles. Germany's Reiner Klimke is in favour of this method. However, his equally famous compatriot Harry Bolt, while agreeing with the principle, feels great care should be taken to ensure the horse does not lose the movement through its back with the increased action of the hind legs. The same message of free forward movement in all training of horses is universal.

The brilliant Hungarian, Bertalan de Nemethy, who has coached the US show-jumping team for twenty-five years and is renowned for his training of young riders, introduced cavalletti to the Americans. The results of his training speak for themselves, with the USA featuring prominently in all major championships for the past twenty years or more. The stylish way the Americans ride is the envy of all serious horsemen throughout the world.

Poles can be used in numerous different ways and sequences, depending on what you wish to achieve. You can encourage the horse's stride to lengthen or shorten depending on the distances at which you place them, and they offer the opportunity for many useful exercises aimed at creating more activity from the horse.

Senior British show jumping coach, Richard Stillwell, is a genius at producing exercises for different problems and is amazingly successful at loosening up varying types of horses that have long since been given up by many as being too stiff or unlevel to work with. He maintains that if you can get the horse loose and working through from behind on the flat with poles and cavalletti, the jumping will follow on naturally with few problems.

As with all forms of training, the initial loosening up period is extremely important. The horse requires plenty of time to do this having usually spent anything up to twenty-three hours standing in a stable. Therefore, allow enough time to walk the horse well and then slowly loosen it in trot and canter before attempting your poles. Start your practice session with easy, straightforward poles then gradually introduce other exercises which you feel would be of benefit. Poles can be worked over in walk, trot or canter; on the straight or in a curve. Cavalletti, however, are best trotted over in a straight line with a long rein, since the horse could strain itself

Above: *Grid work is an excellent way of teaching the horse to think for itself and react quickly over a series of closely related fences. They should be built up gradually as the horse gets used to them.*

Below: *The diagram shows how different grids with varying strides can be set up. Always start with a couple of fences and gradually build up your grid with distances suitable for your horse.*

A Series of Grids with Approximate Distances

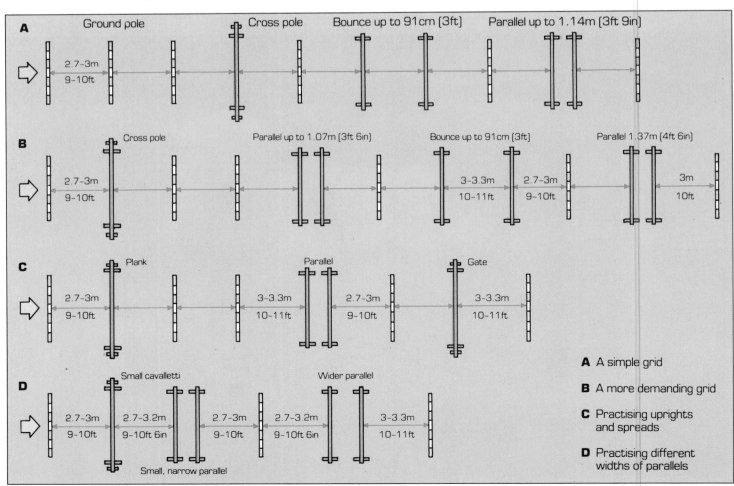

A Ground pole — Cross pole — Bounce up to 91cm (3ft) — Parallel up to 1.14m (3ft 9in)
2.7-3m / 9-10ft

B Cross pole — Parallel up to 1.07m (3ft 6in) — Bounce up to 91cm (3ft) — Parallel 1.37m (4ft 6in)
2.7-3m / 9-10ft — 3-3.3m / 10-11ft — 2.7-3m / 9-10ft — 3m / 10ft

C Plank — Parallel — Gate
2.7-3m / 9-10ft — 3-3.3m / 10-11ft — 2.7-3m / 9-10ft — 3-3.3m / 10-11ft

D Small cavalletti — Wider parallel
2.7-3m / 9-10ft — 2.7-3.2m / 9-10ft 6in — 2.7-3m / 9-10ft — 2.7-3.2m / 9-10ft 6in — 3-3.3m / 10-11ft
Small, narrow parallel

A A simple grid

B A more demanding grid

C Practising uprights and spreads

D Practising different widths of parallels

doing the exaggerated action required for them if they were placed on the turn. The diagrams show some of the many variations and exercises which can be employed. Remember to adjust the distances to suit your horse's stride.

Gymnastic Jumping

This is a particularly useful way of making the horse think for itself and learn to adjust its stride and balance to cope with a series of different fences close together. While gymnastics are good for the training of all horses, it is for the event horse that this is particularly beneficial. With the huge variety of fences encountered on cross-country courses today, the event horse has to be able to think quickly and adapt to the questions being asked of it. The horse will be expected to cope not only with several obstacles with differing strides, but also with 'bounces',

having to jump up and downhill as well as having to stretch out over wide obstacles or shorten for uprights.

The use of gymnastics is helpful for both horse and rider, teaching them to be alert and pay attention. The rider has to adjust his or her balance quickly and be able to ride forward or sit still, depending on the exercise. The horse has to lengthen and shorten its stride frequently, which is excellent for loosening it up and increasing its ability to cope with different types of demands.

The diagram shows a variety of gymnastic exercises, but everyone has their own ideas of what works best. The secret is to encourage the horse to shorten and lengthen between fences over various different stride sequences.

Loose Schooling

This is the ideal way to start the young horse jumping. The horse learns to work out for itself what to do without the rider's weight whilst the trainer has the chance of studying the horse's technique over the fence, which can be invaluable when it comes to further training. Loose jumping is practised extensively in Europe and is featured at all the Horse Performance Sales.

When setting up fences, the aim must be to gradually build up the size of the fences, and to eventually build up a variety of different fences to accustom the horse to these as well as to allow it to judge its own take-off platform. For the timid horse, the trainer can encourage it forward with the whip. But the over-exuberant horse may require slowing down with a greater variety of fences or by shortening the distance a little to encourage it to slow down and think before it acts. Once again, it is extremely important that the distances are right for your horse and, while the diagrams offer a rough guideline, they will need adjusting depending on the natural stride of your horse and the amount and types of fences being jumped.

Above: *Playtime is a very important aspect of training, and if the horse cannot go out in the field, a buck and kick in the school will be a welcome substitute – clearly demonstrated by this big four year old.*

Below: *Confident and alert, this horse looks carefully down this small grid set up in the school with rails and barrels. The sloping rail at the beginning helps to guide the horse into the grid at the start.*

Below: *Springing out over the parallel at the end of the grid, the horse has made nothing of the fence which could be widened to encourage a larger bascule. Extra height can also be used if appropriate.*

Advanced Dressage

The pure dressage horse requires months of basic work before being asked to perform the more advanced movements such as half-pass at trot and canter, flying changes, pirouettes, passage and piaffe. It takes considerable time and patience to train the horse to perform these movements and they should never be attempted until the basics have been thoroughly mastered. The horse must be physically strong and mentally mature enough to absorb the extra demands.

Having established the basics (pages 23–35), these movements need to be introduced.

Travers and Renvers

Useful exercises such as travers and renvers help to increase suppleness and the degree of bend and prepare the horse for half-pass. In travers the rider increases the weight on the inside seat bone and bends the horse around the inside leg so that the horse is on four tracks, with the quarters brought in off the chosen track. It can be performed on the straight, across the diagonal or on the circle usually best started after a corner or circle.

In renvers the horse's shoulders are brought in off the track but the horse is looking in the direction in which it is going and is bent round the rider's outside leg. Both exercises are useful when warming up for the half-pass.

The Half-pass

This is the most advanced form of lateral work in which the horse moves forward and sideways looking in the direction in which it is travelling. Its body should remain parallel to the track with the outside fore and hind legs crossing over evenly in front of the inside fore and hind legs. The half-pass may be performed in walk, trot or canter and the important aspect is to maintain the bend, rhythm and forward movement throughout.

To perform a half-pass the horse must be in collected trot or canter and prepared with a half-halt before asking for the bend and sideways movement. The rider looks in the direction in which he or she wishes to go, asks for an inside flexion and bends the horse round the inside leg with the outside leg used back behind the girth pushing the quarters over. The degree of bend is controlled through the outside hand and leg. Half pass is normally started after a corner

Above right: *The moment of suspension, as the horse takes each stride round in the canter pirouette, requires timing and balance as well as tremendous strength to maintain the rhythm of the movement.*

Right: *The canter half-pass, performed either diagonally across the arena or as zigzags down the centre line, is often required in advanced tests. This rider appears to glide across the arena.*

Left: *The power and elegance of the dressage horse clearly demonstrated. The elevated steps of the passage require great collection and impulsion as well as supreme fitness to maintain the strenuous movement.*

or circle. The degree of angle will depend on the horse's standard of training, but as it progresses this will become more acute, as required for the more advanced tests.

The Counter Change of Hand

This is a movement whereby the horse changes from one direction to another, which must be performed fluently and smoothly. The horse must be straightened for a couple of strides and the bend changed before asking for half-pass in the opposite direction. As the horse progresses it should require only one stride to change the bend from one side to the other. In canter, a flying change must take place to be able to change direction and perform zig-zags down the centre line as required for the Grand Prix dressage test. The evenness of the steps and the maintainance of a three-time canter are essential if these zig-zags are to be performed correctly. The rider must take his or her time, be positive in timing and count the number of strides he or she wishes to take before changing direction. Usually this movement starts down the centre line with three strides in one direction, change, then six strides back across the centre line to the other side, change, then six back across, with three back onto the centre line at the end. This can also be done with four then eight etc. Trailing quarters is a common fault in performing the half-pass, which can be corrected with a half-halt and a stronger outside leg to push the quarters more in line. Quarters leading is another fault when the horse should be ridden forward more from the inside leg. Loss of rhythm may be caused by hurrying the movement, too much bend and lack of balance.

Flying Changes of Leg in Canter

This movement involves the horse changing from one canter lead to the other in a kind of skip action. It takes place at the moment of suspension when the horse has all four feet off the ground before taking the next stride. To be able to perform this successfully, the horse must be straight with an even feel on both reins and in balance. There are various methods of teaching the flying change, but one of the simplest is to ride a half circle and just before returning to the track, and half-halt, prepare to change the bend. At the moment of suspension, ask for the change with the outside leg strongly applied behind the girth thereby putting more weight onto

the inside seat bone, taking a firmer feel on the inside rein. As soon as the horse has responded, the rein must be eased and the horse should be ridden forward. Other ways of asking for a change are when changing through the circle, across the diagonal; when doing a serpentine, changing across the centre line, or when turning across the arena at any marker. In whatever route taken, straightness is the important factor and the rider must take care not to swing his or her weight and so unbalance the horse, lean forward too far, have too strong a leg or hand aids, or be out of time for the move-

Left: *The walk pirouette is well demonstrated here. The rider asks for the turn with the inside hand and uses her legs to maintain and control the circle which must remain small. The horse must not pivot but keep moving correctly on the turn.*

Below: *The power and balance required for the flying change from the right to the left is clearly seen. The rider must change the aids without unbalancing the horse and must keep a soft seat and steady feel on the reins throughout the movement.*

Left: *This interesting sequence of a canter pirouette shows eight different stages of the movement. The rider is keeping the horse balanced and maintains the impulsion with her legs and seat, guiding the horse round on the circle with her hands. It is most important that the rhythm is not lost; the movement must not be hurried, nor the horse allowed to lose impulsion and so run out of the impetus to be able to continue round on the circle. A lowering of the quarters and the flexion of the joints can be seen quite clearly in the various stages of the pirouette.*

ment. Once the horse is quite happy and has mastered single flying changes, it can then be introduced to multiple changes. These may be performed in sequence from any number of strides but four, three, two and one-time changes are required for the various standard international tests. The rider must train his or her horse to perform changes as required, gradually reducing the strides in between. How this is done very much depends on each individual horse and rider but again straightness and balance become even more important and obedience to the rider's aids essential. In one-time or flying changes every stride of the horse and rider's reactions must be in perfect harmony, with the rider's seat remaining very light in the saddle and the leg and rein aids moving in time to indicate the moment of change. It is important that the rhythm and tempo are maintained throughout for the horse to be able to perform this with ease. In early training only a few changes should be asked for, since this is a tiring movement and needs time to be perfected so that the horse can cope with ease.

The Pirouette

This is a highly collected movement whereby the horse's forehand moves round the hind legs creating a full circle. The horse should turn round the inside hind leg in a turn of 360°. The hind legs should remain active, stepping round more or less on the spot. The movement can be performed in walk, canter or piaffe.

To ride the pirouette in walk, the horse must be active and collected and led into the turn with the inside hand. The inside leg on the girth controls the horse, and the outside leg used vibrantly just behind the girth keeps the horse moving round on the circle. The outside rein gives the horse the necessary flexion to keep coming round but also controls the pace. Try to ensure that the horse does not step backwards or deviate off the circle and maintains the correct sequence of steps when performing in canter.

The Canter Pirouette

This is a highly collected movement requiring great impulsion and balance. The rhythm must be maintained throughout. It is a common fault for the rider to try to hurry the horse out of the pirouette losing the tempo, or for the horse to 'die' through lack of sufficient impulsion before starting and being unable to keep the rhythm throughout. To be successful the horse must lower its quarters and flex its joints well so that it remains light in front and can perform the full 360° turn in six to eight strides.

The best way to teach the horse pirouette is to do a small half-circle to start with and gradually shorten the stride and size but maintain the impulsion. As the horse learns how to cope with this, a three-quarter pirouette can be attempted and eventually the full circle. The horse must always maintain

the forward movement and be able to be ridden straight on at any time. The pirouette will eventually need to be performed on the centre line, so it is vital that the horse can come into it and leave it moving straight for the judges to give good marks.

Passage

This is a very collected, slow, elevated trot with a definite moment of suspension. The horse must be highly collected and straight but light in front and not tense, to do this well. The hindlegs should show increased activity and the forelegs should be well lifted. Traditionally the passage is taught as a progression from the piaffe, but many trainers find that teaching the passage first and shortening this into piaffe is better. Either way works well in the hands of an experienced trainer and will very much depend on the horse.

The most difficult part is the transition into and out of passage as the rhythm and tempo must remain steady, and in dressage tests these are what the judge will be looking at just as much as the actual quality of the movement itself.

The rider must sit light to allow the horse freedom to use its back. Ask for a half-halt then use both legs to generate the extra impulsion in time with the steps of the passage. The hands lightly control the horse but must allow enough freedom for the horse to remain balanced and regular. A well-executed passage should present a rhythmic, proud and elevated show of power and obedience from the horse.

During training the rider may need a helper on the ground with a long whip to tap the hind legs further underneath the horse, to enable it to create more powerful steps. The helper can also touch the fore legs as each is lifted off the ground to increase the height and so prolong the moment of suspension. The rider will need to give several short half-halts in time with the strides and balance this with his or her legs to create the springy steps.

If coming from piaffe the horse will only be able to do a few strides in passage to start with and must then be pushed forward into

collected trot and brought back to piaffe and tried again, until gradually the horse finds its balance and can remain in passage for longer periods. This is a very strenuous movement and care must be taken not to overdo the horse during the early stages in order not to worry it mentally by asking too much too soon. Reward the horse frequently and give it the chance of total relaxation from this intense training by going out for hacks regularly and taking care to change the work routine.

Above: *The perfection which has won Anne Grethe Jensen and Marzog so many dressage titles is clearly demonstrated here as they perform a passage at Goodwood during the European Championships.*

Above: *The passage, seen here on the turn, is a very collected, slow, elevated trot with a definite moment of suspension. This most impressive dressage movement requires tremendous strength from the horse.*

Right: *The Spanish Riding School performing their world famous display in their school in Vienna. The horse in the pillars demonstrates the piaffe whilst the other riders do a series of movements.*

Below: *Jane Bartle-Wilson and Pinocchio perform the piaffe during the Grand Prix test. The most collected of all the movements, it requires a trot on the spot with tremendous flexion of the joints and true engagement of the hindquarters.*

The Piaffe

This is the most collected movement consisting of a trot on the spot with moments of suspension between each diagonal step. To be able to achieve such a high degree of collection, the horse will have needed at least three years' training to have built up the necessary muscle power to be able to perform this highly advanced movement.

To be able to perform the piaffe correctly, which is in any case rarely seen in its true glory, the horse must be able to really flex its hind joints, and lower and engage the hindquarters. This will lighten the forehand and enable the forefeet to be raised as much as possible and higher than the hind feet. The elevation, regularity and tempo must be maintained throughout by keeping the horse straight and not pushing the horse out of a natural rhythm.

The way to train the horse for piaffe is best started in hand. The trainer should take both reins in one hand and hold the horse along the wall and encourage it forward with a dressage whip, tapping the hind legs until it starts to bounce a little. Reward the horse and gradually restrict the forward movement, so that the 'bounce' or moment of suspension becomes more pronounced.

The rider can be put on top once the horse understands what is required of it and the same principle applied. The rider must have a light contact on the reins and a very light seat but must give alternate leg and back aids in time to the steps and shorten the trot until a few strides of piaffe are achieved. The trainer can use the whip to again tap the hind legs further under the horse to achieve greater engagement and lowering of the quarters which is very necessary if the piaffe is to be performed correctly.

Work Between the Pillars

In Europe, this is practised much more widely than in Britain or America. It is a method which has been used in the training of horses for centuries to increase balance and rhythm, and is essential for teaching the horse the levade and other 'airs above the ground', as practised by the Spanish Riding School in Vienna and the Cadre Noir at Samur in France. These long established and renowned training schools specialize in the classical school movements and perform displays worldwide, which include such spectacular movements as the aforementioned levade, courbette, capriole etc. These movements are not practised in the competitive field but are the ultimate in man's training of the horse using the horse's natural, instinctive movements and training it to produce these on command.

A fully trained dressage horse is a truly magnificent animal showing power, presence and great obedience. Dressage displays at many of the great shows worldwide have kept audiences spellbound. Perhaps some of the most impressive are those performed in long reins showing all the movements without a rider. Perhaps some of the greatest and most elegant shows of horsemastership have been demonstrated sidesaddle, which is difficult for both horse and rider because there is no rider's leg on the one side.

Below: *Britain's first ever dressage medal was won at the World Championships at Goodwood by Jennie Loriston-Clarke and Dutch Courage. Following his retirement, Dutch Courage has performed spectacularly all the Grand Prix movements in long reins.*

The Show Jumper

I have previously discussed the basic training of all horses, practised fairly universally to a lesser or greater degree, but the show jumper does require some specialist training.

It takes time for the show jumper to build up the muscle it requires to jump big fences and also to create the confidence in its rider to do this unquestioningly. Hours of work must be spent fittening and training the horse to jump accurately and cleanly. This cannot be achieved unless the flat work is sufficiently advanced to produce an obedient and well-balanced athlete.

No jumping exercises will be of much benefit unless the rider understands the importance of maintaining balance, controlling the rhythm/rate, communicating effectively and having a feel for what is happening beneath him or her.

Before looking in detail at training techniques, let us consider the desirable qualities specific to the show jumper.

WHAT TO LOOK FOR IN THE SHOW JUMPER

Every horse has a natural instinct for jumping, and with careful training this inherent ability can be utilized to produce many good show jumpers. There are, however, two factors which can make all the difference between a good show jumper and an exceptionally good one, so it is always best to know what the ideal is, even though this may be very hard to find.

The horse's disposition or character and its cleverness or agility over the fence are what really matter, and to get to the top the horse needs a good proportion of both. If you

Left: *Competing on snow is common in many European countries, particularly in Switzerland. This horse and rider at St Moritz are both looking confidently ahead towards the next fence.*

Above: *This horse is really using its forearms well to clear the fence, with Robert Smith well in balance giving plenty of freedom with the reins. The Cornish double-ringed snaffle is a popular bit.*

Below: *This nice young horse is jumping in immaculate style, showing itself off to perfection in the Young Ireland Horse class. Youngsters are shown in hand and on the lunge before the final at Dublin.*

The Show Jumper

are fortunate enough to find one with these two attributes, you are extremely lucky, but the responsibility of then training and producing this talent in the ring on the day rests with the rider.

When trying a horse, watch it carefully to first see how it jumps over a single fence. Does it lift its front legs from the shoulders? This is an indication of its ability. Does it round well over the top of the fence? Do not be put off immediately if it does not as there may well be an obvious reason, such as bad training, which may become apparent as you see more of the horse in different situations.

See the horse next over a simple in-and-out set at about 7.3 to 7.6 metres (24 to 25 feet) apart and then adjust this to suit its natural stride length. If the horse is sufficiently advanced, raise the second part higher and higher a few centimetres or inches at a time up to about 1.2 metres (4 feet) and watch the horse's technique and its mental reaction, particularly if it is unlikely to have jumped this height before. Should the horse suddenly start to stop, it is worth watching it carefully as this may be an indication that it is a bit 'chicken' and lacks self-confidence.

If you still like the horse, try it yourself to see what it 'feels' like. This is one of the most important points to remember when trying a horse – it must feel right for you and be your type of horse, and temperamentally the two of you need 'to gel' to be able to create that all important partnership which makes up successful combinations.

TOP TRAINERS' METHODS

There are many good show-jumping trainers, numerous bad ones and a few very good ones and I have been lucky enough to have been taught by and have observed a couple of these few at work.

Bert de Nemethy gives courses all over the world and his teaching and theories are simple and classical. The rider must understand the basic principles of straightness and riding the horse forwards on the flat before jumping work is begun.

He emphasizes the necessity of the spine from head to tail being absolutely straight. The rider must be aware of this and know the feeling of the horse going forwards straight.

Obedience is another important factor and to be able to perform well the horse must be able to obey the rider's instructions without resistance. Leg-yielding and shoulder-in encourage the horse to bend its body and, by putting it in position for these exercises, the horse becomes more athletic and supple and so finds everything easier.

The **turn on the haunches** or **half pirouette** is extremely important for the show jumper as this prepares it for the quick turns necessary in jump-offs etc and is an exercise that requires frequent practice. It can be practised in walk or canter anywhere in a school, but is particularly useful as the horse approaches a corner when it is already thinking of making a turn. The horse brings the forehand in off the track round the haunches. Prepare the horse with a half-halt, sit a little deeper on the inside seat bone and apply the outside leg behind the girth

Above: *Robert Smith instructs his assistant on the height required for schooling. Despite being a top rider, Robert's practice fences can hardly be described as grand but they still serve their purpose!*

Below: *The classic start to any schooling session. The ground pole followed by the cross pole makes the horse concentrate and encourages it to fold neatly in front. The higher the cross, the greater the fold.*

Left: *This horse is being schooled over a ground pole placed approximately 9–10 feet (2.7–3 metres) away from the upright to encourage the horse to find the correct take-off spot so that it rounds well over the fence. The sequence shows the horse picking up neatly in front and clearing the fence well behind, even though it appears a little restricted by the balancing rein throughout the jump. The rider's leg has remained in a good, effective position throughout the jump.*

whilst bringing the inside rein inwards to guide the horse round until it is facing the opposite direction. Just before completing the turn, straighten the horse and with even pressure ride the horse forwards. When done from trot or canter, this movement becomes a half pirouette.

Bert de Nemethy's lessons start with a check on the rider's position and correct length of stirrup for the work being done. Starting in walk, he likes to see the horse get into a good rhythm with lively but non-hurried paces and a good even stride. Several changes of direction loosen the horse up well and then exercises to shorten and lengthen the stride are carried out along with leg-yielding and turns on the haunches.

In the lessons I observed, pole work consisted of first walking then trotting over poles, with any disobediences corrected by returning to the walking exercise until the horse was settled enough to carry on in trot. The poles were set at 1.37 to 1.45 metres apart (4 feet 6 inches to 4 feet 9 inches); they should never be wider than 1.5 metres (5 feet). A small parallel was added about 2.9 metres (9 feet 6 inches), or one stride on from the last pole, and the horse was then walked and halted after the fence so that it remained controlled and listening to its rider. Further exercises consisted of jumping parallels at 1, 2 or 3 strides apart, always coming back afterwards to a halt and ensuring the horse remained obedient throughout. The rider's position was watched and corrected with the emphasis very much placed on maintaining the weight over the centre of gravity, keeping the head up and the lower leg position secure at all times.

Bert de Nemethy believes strongly in the correct systematic buildup of flat work before jumping anything too big. When the horse is going satisfactorily, then it can jump bigger fences. Parallels are the best for teaching the horse to round well over the fence and these can be increased gradually in height so that you have a combination of parallels with different strides in-between. Jumping different types of fences is always important for the young horse as well as practising round a course. But if you can train the horse to be obedient to the rider's wishes and perfect its technique over a fence, it is now competitive experience which will help it settle and produce the same style in a competition as it produces in training.

Iris Kellet and her husband John Hall, who run the very impressive Kelletts Riding School outside Dublin, teach on very similar lines but perhaps place even more emphasis on the rhythm and rate of approach into a fence. Flat work is again the priority with the rider's position then being scrutinized and corrected, with the firm lower leg position being used to govern the rest of the body.

Iris fully recognizes the difficulties experienced by a short person when jumping a big fence and encourages these people to make the best of this slight handicap by full use of

Below: *The approach to a fence is so important. In this approach, in which the horse's head is up and has a hollow outline, the horse will not be able to lower its head properly and fold up well in front or get the hocks sufficiently underneath the body when taking the fence.*

their arms and body over the top of the fence, to ensure there is the minimum of interference with the horse in the air and during the landing.

Both stress the importance of being able to judge the correct pace to approach the different fences and combinations and also how to shorten or lengthen the stride; to put in an extra one or ride on enough to leave one out will help to save that valuable second in the jump-off.

THE RIDER'S STYLE

The great Italian trainer, Caprilli, changed the style of the show-jumping rider from the backward to the forward position over fences. This style enables the horse to use itself much more easily over a fence and to use its shoulders and round its back well, allowing its withers to be the highest point over the top of the fence. The priority for the rider, however, is to get in balance so as not to disturb the horse. Keep a delicate feel on the mouth with rounded hands held together just above the withers. The legs must be in the correct place at all times used just behind the girth and must not be allowed to slide around. The rider should feel both seat bones evenly on the saddle in rhythm with the horse's stride. The head must always be held upright and straight, looking in the direction of travel. The shoulders and back must be upright but not stiff.

The balance changes with the movement so it is important that the rider does not disturb the horse's centre of gravity point by being in an incorrect position. The rider must control his or her balance and keep the horse

moving in a steady rhythm with enough impulsion to perform whatever is asked of it. The rider must sit above the centre of gravity at all times. Therefore, as the horse moves on forwards, the rider should move his or her weight forwards a little, and as the horse slows down so he or she should come back to a more upright position. The rider's legs control the speed and impulsion required, but care must be taken not to be too strong with these on a highly sensitive horse while the plodder may need extra motivation through the use of sharper spurs on occasion. The hands indicate direction and regulate the speed. All these factors produce our means of communication with the horse. Many riders use the voice as well, but some trainers say this can be confusing as everyone has a different tone.

Taking the Jump

The rider must make the jump as easy as possible for the horse throughout each phase. He or she should adopt a light but forward seat and maintain a positive attitude during the approach. At the point of take-off, the rider maintains a firm leg position, allows the hands to travel forward giving freedom to the horse in front and remains in balance, going with the horse as it prepares to thrust itself into the air. It is very important at this stage that the rider does not get in front of the movement, which will

Right: *Riding a turn is most important when it comes to jumping since the horse must stay in balance at all times to make a good approach to each fence, many of which come after a corner or turn from another fence.*

Below right: *This horse is trying hard by using its neck and bringing up its withers as the highest point over the jump, but has put a stride in after the pole so is unable to lift its forearms up quickly enough.*

Below: *This American rider is clearly demonstrating the power required by horse and rider on approaching a fence. Notice the strong lower leg position and allowing hand as the horse prepares for take-off.*

Above: *This sequence shows the approach, take-off, moment of suspension and the landing over a simple training fence. The horse has taken off a little far away from the fence and has flattened slightly over the top but has cleared it quite well.*

Left: *This sequence shows the tremendous power in the hindquarters as the horse prepares for the take-off to a big spread fence. Notice how neatly the forelegs are brought up and remain so over the fence.*

unbalance him or her for the landing and interfere with the horse's rhythm over the fence. During the moment of suspension over the obstacle, the legs must remain steady and on the horse. The hands follow the movement through without hindering the stretching of the neck, and the body folds over the top of the fence and starts to become more upright again as the horse starts to descend.

The landing is the most difficult part of the jump as the horse carries all its weight for a split second on first one and then the other other foreleg before its hind legs touch the ground. It is so important, therefore, that the rider does not add to this already considerable strain by getting too far forward at this point. The least interference possible at this stage is most helpful and the rider must follow the horse's movement until the next stride to allow the horse time to rebalance.

In combinations, this attitude of non-interference becomes doubly important, although the rider may need to help the horse with his or her legs to create extra impulsion. But this should really have been done before the combination as a whole rather than at any stage in the middle. This is where experience has no substitute and it is only practice which will teach the rider how and when to create the correct amount of impulsion to negotiate the different types of obstacle.

Pace

The canter is the most important pace for the show jumper and it is important that the horse can be collected and extended with ease and without losing the impulsion so vital for jumping a big fence. The larger the obstacle, the more collection and impulsion will be required to negotiate it. Plenty of time must be spent on the canter to ensure that the horse remains in balance without resistance, whether in a very collected frame or when being ridden forward. For success in the jump-off, the horse must respond quickly and obediently to every command without wasting precious seconds.

Above: *The power and flexibility of the joints can be seen as Pierre Durand jumps this big upright on Jappeloup. The horse uses its head and neck well to help balance itself and pushes off well from behind.*

Below: *Michael Robert soaring towards the camera over some rather flimsy rustic poles. The horse, totally airborne, demonstrates its supreme athletic ability; a good take-off is vital.*

Right: *Ireland's greatest show jumper, Eddie Macken, shows superb style and balance over this parallel. In fact, Eddie is seldom seen in anything less than a perfect position over a fence.*

Riding A Turn

This is very important just before a fence, since how it is done will influence the approach and outcome of that particular obstacle or combination. Maintaining the impulsion and rate is essential and, if your flat work has been steadfastly practised with pirouettes, circles and turns on the haunches perfected, it is now only a matter of choosing the right amount of impulsion to cope with the turn and fence. The rider must be able to feel with ease what is required to do this so that the horse is not asked to make an unnecessary effort through lack of pace and preparation before the turn.

By studying the top riders during their rounds it is possible to learn a lot on how this is achieved and, although there are many variations in style, the influence of the

degree of impulsion required to come to the correct spot for take-off is nearly always the deciding factor.

The take-off

Choosing the correct take-off spot or platform is largely governed by your horse's stride and its degree of training, but the pole and cavalletti work should have helped it to judge this correctly if it has been carefully schooled. If the horse does have a problem then extra schooling is necessary and the following exercises may be helpful.

A placing pole can be put on the ground or a cavalletti (at the middle height to start with) approximately 2.5 metres (8 feet) in front of the fence – this will need to be pulled out further with a bigger fence or a long-striding horse. If the horse tends to get too

close in spite of this, two poles can be placed with the corner of the 'V' just resting on the centre of the jump with the other ends pulled out to form an upside down 'V'. This encourages the horse to take off a fraction earlier. A high cross pole may have a good influence on bringing the horse to the right spot.

Gymnastic jumping is also extremely helpful, as the horse has to think for itself. It is very important that the rider does not interfere or pull back at the horse when jumping, otherwise the horse will never really learn to judge its own take-off which is essential when competing at the top to save time and unnecessary interference from the rider.

THE VARIOUS TYPES OF FENCES

There are fences of every type and description to be found in competitions, but they all divide into the four basic categories: uprights for testing height; spreads – width; water – length; combinations – agility.

Uprights

These fences require a high jump, but it is the ground line which influences how easy they are for the horse to jump. Generally, high fences require plenty of impulsion and collection for the horse to be able to spring upwards with ease.

Planks and gates require great precision since they do not have a solid ground line. Unless the horse is controlled and obedient on the approach, it may get too close and knock the fence. Walls are solid to the ground and therefore easier to jump, but are made more inviting with the addition of a brush or similar filler in front. Sun gates, which are shaped in the form of an ark, require extra precision as they are higher in the middle. The reversed sort which have a dip in the centre are much easier. Sloping rails require great precision and straightness, especially when they are used in a combination, but the centre of the fence is always the most important and inviting place to jump. Upright rails are sometimes painted in such a way as to be either quite confusing or helpful. If you notice some sort of optical illusion as you walk the course, remember that the horse will be likely to experience the same momentary confusion, so help your horse to cope with this when you ride. Stiles, narrow poles and wicket gates require extra obedience and control, but it is the size of the wings which can determine how difficult they are to jump. A narrow fence with narrow wings can be a real test of precision,

Left: Jumping uprights requires great precision and impulsion, particularly at a fence such as this which does not have a definite ground line and is on the airy side. The horse has got amply close to the top but is clearing it neatly behind. The rider, Nelson Pessoa from Brazil, has stayed well in balance but loses some security by allowing the heel to come up and the lower leg to start sliding back. The hands are being used on the neck on landing for extra security.

whereas the same fence can be quite inviting if it has large, wide wings which draw you into the central spot. Rustic fences may have the effect of making some horses rather careless, since their lack of colour makes them look less imposing, especially if they lack a bit of filling. Again, be careful to get your horse's attention.

Spread Fences

These require the horse to jump wide as well as high. Once the fences reach much over 1.2 metres (4 foot) they tend to become quite imposing obstacles and require greater precision and care on the approach. The classic spread fence is the oxer or parallel. If the rails at the front and back of the fence are the same height, as in a true parallel, the horse's accuracy is tested to the limit in requiring a very neat, clean jump. If the front rail is slightly lower, the fence is considerably less demanding. There are numerous variations of spread fence, but whatever the type of fence, be sure to have the right

degree of collection and impulsion and to approach the fence with the right rhythm or rate for the horse to jump it easily.

Triple bars are best ridden like an upright, with precision, but the horse must come quite close to the bottom of this wide, ascending obstacle. Be quite wary of the triple that does not look solid and well filled-in. Ride on more strongly at this sort whilst maintaining the collection.

Spread fences with water trays or ditches underneath can come as a surprise to some horses if they have not previously seen them. Therefore, it is important to accustom your horse to as many different types of fence as possible in its early training. Some cross-country schooling will help with this type of fence.

Water

Although a spread in its usual form, a water jump is basically testing the length a horse can jump as well as its bravery. Many show jumpers are not introduced to this type of

Left: This horse is folding up well in front over this big parallel. The rider is well in balance with a strong leg maintaining the forward movement. It is important to have enough controlled impulsion to jump fences at this height.

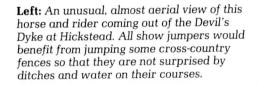

Left: *There are many different ways to jump a fence, but this rider's acrobatics on horseback have not deterred her brilliant little horse from competing most successfully at the top level. Despite the excessive movement of the body, the rider's hands are soft and sympathetically placed throughout the jump. The consistency of the way the jockey rides is vital to a successful partnership, and this one has competed over many different types of courses around the world.*

Left: *The difference in the classical American style is plain to see. American riders have been trained for many years by Bertalan de Nemethy using the classical seat with strong leg and a following hand. His influence has played a major role in the great success of US riders over the last twenty years. Now retired, Bert still enjoys taking clinics around the world. Despite the striking contrast in styles, in both sequences, the horse has cleared the fence with ease!*

Left: *An unusual, almost aerial view of this horse and rider coming out of the Devil's Dyke at Hickstead. All show jumpers would benefit from jumping some cross-country fences so that they are not surprised by ditches and water on their courses.*

Below: *The split second between these two photographs shows how much the horse uses its head and neck when jumping. The reins are quite loose in the first picture as the horse rises up to the jump and then stretches forward taking more rein. Vicki Roycroft's hands slide forward to allow the horse maximum reach, especially important over spreads. Horses at this level usually have to jump water.*

fence until they meet it in competition. This is short-sighted and the horse should be taught to go over and through water from its earliest training, as has already been stated.

Start by teaching your horse to jump over a narrow water ditch then gradually increase the width. Gradually introduce a small brush in front and a pole over the top so that the horse becomes accustomed to the various forms that water jumps may take. Wide open water fences should be ridden at strongly with plenty of impulsion and you should ask the horse to really 'open up' over the fence. It is very important to practise this type of fence fairly regularly until you are convinced your horse will have no qualms should it meet one of this kind in the arena.

Combinations

These require very accurate riding to create the right degree of collection and impulsion for the height and type of fences to be jumped. The position and balance of the rider become even more important if he or she is to help rather than hinder the horse. The distances between the jumps are extremely important as they will affect some horses much more than others, depending on their different strides. For this reason the rider must be able to accurately assess what will be easy or awkward for his or her horse, and whether he or she will need to lengthen or shorten the horse's stride a little to cope with the demands being made.

Above: *A lovely sequence of Anne Kursinski on Starman from the USA jumping a combination in near perfect style over both obstacles. The secure leg position has been maintained throughout. The rider has maintained a good position over both fences and yet has managed to sit up and keep driving forward between the two fences. Notice the sympathetic hands, never interfering but keeping an even feel. The one-stride double requires accuracy and neatness if faults are not to follow.*

Left: *Trebles require even more balance and accuracy than a double since, if approached too fast, the rider can get too close to the last two elements or, if lacking in impulsion, too far away.*

Straightness is essential and increased impulsion will be necessary for most horses if they are not to be found struggling a little to reach the final fence in a treble which may be a big parallel, possibly off a rather long stride. Walk the distances and carefully check how much time there is from the last fence or corner to the combination so that you can prepare your approach to give your horse the best possible assistance.

Doubles are usually designed for either one or two strides in between the fences, and it is the rider's responsibility to ride the horse positively and accurately using the correct number of strides, so that when a treble is encountered the horse is confident and happy to cope with the extra fence without apprehension. A young horse may find a line of coloured and imposing fences quite daunting. Be careful not to overface the horse with these fences, but build up confidence through correct riding and plenty of practice. The practice fences need not be big, but the horse must be taught the correct technique and be happy and confident about jumping them. Gymnastic work and loose schooling will also help to build up the horse's ability, but nothing should be over-done unless the horse is either fully fit or mature enough to cope with the more demanding obstacles.

Problems

They do and always will crop up from time to time. However careful you are, there will always be the odd occasion when you make an error of judgement or some silly mistake which affects the horse in one way or another. It may undermine its confidence if it is inexperienced; its reaction may even shake your own faith in its ability. It may

mean that an awkward jump catching you off balance has actually given the horse a slight strain, so that the pain it felt at the time or later causes the horse to loose its usual flair. Some horses knock themselves badly as they spring off the ground, making them tighten in the air.

All these small, potential hazards should be considered, in addition to the usual, well-known problems of over-facing; incorrect position of the rider over the fence resulting in poor jumping performance; bad positioning of the horse on approaching a fence; the rider not being positive enough over the fences; the rider being too restrictive or over riding the horse into its fences, resulting in loss of confidence, etc. Whatever the pro-

Left: *It can happen to the very best! The moment when it all went wrong. John Whitaker and Hopscotch failed to arrive at an agreement over this fence and ended up very near a fall. However, they cleared it at the second attempt.*

blem it must first be analysed and then acted upon to solve it. Often it is something very simple, but the secret of coping with any problem is to notice it at an early stage before it grows into something bigger. Accept criticism and advice, if necessary, and set about putting the fault right as soon as possible.

If a problem arises while your horse is in public, that is not the best time and place to deal with it. Take your horse home and solve its difficulties there before appearing in public again. People love to criticize and gossip about other people's misfortunes, so it is always best to avoid giving them the opportunity to do so!

From the horse's point of view, a problem in the ring is a very disturbing experience. Since you are not allowed to school the horse when the problem occurs in the ring, the opportunity to sort it out there and then is lost. The result is that both horse and rider leave the ring feeling less than satisfied with a certain degree of confidence lost. If it is

appropriate to jump the practice obstacle to restore the situation, be sure to do so. But this is just not possible on every occasion, so the sooner you and your trainer can get to the root of the problem, the better. Do make quite sure that you have mastered the problem before actually competing in public again. One mistake will not matter and can be put right, but two or more mistakes in the same vein will do no-one any good, least of all the horse. For those aiming for the top, it is worth remembering in the back of your mind that selectors or judges have a nasty habit of remembering your mistakes, however long ago they were committed. So the fewer you are seen to make, the better your chances of catching a favourable eye.

Below: *The rider has allowed this horse to get a little too close to the fence and so does not have much hope of clearing it. But both the horse and rider are trying hard even though this has happened. Notice how the rider has folded well over the fence.*

The Event Horse

The event horse requires much the same basic training as both dressage and show jumpers, but while the other two are 'specialist' sports, the eventer is an all-rounder or 'jack of all trades' as some like to describe it. It is, therefore, this all-round approach that must be adopted from the beginning.

Eventing is a tough sport, so the horse must be 'brought up tough'. Over rugging, bandaging, and general 'molly-coddling' is not helpful to the eventer. Neither is a rigid routine in its daily life – there is nothing routine about the sport so it is just as well to get the horse used to some variation in its life generally. Having said all that, the intention is not to care less for the event horse, but to help it to cope more easily with the work and training, and not allow it to be too 'soft' for what is most definitely a rugged and demanding sport, especially in the colder climates early in the spring season.

FITNESS WORK

We have already discussed the first two stages of fitness work, and the importance of the initial walking and slow work to the eventer cannot be over-emphasized. With the tremendous variations of ground that have to be coped with on the cross-country

Left: *Water requires careful and thorough schooling sessions for the horse to master the technique of jumping in, over and out. These riders are practising over rails, out of this excellent schooling jump.*

Below: *This rider is demonstrating most effectively how to remain in balance with his horse over a drop fence, giving freedom with his hands while maintaining a firm leg position, which is essential for security.*

Above: *All young horses should be accustomed to water, so that it becomes second nature to them. Standing in running water is also very beneficial to the legs, especially after jarring or bruising.*

course, the strain taken by the horse's legs can be considerable. Therefore, a good grounding at this stage will pay dividends later on when so many horses fall by the wayside later in the season.

Remember when trotting to keep the pace slow to really give the muscles a chance to extend and contract so that they build up the maximum amount of elasticity. Fast trotting will only jar the horse, and if trotted on hard for too long at this pace, the horse will start to shorten its stride. This may even affect the horse's jumping as it braces itself against even more jarring on landing after the fence.

When you are out hacking, try and make the effort to accustom your horse to all types of ground and different going. It must be just as good going uphill as downhill. Over rough ground, the horse must sort itself out and become adept at coping with wooded or stony tracks, and be made to go through trappy or narrow places as well as over or through water and ditches. It must be encouraged to be bold rather than timid and at all times obedient.

OBEDIENCE

Obedience training should start in the stable and applies to all horses whatever their role in life. It is so easy to make the horse listen to you when mucking out. Teach it to move 'over', to go 'back', to stop with a 'whoa' when you are doing its box; be sure it responds when you ask. A few weeks of training the horse in this way, making sure your commands are carried out, will teach your horse to respect you from the start. The horse should also understand the word 'no' if it is doing anything wrong, just as much as 'good boy/girl' whenever it is rewarded. The tone of your voice can communicate quite a lot – sharp meaning you are displeased or require some action; quiet and caressing as a reward. Be sure to always use the same

Top: *The shoulder-in, demonstrated here, is one of the most useful suppling exercises whereby the horse bends its body and moves forwards on three tracks, looking away from the direction in which it is travelling.*

Above: *The rein-back is used regularly in all training, being particularly useful as a re-balancing exercise. Diagonal pairs of legs should step back evenly in sequence, and the horse must stay straight.*

Far Left: *The half-pass is the ultimate in lateral work. This young rider is concentrating hard on moving the horse across the arena; the off foreleg crosses over the near foreleg as the horse steps sideways.*

Left: *Continuing in half-pass, the hindleg can be seen crossing in front of the near hind. The bend is not quite enough, but the horse is always looking in the direction in which it is travelling.*

words to make the horse understand them, so they will become doubly useful when you are riding. But be consistent and use them when you require some reaction from the horse. Make sure it responds every time, even though it may take a little time for the horse to learn at the start.

FLAT WORK

The flat work will vary depending on the stage of the horse's training and the standard being aimed for.

The novice horse will be expected to perform all the basic movements at working trot and canter with obedience and accuracy. Obedience, straightness, correct halts and turns and circles are what the judge would most like to see at this standard, with the horse maintaining a good outline and rhythm throughout.

At preliminary or intermediate standards, the tests require a slightly more advanced outline with the horse going consistently well on the bit during working and medium paces. Leg-yielding and shoulder-in are required in many tests, as well as halt and rein-back and the simpler versions of counter-canter loops and simple changes through walk.

For the advanced tests, the horse should be able to perform on the flat at the same standard as a medium dressage horse. The outline should be raised and more collected so that the horse can produce all the different walk and trot paces showing a distinct difference between each. It will also be expected to show collected, medium and extended canter as well as more advanced counter canter in the form of serpentines or 20-metre (65 feet 6 inches) half or even full circles. The horse must be capable of producing half-pass at least half-way across the arena within the distance of two markers in trot, with a halt, rein back and canter strike off to be expected in most tests.

The work for all this has already been mentioned. But the rider has an additional problem with the event horse in that the horse is not being trained for dressage alone. It requires quite a subtle approach if the horse is to remain calm and sensible for dressage, while also being schooled to jump at speed for the cross-country and be fit enough to do so.

Schooling

It is important to keep the eventer occupied in its work but not to bore it. Schooling sessions are generally best done after the horse has been out on a hack and is well settled. Insist on some good, obedient work remembering all the time the basics of straightness and free, forward movement in all paces. The horse must be able to shorten and lengthen in all paces and this becomes even more important for the eventer as it approaches large, solid obstacles on the cross-country at speed. Practise this at every session as well as the lateral movements, depending on the standard for which the horse is being trained.

Your schooling always needs to be aimed a stage higher than your competition level, so

Above: *Schooling can be done anywhere on flat, well-drained land, and arenas can be laid out in many different ways. This one, marked out with pegs covered by plastic bottles, is a very effective improvisation.*

Below: *This lovely athletic jump out of a water obstacle demonstrates the importance of schooling and fitness for the tough sport of eventing, if the horse is to cope easily with the varied courses of today.*

that if all goes well you will have done your basic groundwork and the horse will be properly prepared to cope with the next stage. There are often occasions when you find you have qualified for certain championships which are aimed at horses ready for the next stage. In some cases, the horse is not sufficiently prepared in time and is over-faced by the competition.

One of the problems of doing dressage at an event is the atmosphere, and the often distracting influence of the cross-country course running rather too close to the arenas, or at least the commentary for it booming away all day long. It is worth training your horse with the radio blaring at times so that it becomes used to the noise, and if possible do not always work on your own. Your horse must learn to concentrate with other horses around whether these are jumping or not. Make the effort to get it used to all these typical types of distractions.

The looseness of the paces and rhythm must be worked on regularly and, perhaps more than others, the eventer must be really well loosened-up before and after its work. Starting and finishing on a long rein, encouraging the horse to stretch down in a slow trot and at the walk, is excellent for preventing

Right: *Practising jumping in and out of water is an important part of cross-country training. This rider is a little too far forward but has a firm leg position and is giving plenty of freedom with the reins.*

Left: *This rider has met the bank on a good stride and is in a very good position to be able to ride the horse forward so that it is well balanced throughout. The horse is being ridden forward strongly and has made a good jump off the bank landing well out. The rider is perfectly positioned to be able to ride the horse forward into the next stride without having put too much weight onto the forehand, which might have resulted in a rather crumpled landing. The rider's position is vital at these fences.*

Left: *The same rider and jump, but in this sequence the rider is slightly too far forward throughout and, particularly in the last two photographs, can be seen rather in front of the movement pushing the horse into a steeper landing. Banks and steps require plenty of impulsion so that the horse jumps well up onto them. A series of uphill steps must be ridden boldly as the horse will land a little shorter on each one. Downhill steps or banks require the rider to keep in proper balance throughout.*

muscles becoming too tight. Some horses are slightly prone to this, with the result that all their work, including the jumping, does not have the full elasticity which allows them to shorten or lengthen to the maximum. The well-trained horse should have been schooled in such a way that it is able to utilize its body and mind to maximum effect.

CROSS-COUNTRY TRAINING

This should begin early and can be done alongside general jump and gymnastic training. You can start quite simply by accustoming the horse to water from the earliest days. The horse must learn to go through puddles not always around them, it must go through muddy patches and be quite happy about going down into dips or small quarries. Ditches need frequent practice until the horse is fully confident that they are not as frightening as they sometimes look. Very often there are nice little calverts on the side of the roads which are a good size to pop over with a young horse, if it is safe enough, and you have a decent verge and a quiet road. Always check everything carefully, particularly with a young or inexperienced horse, so that you build up that all-important confidence. This is particularly important if the ground is wet or boggy; there is nothing more frightening to a young horse which rarely goes into a messy-looking place, than to end up struggling out of a full-scale bog. Beware also of water or ditches – be sure you know

they are safe and that they have a good bottom before making your youngster tackle them. A fright at this stage could influence the horse for the rest of its life.

As far as jumping bigger cross-country fences goes, this will very much depend on how the horse is progressing with its general jump training and its state of fitness. Do not be tempted to jump too much too soon until you are sure the horse is physically fit enough and you have taught it enough to be able to negotiate ins-and-outs, parallels, bounces, fences on an angle, etc. Cross-country fences do not fall down if you hit them, but you and your horse could, so it is in your own best interests to prepare your horse sufficiently beforehand.

Cross-country schooling sessions, where you can actually go and jump a whole series of fences at one time, are the ideal way of giving your horse the necessary experience. The fences do not need to be very big, but must be solid and safe. Any fence that has not been jumped well or the horse is worried about should be jumped three or four times until you are sure it fully understands how to negotiate that type of obstacle. With combinations, it may be useful to jump part of it first, such as with a coffin. Sometimes getting the horse over the ditch first and then tackling the 'out' works wonders, rather than confronting the horse with the whole thing in one go.

With young horses I never mind encouraging them with a lead from a more experi-

enced horse on their first couple of schools, but they must always finish up by doing it themselves and must never be allowed to rely on getting a lead. I do think this method is extremely useful in building up confidence and it is also worth remembering that the horse, being a herd animal by nature, finds this very encouraging. It often avoids what might otherwise become quite a battle over certain fences which appear horrific to some horses. For instance, some logs frighten horses so much that they will not go near them to start with. There is a theory that these fences remind them of large, lethal snakes or crocodiles, which instinctively means danger! Who knows what our now heavily domesticated equine friend thinks, but the fact is that we now expect it to perform over these and other much worse horrors unquestioningly. So whatever way we can use to persuade the horse that these obstacles are in fact harmless, the fewer battles we will have and the quicker it will gain in confidence. I have always found a

Below: *This horse and rider are practising over a coffin, a classic event obstacle consisting of rails to a ditch to rails out. The ditch is often sited on a downhill approach, as in this case, and the horse must be neat over the rails in if it is not to peck or stumble towards the ditch. This fence has adjustable rails and is ideal for use as a practice fence, since all or parts of it can be raised or lowered.*

Some Typical Cross-country Fences

Above: *Trakhenas require strong forward riding; riders should look and think ahead rather than peering down into the ditch.*

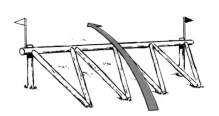

Above: *Zigzags vary in design but need riding a little like spreads. Do not ask for too big a stand off but keep straight.*

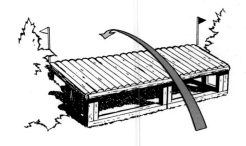

Above: *Pheasant feeders may look a little spooky and can be deceptively wide. Ride on strongly but keep a good feel on the reins.*

Above: *Pallisades vary according to their siting but should be ridden in a balanced, forward manner with a well-studied landing.*

Above: *Bull finches can be quite confusing for the horse, especially if thick, so be very positive and practice beforehand.*

Above: *Log piles, a standard fence, rarely cause problems with their solid appearance. Ride with accuracy and boldness.*

Above: *Zigzags over a ditch require some thought to choose the most inviting part. Bold, positive riding is important.*

Above: *Tyres may seem spooky to a young horse and are presented in many ways, but rarely cause problems if positively ridden.*

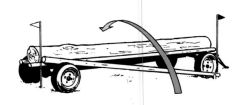

Above: *Timber wagons jump well with bold, straight riding. Aim for the part with the most obvious ground line, if possible.*

Above: *Tiger traps come in various guises but usually have a ditch underneath. Ride forward strongly and look ahead.*

Above: *Coffins are a test of obedience and athleticism and should be approached steadily but with much forward impulsion.*

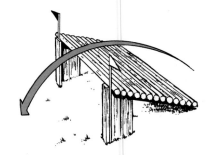

Above: *Sloping pallisades with drop landings require balance and impulsion. The rider must not tip forward on landing.*

Uprights

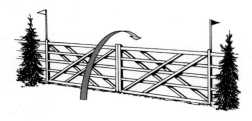

Left: *Gates on a cross-country course need treating with great respect. Set your horse up well and jump accurately and straight.*

Right: *Rails with a drop landing should be ridden at steadily with the horse well on its hocks and listening to the rider.*

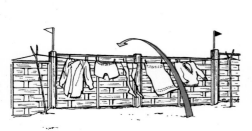

Above: *This upright fence with 'spooks' must be respected like any vertical jump but should not cause problems.*

Above: *The steps to this stile act as a ground line making it more inviting. Aim for the step to make the horse stand back.*

Above: *This uphill log pile needs strong riding to give the horse the necessary impulsion to clear it with ease.*

couple of sessions with another horse most useful for the young or slightly apprehensive type of horse which requires plenty of encouragement.

Cross-country Fences

Every type must be practised so that the horse understands the technique required for the different fences. Once the horse is confident and jumping combinations fairly slowly and neatly, it must then learn to jump them equally safely at cross-country speed. It is the consistent rhythm which will become so important when the horse reaches three-day event standard. A steady rhythm throughout a course will take half as much out of the horse as those seen galloping off madly across a field, only to be hooked right back for a fence which is then 'show-jumped'. This method is totally unprofessional and tiring for the horse, quite apart from defeating the whole object of cross-country riding which is to negotiate the fences fast, cleanly and safely with the minimum amount of stress to the horse.

As with show jumping, the fences come in a huge variety but the important aspect is the speed and degree of balance and impulsion required to clear them successfully and safely.

While collection and impulsion are important for the show jumper, it is more speed

while maintaining the horse in balance with the right amount of impulsion that is important for cross-country. The centre of gravity is much further forward with a galloping horse and the rider is forward over this point, but as horse and rider approach the fence, the rider must push the hind legs more underneath and come more upright to lighten the forehand before the fence. Only the most essential adjustments should be made to the horse's pace, except when riding the trappy or technical combination which will require a certain amount of collection and impulsion beforehand.

Some of the different fences to be found include: uprights, spreads, banks, combinations, water and ditches, fences to be jumped through, corners, angled fences and bounces.

Upright Fences

These always need treating with caution on the cross-country. However innocent they may look, to jump an upright safely at speed means that the horse must jump cleanly. Prepare the horse well and be sure it is not on its forehand, but has the impulsion well underneath itself between your hand and leg. Try and take off at a sensible distance from that particular fence. The solid obstacle will be treated with much more respect by the horse than a couple of flimsy

looking rails, and take especial care of those with a false ground line.

Study the approach, especially if it is in heavy shade and is not going to look particularly obvious to the horse. Also, if it is on a downhill slope, the horse should not take off too early thus increasing the jar of the landing phase, nor too close so that it just catches the top, resulting at best with a 'peck'.

Generally speaking, all uprights require a little extra balancing of the horse and treating with enough respect to ensure they are always correctly assessed and cleanly jumped with ease.

Spread Fences

These tend to be the eventer's favourite. There is nothing more thrilling than galloping safely over a big, inviting spread fence whether it be solid or a good double-brush type with ditch in front. The horse requires the speed and impulsion to jump these cleanly and with ease, but again careful assessment of the approach to be sure of being straight is important. Angling a spread is not recommended since this results in increasing the width, especially if it consists of big parallel bars. These must always be jumped straight and with plenty of impulsion in the same way as tables or other wide, solid fences or big hedges.

Left: *This excellent sequence shows how the horse has taken off well outside the wings and the sheer momentum of speed is carrying it effortlessly over the fence, with its rider staying well in balance throughout. The art of jumping steeplechase and cross-country fences at speed is what will ultimately make a successful event partnership. The position over the fence when jumping at speed is a little more upright and braced so that the rider is well-placed to cope with the unexpected.*

Spread Fences

Above: *This spread of parallels is well-framed by the two trees which helps to make it much more inviting.*

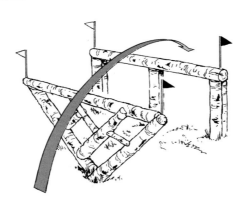

Above: *Another spread best jumped where there is a ground line. Because of the optical illusion, be sure to keep straight.*

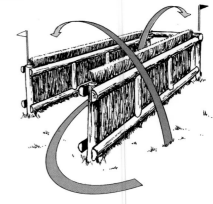

Above: *This double brush has an option: the longer but single rail part may be better for the unfit or the horse with less scope.*

Above: *Wide and square solid fences such as this must be jumped straight and with some respect. A stand-off must be discouraged.*

Above: *A nice inviting fence, but rounded bales are big, even when sunk into the ground, so ride with plenty of impulsion.*

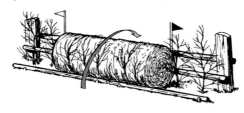

Above: *A sloping garden stand may be full of very brightly coloured flowers so be positive with a spooky young horse.*

Above: *Uphill square log piles require neat accurate jumping but must be approached with plenty of impulsion.*

Above: *Open ditches and big brush fences should be ridden at strongly, but always keep the horse balanced into them.*

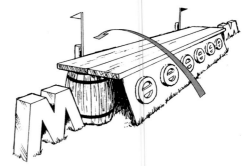

Above: *Sleeper piles or tables are solid and imposing. They require respect but should be ridden at strongly.*

Be sure you do not allow your horse to stand off at spreads; it should be encouraged to take off as close to the fence as possible without getting underneath it. Spreads going downhill require the same principle of controlled impulsion, whereas those on an upward approach need really strong riding to be sure the horse has the necessary impulsion to clear them. The size of the fences and the horse's stage of training make a great difference to how these are ridden, but spreads do require bold, straight riding.

Combinations

They come in such a huge variety of different stridings nowadays that it is difficult to divide them into any set type, but generally all require careful assessment to work out the best method and speed of approach for your particular horse's stride. Accuracy and control are the all important factors. Make sure you ride them throughout; do not set the horse up for the combination and then leave the animal to its own devices. It is at exactly this point that the horse really needs the most help.

Whether the combination takes the form of a 'bounce', which requires a really collected 'bouncy' approach, or a fence that demands a series of different strides, your planned route through the obstacle must be precise and positive. If necessary, line up the fence with some easily identifiable object before and after the fence, get onto that line then stay on it throughout the fence. This same approach is also necessary for **a corner** or

Combination Fences

Above: Raised logs are usually fairly solid looking despite the lack of ground line, but you must meet them on a good stride.

Above: This jump in and out of water has an alternative but time-wasting approach to the first element. Ride water quite steadily but with enough impulsion to ensure the horse will go first time.

Above: Square and solid tables or bars are often found at the end of courses and must be treated respectfully but ridden well.

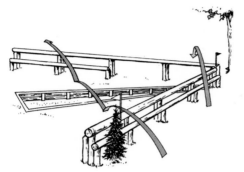

Left: This jump can be ridden as one by going straight over the corner, which requires accurate and bold riding, or on the left to jump the rails, ditch, then rails out slightly on the angle.

Below: This combination incorporates either a bounce downhill or a longer alternative avoiding the bounce. The horse must be well balanced and on its hocks before the fence, then ridden forward strongly and straight.

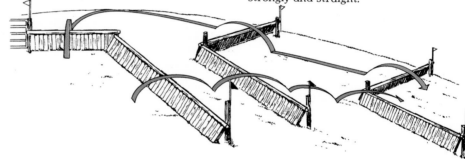

Above: A variation of a big open ditch. Ride such fences strongly and boldly so the horse has the momentum to clear it easily.

Left: This rider is coming into this rather artificial but ingenious fence perhaps a little lacking in impulsion, since the horse is backing off and not really finding it as easy as if it had come in with a bit more pace. It can be very difficult to get the approach just right when there are several elements to an obstacle; each horse will react a little differently. The riders that have developed a real partnership with their horses show their experience by making it look really easy.

Combination Fences

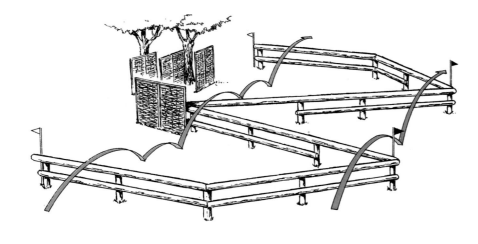

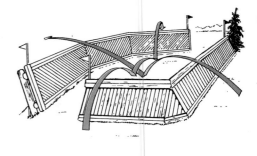

Right: A sunken road with quite a steep landing, if you ride straight on, and a longer route on the left. Here, competitors are able to choose a route to suit the experience and ability of the horse.

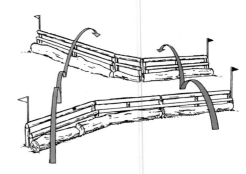

Above: A similar type of fence but filled in may appear more imposing to some but be helpful to others. A bounce or one stride, it has a downhill landing over the second element which requires essential balance.

Top: Combination fences such as this require careful thought as to which route would be best for that particular horse: two corners or the three easier elements on the left allowing more room.

Above: A combination with two options, one incorporating four jumping efforts including a bounce but all on the direct line; or a simple but longer option on a tight turn with a stride between fences.

Above: A bounce option going straight is rarely a problem with an experienced horse and this fence offers one stride on the angle for those that require extra room. However, a run-out could catch the unwary.

Above: *This double coffin can be approached either in the middle or on either side, all presenting different problems over the way the ditches may be jumped. A bold, obedient and athletic horse is best for this fence.*

Left: *This picturesque obstacle presents a fairly straightforward one or two-stride in and out, but some competitors with spooky horses need to ride on strongly if their horse is not to catch them out.*

Above: *A bold, neat jump into this water requires balanced, bold riding. This rider has a firm leg and is in a safe, strong position to cope with any eventuality. She is landing well ready for the next jump.*

Left: *This interesting sequence shows the complete take-off, jump and landing over a large corner fence. Notice how far the hocks have come underneath before the actual jump. The rider has remained well in balance ready to ride on to the next fence.*

Combination Fences

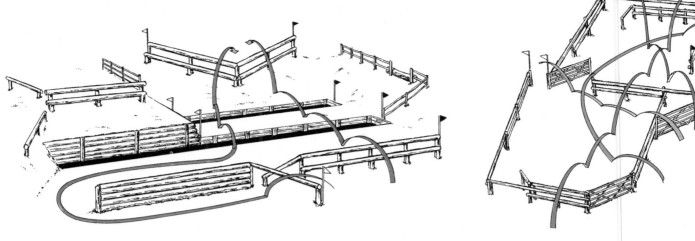

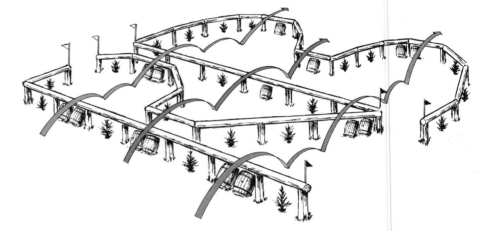

Above: *Double coffins require accurate riding and their severity depends on the ground and the approach. Some have flat, others steep ground into them; this and the speed must be taken into account.*

Above right: *An interesting fence providing several routes. Careful thought must be given to this type of obstacle to ensure that the flagging is properly worked out and ridden through in the right direction.*

Right: *A more complicated fence giving less room and requiring extra agility but having three obvious routes involving a bounce or strides in-between the various elements. Controlled impulsion is required.*

jumping **angled rails.** Once you have got set up for the fence then be really positive and boldly ride forward sticking to your straight line throughout.

Coffins are the classic form of combination fence requiring an obedient and bold horse. Depending on their siting, they require a bouncy, controlled approach but with plenty of impulsion to ensure the horse does not stop at the last moment on seeing the ditch. An athletic and supple horse is required, so grid work will help a lot towards making the horse neat in front to jump this type of fence with ease.

Banks and Steps Uphill

These require an enormous amount of impulsion to enable the horse to cope easily with the effort of jumping upwards. Inevitably, the type of fence and the approach to it are all important, and jumping onto one bank is much easier than going up a series of steps, which asks for several sustained efforts as the horse springs up from one to another. The rider must be aware of the necessity of keeping the horse going forwards throughout to help compensate for the inevitable shortening of the stride the further the horse goes up the steps. At all times, care must be taken not to get left behind but to stay forward in balance with the horse, driving it on.

Steps Down and Drop Fences

These require balance and the right degree of impulsion so that the least possible strain is put on the horse. The degree of difficulty of steps very much depends on their size and the horse's own technique over them. Some horses tend to lower themselves down very neatly, which is the ideal way to take them, so long as they do not waste time doing so. Other horses take great leaps, which not only jars the legs but also sometimes causes injury, since the horse is more likely to strike into itself. It is, therefore, best to practice over small steps until the horse has learnt to be less exuberant. A bold jump outwards off a bank is fine and is to be encouraged, especially off a Normandy Bank where going too slowly and landing too steeply can spell disaster. Ride on and off boldly so that the horse jumps well out and safely clears any ditch or steep landing which is often presented on the far side. Fences with drop landings should be ridden at boldly, but the rider is usually best leaning back in balance allowing the horse just enough but no more rein than is required. The rider's legs must be pushed a little forward to help him or her stay in balance; at no time should they be allowed to go back causing the rider to tip forward past the point of balance. Those fences that have landings which continue on downhill require a steadier approach and

Banks and Steps Up and Downhill

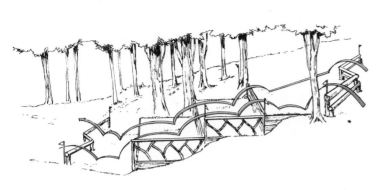

Above: *Fences which include jumping steps downhill require controlled impulsion and straightness. The rider must not get too far forward at any time.*

Above: *This fence has two obvious routes, one with a bigger drop off but is on the way to the next fence. The other is less demanding but involves some tight turns.*

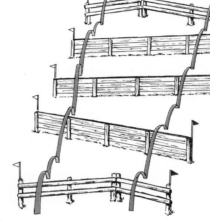
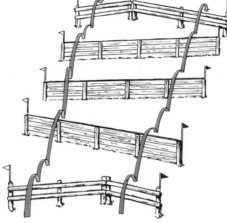

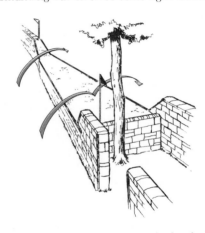

Above: *An imposing drop such as this tests obedience and agility. If the landing is sloping, a steady approach is best to prevent the horse over-jumping downhill.*

Above: *Jumping up steps requires tremendous impulsion which must be maintained to the top, so very strong riding is necessary up both routes of the obstacle.*

Above: *This type of fence can be banked or jumped over in one, but the rider must be prepared for the horse to make its own arrangements. Be ready to sit tight!*

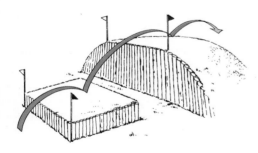

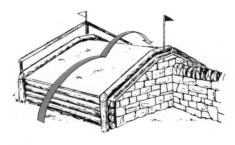

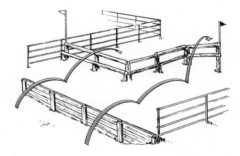

Above: *A smaller followed by a larger bank. Positive riding with plenty of impulsion makes the leap easier for the horse, giving it the necessary impetus.*

Above: *An ascending bank such as this must be jumped strongly so that the horse gets well on top before steadying and popping off nicely balanced to continue the course.*

Above: *A step and rails with or without a stride requires sufficient impulsion to make it easy for the horse to negotiate. The size of the step up can be influential.*

Left: *The rider has approached this impressive uphill obstacle with just the right amount of impulsion to make the fence easy for the horse. The whole jumping action shown in this photographic sequence looks deceptively easy because the horse looks confident and happy about negotiating the obstacle. The rider has remained in balance and in a good position throughout, maintaining a strong leg position. The latter is the real basis of good and safe cross-country riding.*

Fences to be Jumped Through

Above: *Jumping through fences such as this barn requires accuracy and ability to adjust to a change from light to dark.*

Above: *Some horses duck their heads when jumping through fences especially if it seems quite low or the 'lid' rather solid.*

Above: *This one is very high but narrow so the rider must keep the horse between hand and leg to ensure it remains straight.*

Above: *The seat helps this fence as it encourages the horse to take off at the right spot, but the top is not very high.*

Above: *This fence has made clever use of the natural line of trees with effective trimming. It may be dark between fences.*

great control while maintaining the forward impulsion. The horse should learn to pop over them neatly with the minimum amount of effort with the rider keeping fairly upright avoiding getting the weight too far forward at any time.

Jumping Through Fences

This seldom causes a problem but some horses do need practice as they find them a little confusing. If the 'lid' is high there is less

Left: *A lovely jump through this obstacle which has a high lid and is not worrying the horse at all. Some horses may feel cramped and duck their heads and not pick up neatly in front if the lid is too low.*

Water Fences

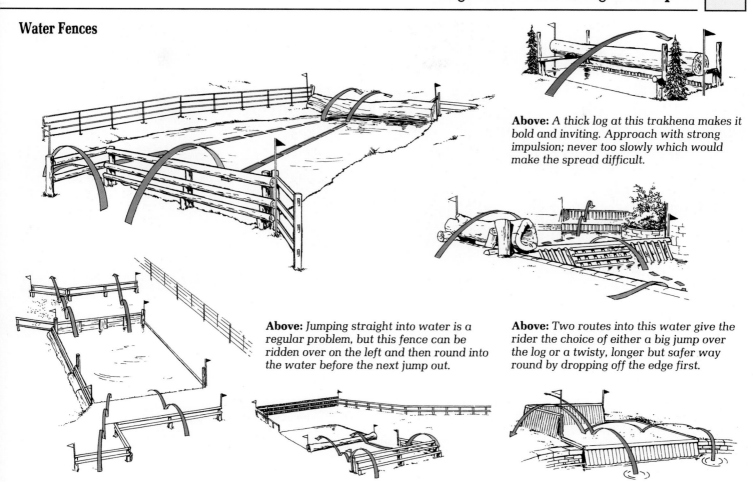

Above: *A thick log at this trakhena makes it bold and inviting. Approach with strong impulsion; never too slowly which would make the spread difficult.*

Above: *Jumping straight into water is a regular problem, but this fence can be ridden over on the left and then round into the water before the next jump out.*

Above: *Two routes into this water give the rider the choice of either a big jump over the log or a twisty, longer but safer way round by dropping off the edge first.*

Above: *A bounce in and out of this water is the quickest but not necessarily the safest route. An extra stride may be safer, especially with inexperienced horses.*

Above: *Two different ways over the first element give this fence an option, but the log into the water and the hedge out have to be jumped. The straight way may be best.*

Above: *The bounce out is quite close and upright allowing no room for error. The less experienced may prefer the longer option – out right before jumping left.*

chance of the horse tending to duck its head, but with low ones the horse may do this and also fail to pick up its legs quite as high as it should. Take care to set your horse up and keep hold of it with this sort of obstacle. The lower and larger the 'lid', the more your horse must be made to appreciate the fence underneath and learn to round just as well over this sort of obstacle as any other. Generally ride on but keep hold of your horse through this type of fence.

Water

This is the fence spectators love to watch, but at which eventers dread making a fool of themselves! The approach is all important since it is the speed at which the fence is jumped that is essential. The 'drag' of the water can be considerable so the depth plays a big part in deciding on how best to jump the fence. If the water is deep and the approach fence is big with a drop, you will require enough speed and impulsion to be able to jump the fence clear without going too fast so that you are 'tripped up' by the drag of the water. Check carefully for any soft patches or holes; these do have a happy knack of appearing after several horses have been through. Fences in the water can be a problem because of the spray, so steady up once in the water to allow the horse time to see the fence then ride boldly forward. Make sure the horse sees the 'out' part of a water jump, set it up well and be really positive in riding it out. It is very easy to loose impulsion once

you have got into the water, so if it is a straight-forward exit, keep riding the horse on throughout. The rider should stay fairly upright and is generally best leaning back when entering water but must be positive and keep the horse going forward throughout. Most water fences are best ridden at a sensible pace with plenty of controlled impulsion.

Coping With Problems

Inevitably, problems will crop up from time to time and these are often due to lack of confidence following a fall on the cross-country. Hitting a solid cross-country fence can be quite an unnerving experience and if this results in a fall it is very important that

Left: *This young horse and rider are jumping the in-and-out of this water fence in a nice way, but because the rider is riding a bit long, she does not have a very strong or secure leg position to cope safely if the horse stumbled or pecked. She is riding quite fast and the spray could mask the horse's view out of the fence, especially if it was less significant than this solid log out. Once safely in the water, the horse should be rebalanced and then ridden at whatever is presented.*

neither horse nor rider are given too long to brood over it. Ideally, if you have remounted and finished your course a lot of the damage done will have been restored along the way in any case but it is likely that you will still have that niggling doubt. Think carefully about what you consider the problem was in the first place. Was it a wrong approach – not straight, too fast, too slow, not enough impulsion? Had you not taken the deep going into consideration and ridden with extra impulsion to cope with this? Were you out of control, in which case you may need to reconsider your bit for this phase, or was it too strong and the horse was fighting you instead of concentrating on the fence? Was it bad technique over the fence on the part of the horse – was he dangling in front? Did your boot come off or a bandage, bringing the horse down? Next time, stitch or tape them carefully to prevent this. Whatever the problem, make quite sure you recognize and analyse it and set about putting it right before the next event.

Psychologically, it is a good idea to have a school before the next outing and jump that

Above: *Problems can occur at any time on a course, but many a rider has a healthy respect for ditches! It appears that this rider did not ride on enough and therefore lost the necessary impulsion to clear the ditch and hedge – with disastrous results.*

type of fence a couple of times again so that there are no niggling doubts left to build up into a major worry. Make quite sure in your own mind that you were in fact tackling the fence in the right way.

Lack of control can give rise to all kinds of problems which are quite dangerous, so your braking system needs very careful thought if there are any problems in this direction. The use of flashes, grackles and drop nosebands may be all that is required, along with running martingales or the attachment to your breastplate. These all help keep the horse under control and improve steering, especially the latter.

The choice of bit is always a difficult one, especially on the cross-country, since control

Right: *This rider, despite hanging on with arms and knee, has reached the point of no return! A peck on landing over the first element of this downward combination tipped her too far forward, possibly due to an insecure lower leg position.*

is essential but it is something that has to be experimental. What may suit one rider is hopeless for another because of their hands on the end of the reins. While one may ride with plenty of leg and be able to keep the horse between his or her leg and hand, the other may be all hand and so require a bit that is kind enough to compensate for this and yet gives the necessary control.

The rubber gag is quite a useful bit for those that can ride in them correctly, being sure to 'give' and 'take' rather than pull incessantly at the horse's mouth. They certainly help to get the horse off its forehand and there are numerous variations, but it is not a bit for the inexperienced rider. The Dr Bristol, Waterford, Scorrier or Cornish snaffles have been used with success and, although generally I am in favour of some

sort of snaffle for cross-country because of their relative simplicity, the double bridle should certainly not be discounted.

Sometimes a different bit may be used just for two or three outings to teach the horse a lesson in obedience and then the rider reverts to the original. This is often very successful. Control is vital – without it you cannot safely compete. There is nothing more frightening than galloping flat out down a hill towards a large obstacle knowing you are quite unable to set your horse up to jump that fence safely, so try out your braking system carefully in your schooling sessions. Do not forget, however, that some horses settle very quickly after the first two or three fences once they are on their way. Others may be fine until they get a little tired and then start pulling away from you with their heads on the floor. This is the worst type of horse as it will catch you out when

you are also getting tired, which just goes to impress on us all the importance of rider fitness.

This is vital for the event rider in particular as it is more difficult to get your breath at speed. Be absolutely certain that you are fit enough to handle a really strong, fit horse. Do not slack on your daily riding to get fit – plus the running, swimming, exercises and correct diet which play an important role in keeping your horse under control so that it is a safe ride, especially on the cross-country.

Running out and refusals are usually caused by an incorrect approach, confronting the horse with a seemingly insurmountable problem. Always look at your fences as if you were seeing them through the horse's eyes as well. Remember, you know what you are jumping; the poor horse does not. Think carefully about your initial reaction to a certain

fence. Does it look imposing, in which case remember to ride on at it; confusing, because of a seemingly huge jumble of poles, in which case keep steady with plenty of impulsion to give the horse a chance to work it all out as it gets nearer. Wide fences must be ridden on at, whereas uprights need careful approaches. Have you been doing this consistently or have you had a series of near misses which have finally unnerved the horse?

Other reasons for this sort of problem may be that the rider is simply not keeping the horse going straight between hand and leg, allowing it to wander off course at the crucial moment; not lining up carefully enough for combinations; over-estimating your horse's readiness to do what you are asking. You may be asking too much too soon, in which case it is essential not to do more with that horse at that level until it is more experienced. Over-facing is one of the main reasons of failure. The other is lack of fitness so that the horse is physically incapable of doing what is expected through weakness and lack of proper preparation. This is inexcusable since it means the rider has not done the groundwork and is also not able to 'feel' when the horse has reached a certain level of fitness or, if on a course, has not ridden it in a way that enables the horse to compete without undue physical strain. Even if the horse is not that fit, the true horseman should be able to pace it so that it can get round safely without wearing it out completely on a one-day event. This is where experience counts, and the more of this you can accumulate the better horseman you will become.

Riding at Speed

This is really what cross-country riding is all about. To do this successfully the rider must be positive and forward thinking at all times, should ride with shorter stirrups and a tighter rein to give more leverage and control and keep the horse in balance and at a good rhythm throughout. The horse requires quite

Left: *This very dramatic photographic sequence taken at Burghley fully demonstrates how a slight miscalculation on approaching a big fence can mean disaster. The take-off was too close and the horse was unable to free its legs enough to push itself out of what was a very nasty situation. The roping on the fence poles enabled the fence to be quickly dismantled, so that the horse was released from its uncomfortable position. The rider did well to keep hold of the reins.*

Left: *At the best of times a downhill jump is difficult, but this bounce at Gatcombe on a very steep slope requires an athletic, neat jumper to produce a clean jump. This horse has lost heart on take-off and left one leg behind, screwing badly as a result and sending the rider hopelessly far forward. With such a mistake at the first of the two fences, there is no room to recover and the rider is on her way to a painful fall. The horse needs to be experienced to tackle a fence of this type.*

a lot of practice jumping at speed, but this must not be attempted until it is proficient and has mastered the technique necessary to cope with the different types of fence. The rhythm and evenness of the stride and choosing the most direct route between the fences are what make up time rather than actual speed, but it takes a lot of practice to train the horse to gallop in a relaxed and easy manner to be able to achieve this.

Galloping

This is the final part of the fittening programme and how much, how far and how fast keeps the experts arguing incessantly. However, the fact remains that every horse is different with differing requirements to reach peak fitness, and only experience will tell you what will be right for any particular type of horse.

I personally gallop my horses much less than I used to but canter them slowly quite frequently. The saying that 'speed kills' does seem to be universally accepted amongst riders and trainers worldwide but some sort of fast work to clear the lungs and to give the horse its final fittening work is essential to bring it up to peak fitness.

Certain points must be remembered when galloping to ensure your horse is given the best possible chance of reaching its peak:

1 Never gallop a horse until it has done at least six weeks basic fittening work.

2 Gallop only on good ground and keep the horse balanced between hand and leg and under control at all times.

3 It is better to gallop little and often and gradually build on your work programme rather than over strain the horse by doing single long stints.

4 Be sure your horse is well shod and well protected when considering doing fast work.

5 Warm your horse up gradually before galloping and then allow plenty of time for it to cool off and its heart-rate and breathing to return to normal before putting it away.

Remember, it is the recovery rate which will tell you how fit your horse actually is. Watch how quickly it recovers each time you give it fast work and check its breathing to see how quickly it returns to normal. There should be a steady improvement in this rate each time you 'work' the horse, until you are satisfied it is fit enough to cope with the standard of competition you are aiming at.

Interval Training

This consists of several work periods spaced between rest periods with the work periods being gradually increased as the horse becomes fitter. This method is used fairly extensively and was devised by the Americans, adapted from interval training methods used by athletes.

The idea of this method is to build the body up to cope with repeated small demands

made upon it. A programme of work and rest periods is carefully devised so that the horse does not quite recover before the next work period begins. The work period must not involve too much stress but just enough to ensure the cardio-vascular, respiratory and muscular systems are placed under enough pressure to develop over a period of time. Eventually the work period increases and the rest period is cut back to the minimum as the horse increases in fitness.

It is very important that the horse is not overworked and interval training should not be practised more than once every four days. The same important periods of warming up and allowing the horse time to cool off properly after work are an essential part of the training programme. The number of work periods usually starts at about three in

Above: *Fitness is so important for the event horse and a careful training programme is essential if the horse is to cope with this demanding sport. Cantering is a vital part of the fittening process.*

number, with the duration starting at about three minutes and gradually building up to 10–12. The rest intervals usually start at around four minutes and as the horse gets fitter go down to a minimum of one minute. The speeds are the most flexible part of the system. To start with, the pace may be a slow canter and can then be gradually built up to cross-country and steeplechase speeds of 570–690 metres per minute.

Horses with a history of leg problems should not do too much fast work and preferably be worked up a hill which puts less strain on the legs. They are better working for longer at a slower speed.

Swimming

This can be an excellent way of putting the finishing touches to peak fitness and many horses have benefitted from this type of work which uses the heart, lungs and muscles without putting strain on the legs. The horses generally enjoy the change and five minutes swimming is the equivalent of 1.6 kilometres, (1 mile) fast gallop.

As with any training, it is important to introduce the horse to swimming gradually; a couple of short swims to start with will be more beneficial than too long at one time in the pool. The horse uses many new muscles when swimming and must not be asked to do too much at once. It is an excellent way of strengthening the back muscles which come quite prominently into play in the pool. Swimming is very strenuous on the horse and

Below: *Despite a rather hollow performance, this horse is going well and the rider is displaying dash and determination even if it is not very stylish. Experience helps the rider to concentrate more on style.*

it should always be remembered that, although the actual time in the pool is short, the quality of work has been tough. Some people like to walk the horse for 30–60 minutes before swimming to loosen it up and give it a longer time out of the stable, which must be good for the horse if this is a practical thing to do.

Fitness is absolutely essential for all competition horses and short cuts must never be taken. It takes time and experience to be able to estimate the amount of work required by each horse and what type is best for it, but at the end of it, if the horse looks and feels well and is not being strained by the work given and remains content and happy in its work, it is more than likely in good shape. A bright eye, healthy coat, hard, well-toned muscle and cold, clean legs are what is required for the fit horse.

PSYCHOLOGY

This is just as important for horses as it is for humans and plays a very large part in the preparation of competition horses. If everyone remembered the saying 'to know him is to understand him' there would be far more top combinations around winning medals, etc. But too often we forget that, like us, the horse has feelings and is very sensitive to atmosphere and the attitude of the rider.

Unfortunately, the horse cannot tell us what it is thinking. If only it could, how simple riding and horsemanship would become! Our only means of realizing a little of what it is feeling, therefore, comes by observing obvious signs. The horse's eyes are very expressive and convey quite a lot, as do the action of the ears in the same way. The horse's attitude and behaviour are the other main indicators and correct analysis of this is very important. So often people fail to observe their horse's attitude and general facial expression, missing vital signs which convey some idea of whether the horse is frightened, apprehensive, obstinate, in pain, nervous or timid.

The eyes will give you most of these signs quite clearly, along with the action of the ears, and will tell you a great deal about what your horse is thinking.

The ears may be flickering in a worried apprehensive way; pricked forward in enjoyment and confidence; questioning with one then the other going forward then back; back in fear, anger or worry; tight back in sheer obstinacy or real anger.

The way of standing can indicate the horse's mood and temperament. The obstinate horse will position itself so that it is well-braced on its front legs and ready to lean back in a typical 'bolshy' stance should it be pushed, such as when entering a horsebox. Stance may also indicate foot irregularities or pain. Check out any change from the normal.

The nostrils can be useful indicators of a problem and are very expressive if the horse is uncomfortable. They often look pinched and puckered if the horse is in pain or cold.

Above: *Understanding the horse is probably the most important aspect of riding. One must be able to assess how the horse thinks by noticing its reactions. Ears are very expressive and can tell you so much.*

Below: *Swimming can be of great benefit to the horse, especially if it has had leg or other training problems, where too much work could be harmful. Apart from improving breathing it helps strengthen back muscles.*

They look very pinched if the horse is dehydrated. They are wide and flaring in apprehension or excitement. High blowing and loud snorts are also expressions of excitement, feeling well and enjoyment.

The tail is another useful indicator. If it is carried loose and swinging, the horse is generally relaxed. Tightly clamped is a sign of tension and nervousness; stiffness may mean apprehension; pain or stiffness could indicate some back problem. Raised up in the air is usually a sign of freshness and excitement and is often seen when a horse is first turned out. Sit tight if this happens when you first get on – you have an exciting ride!

Character

Watch your horse and really get to know its character. Is it the type that needs coaxing along with soothing words and several expressions of encouragement, such as patting and praise with the voice? Perhaps it needs bold riding, always being driven forward firmly with the legs as it tends to be a bit timid. Again, words of encouragement will also help. Does it need plenty of time to loosen up because it is the tense, rather stiff type and mentally and physically requires a definite period of time to loosen and soften before it is capable of being asked for proper work? The apprehensive or sensitive horse will require quietness and plenty of initial work so that it has built up confidence to take on whatever is being asked and always needs words of encouragement.

The Competitive Scene

Competing in Horse Trials has taught me a great deal about life. In fact, riding horses has been my *real* education. My 'term' with them has lasted for seventeen years now, and I dearly hope it will continue.

Sport is a healthy occupation. It not only tests your physical capabilities but your mental capacity as well. As for horses, they are – like people – all individuals. Subsequently, they need care, attention and treatment specially tailored to suit their own unique set of characteristics. Industries employ and deal with people of varying qualities; there is little difference between the training of horses and the management of personnel. Our sport produces many successful teams that win medals because of the comradeship between the team members. Every sportsman or woman would like to win as an individual, but if you can win and help others in an unselfish way, the reward is greater.

My favourite quote keeps my riding life in perspective: 'The horse already knows he is a horse – the art of horsemanship lies solely with the rider.'

Virginia Leng

General Preparation

Competing is what equestrian sport is all about. It is the competition itself that makes the days, months or years of preparation, fitness work and training worthwhile. The build-up to an event is considerable taking into account the length of time spent in fittening the horse, its schooling so that it is properly prepared to do what is expected and then the important little outings used as warm-ups for the first serious competitions in the calendar.

PLANNING YOUR COMPETITIVE PROGRAMME

This is the first consideration. At the beginning of every season, you should have a good idea of what you are aiming for and then set about planning each horse's individual programme according to what you think it should be able to achieve. Always have an alternative itinerary in your mind in case things do not quite go according to your original plan because of some sort of problem along the way. The experienced horse can be expected to do a lot more than your young, aspiring star. The latter will need mileage to increase its confidence at this stage.

Before the season starts, check that you and your horses are registered for all the right societies and groups necessary for whatever you are planning to do with your horse. Be sure your flu vaccinations are legal and up-to-date, signed and stamped and that you have a photocopy of each to take round to the competitions with you.

Check that you have entry forms, schedules and any other information necessary to hand and that you know when and how to enter the various competitions planned. The equestrian scene is now so popular that many are being balloted out. The first entries to be balloted are those that are incorrectly completed or late arriving, so be sure you do not join these and wreck your chances of acceptance.

CLOTHES, TACK AND EQUIPMENT

Clothes can be quite a problem, especially for the event rider who requires different outfits for the three phases of the event. At the end of each year it is worth thoroughly checking over everything in case coats, breeches or boots require any major repairs. Take the opportunity to sort out your gear before the new season gets under way.

Remember to check that you have all the **right** equipment, especially as you move up to new standards in dressage or eventing. A hunting cap is fine up to medium-level dressage, but the top hat and tailed coat are generally used for competitions above that level and for the dressage phase of advanced eventing. The rules regarding safety harnesses for hats when jumping tend to change fairly regularly and it is now compulsory for

Left: *The strength and power of the show jumper, along with the concentration of the rider, is clearly demonstrated by Hermann Van den Broeck on Wellington from Belgium, as they clear this Olympic fence.*

Top: *The smile of victory from Gail Greenough of Canada as she faces the press after a great win at Aachen. Good public relations are important to encourage owners and sponsors to participate.*

Above: *Emma Jane Brown takes Bill Brown over this parallel in the practice ring at Hickstead, clearing it well in front. Care must be taken to ensure the ground line is not false on the take-off side.*

General Preparation

Above: *Determination gets the rider a long way but in all competitive riding a stick should be carried. Check its length to ensure it does not contravene the rules. Dressage whips are not always allowed.*

Below: *Turn-out of horse and rider is very important, particularly in dressage where so much depends on overall impression. Light-coloured gloves and spurs are compulsory in advanced classes.*

a harness to be worn in all jumping events in most countries. The type is important and now is the time to check that your old favourite does in fact conform to the latest regulations.

When buying **whips and spurs** check that they also fulfil the requirements laid down in the various rule books. Generally whips may be any length for dressage, but they should not exceed 75 centimetres (30 inches) or be shorter than 45 centimetres (18 inches) for jumping.

Spurs should only be worn in the traditionally correct manner with the curve on the neck of the spur pointing downwards and this should not exceed 3 centimetres (1.2 inches) in length. The buckles must be on the outside with the points of the straps pointing downwards. Unfortunately, even at the top level, you occasionally see spurs worn incorrectly which is the height of unprofessionalism.

The rules about spurs and whips are much stricter in Britain than in the rest of Europe, so make quite sure that you know the national rules governing these in each country. In FEI international competitions, all rules regarding dress and permitted saddlery are to be found in the set of rules relevant to the type of competition you are going to be riding in: the type and colour of gloves, breeches and stocks (hunting ties) for the different events. These may seem small and somewhat insignificant details, but the rules are being tightened up considerably since, unfortunately, more and more are being broken either on purpose or through ignorance. No sport can survive for long if discipline and standards are not maintained at all levels.

The following check list may serve as a useful reminder when checking through your kit at the start of the season.

CHECK LIST

General for Rider

Hats – with harness for jumping or cross-country with correct coloured covers

Coats – tails if doing advanced dressage or advanced eventing

Breeches – white or fawn depending on type of competition and coat worn

Black boots or **top boots** with appropriate garters, straps and covers

Shirt, ties and **stocks** – as appropriate for the type of competition and dress

Gloves – several, light coloured or white as appropriate for dressage

Spurs – various for dressage/jumping

Whips – various for dressage/jumping

Hairnets and **hair pins** – several

Stockpins and **safety pins**

Back protector – essential for cross-country

First-aid kit

Sewing repair kit

Hangers and **clothes bags**

Hat bag or **box**

Stop watch – for eventing

Paper and **pencil** – for notes

Elastic bands

Safety pins

Sellotape

General for Horse

Saddles – as necessary for each type of competition

Bridles – as necessary for each type of competition

Girths – as necessary for each type of competition

Irons and **leathers** – extra strong for cross-country

Surcingles and **Martingales** – as necessary

Breastplates/girths – for all jumping work

Saddlecloths and **numnahs** – a variety and some spares

Boots/bandages – for protection as necessary for exercise and competing

Over reach (bell) boots – include spares

Studs and **stud kit**

Spare set of **shoes**

Grooming kit

Lunging kit

Side reins

Tack-cleaning kit

First-aid kit

Buckets, sponges, scraper – for washing down

Water buckets – keep one out for journey

Haynets – including one for journey

Manger

Hay and **food** – with supplements if used

Mucking out kit

Skip

Rugs and **blankets**

Anti-sweat rugs and **coolers**

Waterproofs

Headcollar and **rope**

Travelling boots/bandages

Tail bandages

Full water carrier – for journey

Left: *Dual World Champion, Bruce Davidson, waits patiently after winning at the Stockholm international three-day event. He has won numerous events and been the backbone to many US teams.*

Below: *A well-stocked, first aid case. This is essential when travelling and competing. However, be sure to call your veterinarian should any serious problems arise, or if you are in any doubt.*

Above: *A huge leap being taken as this horse stands off on take-off to this solid and imposing uphill jump, making it a very big fence indeed. It is important to get as close as possible to uphill fences.*

TRAVELLING THE HORSE

Horses now travel tremendous distances to and from competitions and seem to have adapted remarkably well to the stress this sometimes involves. There are a few points, however, which can make a considerable difference to the horse and how it may perform after a journey. Long journeys, especially those involving travel on bad roads, or air and intercontinental travel, need careful planning and preparation of the horse, as outlined below.

Protection

This is very important and depends to some extent on the type of vehicle being used as to which part of the horse becomes more vulnerable. The horse must be adequately secured to prevent it trying to turn or look around and from biting other horses – a favourite pastime of some horses! If the box is rather low or the horse is nervous and if there is the slightest likelihood of it hitting its head, a poll guard should be fitted to the headcollar. The best type protects the vulnerable front of the top of the head, the part most likely to be affected. Poll guards are recommended when horses travel by air as the entry into the plane is quite low.

Below: *Another fence where the horse has taken off quite early making the fence bigger than necessary. Horses, however, make all fences look deceptively easy so long as the rider remains in balance.*

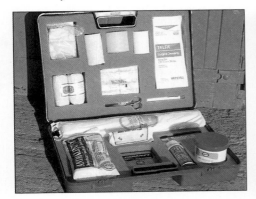

A Travelling First Aid Kit

Thermometer
Wound spray
Wound powder
Dressings/poultices
Bandages and gamgee
Kaolin plastic
Brown paper
Scissors
Salt or Antiseptic solution

Above: *A basic list of useful items to be included in any travelling first aid kit. Take care, however, to check that anything you use on your horse at the competition does not contravene the rules.*

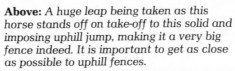

Leg protection is very important and the type used is a matter of preference. There are numerous travelling boots on the market today, many of which incorporate protection for the horse's knees and hocks. These are the best type, so long as they are not too hot and the fastenings, usually made of velcro, stay secured. This depends on how well they have been cared for. Avoid the type made of plastic which, although easy to clean, tend to make the legs sweat – not ideal for the horse. Bandages well put on over good gamgee or other cotton wadding are more supportive and difficult to improve on but do require knee caps and probably hock boots for some horses.

The knees and hocks are very vulnerable, especially on horses facing front or backwards. Knees take a considerable amount of knocks if there is a lot of braking, especially sudden braking, on the journey. Bad turns into competition sites are a prime cause of horses getting big knees as they struggle to keep their balance.

Above: A good way of relaxing or loosening up the horse after a long journey is to put it on the lunge. Some horses need a lot of work to make them reasonably sensible for dressage. A good groom is invaluable if he or she can do this on arrival.

Right: These three horses are quite happy being tied up at the side of the horsebox. It does make life considerably easier if the animal is taught to be tied up and behave from an early age. Nothing is worse than a difficult horse at a competition.

The tail can get badly rubbed if not well protected, especially with big horses being squashed up for a long time. A soft tail guard may help. Horses travelling for a very long time are best left without a bandage in case this is put on too tight and interferes with the circulation. There have been many distressing stories of horses literally losing their tails because of this which leads to gangrene in bad cases.

Travel Stress

This is at last being recognized as something that needs treating seriously. We all know the hassle involved with any type of travel and how tired one gets after a journey of any sort. For the horse this can be just the same, plus one must remember the dehydrating effects, especially in hot weather, and the mental strain, which also takes a lot out of many horses. Some horses remain quite unperturbed by the preparations involved in taking them to a competition. Others get extremely worked up, go off their feed, fidget before, during and after the journey and arrive at the competition as a bundle of nerves with half their necessary energy reserves wasted.

There are many ways to help ease the amount of stress associated with travelling, although little can actually be done to change the horse's reaction to it and the competition.

Above: Ready to travel, this horse is well protected for the journey with knee and hocks covered. A lot of the stress can be taken out of the journey if the driver takes care on the corners and when changing gear to give as smooth a ride as possible.

Right: With quiet, sensible animals it is often best to get to the show first to beat the traffic and then plait them up on site. This particular horse seems quite happy having its mane and tail done at the same time, but not all are so easy on the day.

The Way the Horse is Driven

This can make a considerable difference. Smooth braking and acceleration should be top priority. The box or trailer should not be driven too fast, especially on minor or on winding roads, and all corners should be approached slowly allowing the vehicle to gradually slow itself down, if possible, rather than using the brakes. Swinging it round corners will throw the horse off balance and make it tense and worried. Only on good straight highways and motorways is it safe to travel fast. Most modern vehicles

will run extremely well in these circumstances giving a steady, smooth ride. But trailers must never be driven too fast in case they develop a swing. This can be very frightening for horse and driver and may well result in disaster.

Always allow plenty of time for your journey; you never know what hazards may face you on the way with traffic, road works etc causing unexpected delays. If you have to cross borders, remember to have all the necessary papers, documents and veterinary certificates ready signed, dated and stamped. Be prepared for lengthy waits since many borders are notoriously lax in their methods of helping you on your way.

Ventilation

Be very careful not to let the horse get too hot and unnecessarily dehydrated by putting on too many rugs. Some boxes are very badly ventilated and get very stuffy. If this is so, talk to your local coachbuilders or carpenters and see if improvements can be made. There are many effective vents which can be quite easily installed. The electrically operated ones are good; you can turn them on or off as required. Be careful in cold weather that your horse does not get chilled when travelling – this can be just as bad as getting too hot. A cold draught on the back can cause a lot of unnecessary stiffness leading to a bad performance.

If it is very hot, try and park in the shade and open all windows and ramps to encourage circulation of air. Likewise in the cold, keep everything shut to prevent chilling.

Sea or Air Travel

If travelling by air or sea or making a long journey, the horse should be given a low-energy diet for 48 hours with a mash the night before travelling. It should then be starved for 6 to 8 hours before boarding. This has been found to be beneficial since it encourages the horse to settle into a good haynet once en route.

Travel Sickness

This has often been a problem and at the present time considerable research is going on to investigate the causes. Sponsored by the International League for the Protection of Horses, the FEI is actively working on the problem under the chairmanship of Charles Frank MRCVS. The signs shown include increased temperature and heart rate, colic,

Above left: *After a busy schooling session, these horses are being washed down and made ready for the return journey. The art of travelling is to keep everything tidy and in its logical place for when you next require it, so that it is easy to find.*

Left: *This very big horse has extra protection, with a tail guard and padding on the head to protect the poll. The amount of rugs needed depends on the weather and how much the horse sweats. Note the open ventilation ducts along the side of the box.*

diarrhoea, pleuropneumonia and occasionally death. If the horse can lower its head, it is helpful in allowing nasal secretions to drain. Some horses develop quite considerable nasal discharges from travelling, often caused by a slight allergy to dust and the confined area generally. On arrival these horses are best encouraged to put their heads down to let this drainage occur naturally. Discuss the problem with your veterinarian to see if drugs can be safely given to alleviate the problem.

Ventilation is known to play a big part in how well a horse travels and this is one of the many aspects being researched. But your shipping agents should be well experienced and able to tell you what is required and how, when or where you should feed and attend to your horse. Do ask them for any information with regard to the horse's welfare and any paperwork required. They will often handle this for you as part of the service and the top horse transporters are keeping up-to-date with the latest research and recommendations to minimize the effects of travel stress to the horse. This will be particularly helpful in assessing how much time is required, after a long journey by whatever method, for the horse to recover prior to competition exertion.

FINAL PREPARATION

This includes tidying up your horse so that it looks its very best on the day; cleaning all necessary tack and travelling gear; preparing the food ready for transport; checking through first-aid kits, your own clothes, boots and hats; planning your journey and deciding the route; making sure the horsebox is ready to travel, topped up with fuel, oil and water and the tyre pressures checked.

Trimming

This is important, since a neat, well-presented horse immediately gives a good impression. This is particularly important for the dressage horse and, of course, the eventer. The jaw should be neat and tidy and heels trimmed. Some people trim the whiskers. Others prefer not to, believing they are used as 'sensors' by the horse. Neatness is the important aspect and all competitors should be proud to show off their horses to their best advantage.

Manes and Tails

Manes and tails should be clean; nothing looks worse than a dirty plaited mane or tail. Tails should be carefully pulled, plaited neatly or left full, as some people prefer. Either method is fine so long as they look tidy. In Europe and the USA the tails are left fairly long whereas in Britain the 'bang' tail is preferred, cut straight approximately 10 centimetres (4 inches) below the point of the hock. Full tails are not generally seen in dressage since it is rare to find one that has not been interfered with, looks good and does not detract from the overall picture of elegance. Pulled or plaited tails undoubtedly enhance the looks of most horses.

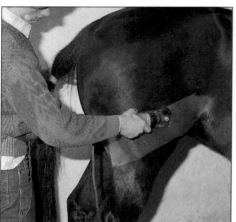

Above: *The importance of that final tidy before entering the ring cannot be over-emphasized. Any part of the turn-out that is lacking may contribute to spoiling an otherwise immaculate performance.*

Left: *Clipping is quite an art, to achieve a good final result, and is essential for horses working hard and likely to sweat. Eventers and show jumpers go for the hunter clip; a full clip for dressage.*

Below: *Plaiting can take time to perfect, and for dressage it is worth studying your horse's neck to see if you can improve its appearance. Braiding with black or white tape or plain plaits look best.*

Plaited or braided manes are an accepted method of competition presentation. The plaits should be even, rounded and flatter the horse's neck. A horse with a poor neck should have its plaits built up so that they sit on top of the neck rather than being pulled down thus accentuating this weak point. Braiding requires the same evenness and the braids are best done quite small, but this method is not so good for the horse with little top-line to its neck. Braiding is usually done in either black or white giving a pleasing, professional look. Other colours are not favoured in the horse world.

There is no doubt that a well plaited or braided horse can make a tremendous difference, so be sure that you or your groom are accomplished at doing this. It may just add that extra, vital mark when the judge is considering the general impression marks at the end of a dressage test.

Grooming

This is one of the most rewarding aspects of general horse care and how your horse is presented again gives an indication of your standards and general horsemanship. A glossy, gleaming coat enhances the horse's looks and is an indication of good condition and fitness, which is something the veterinarians will be taking into account during the three-day event inspections. Nothing looks better than the dressage horse performing with a beautifully groomed coat, perhaps accentuated with shark's teeth, diamonds or other patterns on the horse's quarters. The show jumpers also take great pride in their horse's turnout and the hard-working grooms are always busy behind the scenes making sure their charges are presented to their best advantage.

A good grooming and that important final wipe over with the stable rubber to give the finishing touch will ensure that the judges award you top marks for presentation wherever appropriate.

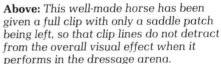

Below: *Grooming to produce a gleaming, glossy coat indicates a fit and healthy horse. The plaits at the bottom have come undone; it is well worth the groom keeping a plaiting kit close at hand.*

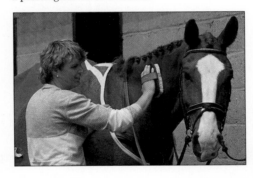

Below: *Picking out the feet and the checking of studs, if used, should always be carried out before competing to ensure the horse enters the ring well prepared and ready for the job required of it.*

Above: *This well-made horse has been given a full clip with only a saddle patch being left, so that clip lines do not detract from the overall visual effect when it performs in the dressage arena.*

Clipping

Clipping for competitions very much depends on the climate and your horse's coat. Generally speaking, the less coat a horse has the better for its welfare if it is doing demanding work and likely to sweat a lot. Most horses, however, have a very fine coat in the summer so rarely need clipping then, but for the horse likely to compete throughout the colder months clipping will be essential. The hunter clip is usual for jumpers and eventers whereas a full clip is perhaps more aesthetically pleasing for the dressage horse.

Some eventers clip their horses between the dressage and cross-country phases of a three-day event. Personally I think this just adds stress to the horse, not only mentally but physically, since inevitably it takes a few days to adjust to the feel of being without the warmer coat. If the coat is fine already, there is little point in removing it at all, especially as after the competition the horse is likely to be let down for a period of rest. If the coat is too thick, it should have been clipped some time beforehand.

Shoeing and Studs

These must be carefully worked out before your competitions start. Your horse should have been regularly shod throughout its fittening work, and during the competitive season shoeing every 3 to 4 weeks is essential to be certain that the horse will always be in good shape. Try and avoid having your horse shod less than 3 or 4 days before competing in case you find it is slightly sore afterwards. Be particularly cautious if your horse is known to have sensitive feet and you have a big competition looming up. Go through your programme carefully and book your farrier in plenty of time for important dates. Get him to make up a spare set to take around with you in case of a problem at any time. Check that you have plenty of studs of different shapes and sizes to use in different ground and be sure they are in good condition. Last year's studs may well be worn out and due for a change. As with all equipment, your stud box should, in any case, be checked and cleaned out regularly, and studs oiled as necessary.

Check your horse's movement regularly to see if it is in need of any change in the way it is shod. Is the horse brushing more or knocking itself or forging? If so, discuss the problem with your farrier and see if some slight adjustments might be helpful such as feather-edging or setting the shoe in or back a fraction. A little can help a lot when it comes to corrective shoeing.

Vaccination Certificates or Passport

These are essential in most places now and rules and regulations are getting stricter all the time, so do not forget them. You will, hopefully, have checked regularly to ensure all are kept up-to-date but make absolutely certain you know when your horse requires its booster. Do not let it run too late and find it then interferes with the horse's programme. If necessary, give it a few months early so that you need not then worry about it affecting your planned season ahead.

If moving from state to state or to other countries, make certain you have the necessary certificates or the horse's passport as required.

Checking Your Tack and Equipment

This always needs a little forethought, depending on whether you are going away for the day, a night or for some time.

Day trips to competitions are relatively straightforward and require only the basics with regard to 'extras' such as food and bedding. However, water, a good haynet and a feed should be taken.

Tack should all be carefully checked to ensure it is all there and that you have the right curb chains, martingales, breastplates, etc – they must be the right size for the horses being taken – and the permitted bits and nosebands allowed for dressage. It goes without saying that it must be all clean and a credit to your stable. Take a spare bridle and any other bits and nosebands which may be useful if you have a slight problem. It is worth having too much rather than too little if you can fit it in. Lunging tackle is always

useful to have in the box, especially if you are taking two or more horses, as one can be lunged while the other is being ridden.

Remember that weights and a weight cloth may be required for eventing and show jumping in advanced competitions. If you cannot check all the kit yourself make a list of tack and equipment that you want to take with you so that your groom can check everything off for you. Keep this in the tackroom or somewhere handy so that it is readily available. Remember to add to it as you acquire different horses which may need different items. All horses tend to need something particular to keep them going at their best, so it is prudent to have everything to hand.

The Day Before the Event

This is when the general preparation, packing up and last-minute cleaning take place. I am not a great believer in washing the horse

Left: *Vaccination certificates or official FEI passports are required for most top level competitions. It is essential to keep these up to date and to check for any special requirements in plenty of time before competing or travelling abroad.*

Below: *After exercise the day before competing the horse should be washed, if necessary, but not if it is cold. The tack and equipment should be checked through carefully. These hard working grooms are busy sorting the tack before cleaning.*

the day before it competes unless it is a really warm climate. However, manes and tails and the legs from knees and hocks downwards all benefit from a wash, especially the legs. These often tend to be forgotten, but a good wash to remove accumulated dirt and sweat which builds up under boots should be carried out once or twice a week to keep the legs in good shape, especially if the horse sweats a lot. It is important to remember to dry the heels carefully after their thorough washing.

Stud holes need cleaning out and tapping so that they are quick and easy to do on the day. Many people put in dummy studs or very small road studs to help towards a quick change on the day. This is acceptable if it is a short journey and your horse is travelling on thick, rubber matting, but it is unwise if the floor is hard or the travelling time long as the horse will not be standing quite square, thereby putting unnecessary strain on its

Right: *For advanced eventing and international jumping, weight has to be carried. Check to see that the weightcloth fits under the saddle correctly and the amount of lead required is available. Mark your own lead as it is often 'borrowed'!*

Left: *In hot climates, hosedown facilities are commonplace and help to refresh the busy competition horse. These horses are being hosed at the back of the stables at Spruce Meadows. In colder countries, it is important that the horse is not chilled.*

legs. Better to pack the holes with oiled wadding or cotton wool which can be removed very quickly. Give the feet a really good picking out, brush and oiling. This will save you the time and the mess of applying a large amount of oil actually on the day of the competition.

Pack the lorry carefully so that the weight will be as evenly distributed as possible. It will travel much more steadily this way, quite apart from being more economical to run. Whether you travel your horse with a haynet rather depends on what it is expected to do on arrival, its temperament and how it travels. Generally, most people do not if they are going on a day trip, but if your horse is not competing until late in the day a small net will keep the horse contented until nearer the time when it can be remove it. Some horses cough after travelling with hay, so with these it is best to remove it altogether or give them a little pre-soaked hay or haylage. Check that the horsebox is full of fuel, oil and water for the journey, that the battery is well topped up and that tyre pressures are even and correct.

Make sure your own riding kit is put in and that you have all the necessary tickets and information for the show plus any flu vaccination certificates or passports, height certificates for ponies and any other paperwork.

It is always a good thing to have the rule book for your sport with you. If you are involved in dressage or eventing, be sure to have a copy of the tests so that you can make a final check over them before you set off on your horse.

Above: *Check and clean out stud holes the day before competing to avoid delay on the big day. The studs used will depend on the ground conditions.*

Above: *Care of the feet is an essential daily chore which is vital to the horse's soundness. Regular picking out and daily oiling will keep them in good condition.*

General Preparation

The Back-up Team

Your back-up team is vital, and whether this consists of just one groom or several it is imperative that you all work together as a team, each knowing exactly what is going on; when to have horses ready and where they should be at each stage of the competition. Be careful to brief your groom thoroughly and leave your times on the schedule in a prominent place, as well as numbers. If there are any tickets or passes required, do ensure you give your groom one before they get stopped at the crucial moment trying to get your horse to you! Also, do not forget to check that he or she has enough money or food and coffee in the horsebox to last through the day. Grooming at competitions, especially if there are several horses to cope with, can be long and exhausting with inevitable crack of dawn starts and late finishes.

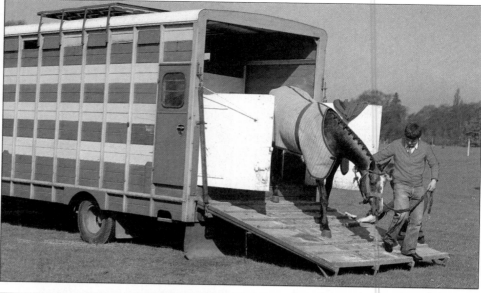

Owners and Sponsors

Owners and sponsors obviously expect to see their horses compete whenever possible, although not all may be able or wish to come to every outing. Do remember to inform them of the horse's intended programme and what you are aiming for and include them in the day as much as possible. Be sure they have the necessary passes, know where to go, the times their horse is due to compete and are generally given a good time. They are paying the bills and need to enjoy their outings if you are hoping that they will continue to do this. They must understand that there will be good and bad days, particularly with young up-and-coming horses, so do take the trouble to explain why you are doing things a certain way or keeping the horse back at a certain level. Try and find the time during the day to

Below: The snow of St Moritz is a big contrast to the heat in many other countries, but the horses seem to cope. See how the snow has been banked up to make an effective barrier to the collecting ring.

Top: Unloading at the show must be treated with caution, especially with young horses which may play up or fret if left by themselves. Check with your groom or back-up team if this situation is likely to arise.

Above: The collecting ring is usually a very social spot for the grooms who rarely have time to stop and chat. There are often long gaps in-between the jump-offs, especially if there are big entries.

bring them to see their horse at the horsebox, introduce your groom and let him or her tell them what a little gem (or otherwise!) it is to look after. Most owners love to be involved in the day and if this is the case, let them join in the preparations if they are experienced or it is practical. They are wonderful at holding on to horses while studs are being put in or taken out and boots or bandages are being put on. They are often pleased to lead the horse round to cool off after its round or a wash down.

Some sponsors may not in fact know very much about horses but it is up to you to explain as much as possible to make the equestrian scene interesting and enjoyable for them and their friends or clients who may also have been brought along to watch. One thing many people forget to brief their sponsors on is suitable clothing and footwear for equestrian events. If it is likely to be their first venture to a horse show, make quite sure it is not their last, as they step through mud and dirt in delicate high heels, for example. Try and introduce them to as many people as possible, explaining who everyone is and how they fit into the scene. If necessary, explain what the judges are looking for in a dressage test, which is a complicated enough procedure in itself; tell them the scoring system for show jumping, which at least is easier to understand. The eventing system needs to be explained in a little detail to show that the scores from all three phases are added together to give the total and the horse and rider with the least penalties are the winners.

Most riders are very good with their owners and sponsors but it is very difficult during a busy day to give them the time they expect or deserve. So it may be a good idea to arrange a day at home when the horse can be put through its paces and really shown off with a good lunch and video show laid on. Find out if your owners are happy or if they would like to do or see more – a few hours of your time and perhaps a talk at the sponsors' showrooms will help a lot towards keeping their support. This is becoming more and more worthwhile in today's increasingly expensive equestrian sports.

Aiming for the Top

To recap, competitions in all three sports can be divided into junior, young rider and senior grades. There are numerous different classes for each age group, as well as classes for children on ponies, which have international status and come under the FEI umbrella.

Most countries have their own national rules for different standards, culminating in some type of national championships. Internationally there are championships each year centred around the Olympic Games. World Championships slot in-between these,

Above: *This pony is performing the extended walk across the diagonal. The walk is the first pace to get right. If bad, the judge will tend to look for other training faults, so aim to perfect this pace.*

Below: *The extended canter across the diagonal is nicely demonstrated here. Be sure to inform your owners and sponsors of the dates and times you are competing so that they can make plans in plenty of time.*

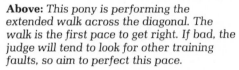

also on a four-year cycle. Regional championships, such as the Pan American games and European Championships, take place in two-yearly cycles in-between the Olympics and World Championships. Apart from the Olympic Games, most championships are offered to the winning country for the following event so long as they are willing to hold it, and these are then approved by the FEI who nominate the officials to preside over these competitions.

It is every rider's dream to compete at the top one day, but the road to that goal is long, slow and hard. Whatever sport you decide on, the training is a continuous process to build up the muscle and mental confidence to achieve your ultimate aim. The dressage horse takes literally years to build up the necessary strength and power to perform the tremendously collected movements required for the top level. Show jumpers reckon that three years is necessary to bring a horse from novice to the standard required for top flight show jumping, and eventers likewise, if all goes well.

The start, however, is perhaps the most exciting part as the horse can make enormous progress in just a few outings if it is trained sensibly and conscientiously towards a steady build-up of confidence and ability for future competition work.

The Dressage Scene

Dressage is increasing in popularity dramatically in Britain and the USA where, up to a few years ago, it was looked on as a rather eccentric or geriatric pastime. In mainland Europe, however, dressage has been extremely popular for years, commanding large audiences, big prize money and expensive horses. From an early age, European children ride horses and are taught the importance of the independent seat, spending hours perfecting the sitting trot, whilst many of the British have been far more interested in Pony Club mounted games. This dedication to the art of dressage is reflected in the success achieved by European riders, especially in Junior and Young Rider championships as well as many adult competitions.

THE CLASSES

These are designed to suit every level of horse and progress from the novice standards to the advanced scene. In mainland Europe and the USA nearly all tests are designed and ridden in the large arena of 60 × 20 metres (197 × 66 feet) even at the lower levels, whereas Britain tends to confine all its lower standard tests to the small arena. This hardly seems conducive to encouraging the horse to go forward freely in the early stages and does make one wonder if this is not in some way to blame for Britain's comparatively slow progress in this discipline. At the lower levels, the basics of straightness and free forward movement are expected to be demonstrated. The regularity and freedom of the paces, activity, suppleness and balance of the horse, acceptance of the bit and obedience to aids are taken into

Above: *The therapeutic value of riding is recognized worldwide. Undeterred by her handicap, this young girl is performing well keeping her pony straight up the side of the arena and enjoying every minute.*

Below: *Starting at the bottom with a happy and honest horse in novice tests is where most future champions are to be found. It is where the seeds of greatness are sown, but few reach their true potential.*

Below: *A nice working trot with horse and rider well in balance. The rider has a good firm leg position and is riding the horse in a good outline for the medium standard test as he works down the centre line.*

Left: *Kyra Kyrklund and Matador from Finland demonstrate all the grace, power and beauty that makes a great dressage partnership. Immaculate turnout of horse and rider completes the impressive picture.*

into consideration along with the rider's position. The movements depend on the standard but obedience and accuracy throughout the whole test and the transitions from one pace to another, which may be progressive up to elementary standard, will be carefully assessed in relation to that horse's standard and way of going.

In medium standard tests there will be more emphasis on collection and the correct outline of the horse and how it copes with the medium and extended paces. Lateral work should be showing suppleness and elasticity. The hindquarters should be actively engaged, producing a lightness of the forehand, which will show that the horse has been correctly trained up to this level. The tests should be flowing and pleasing to watch with the movements accurately and correctly performed without stress.

By the time the horse has reached the advanced standard, it is expected that it will have attained a high degree of athletic ability enabling it to perform with maximum collection and extension in all paces as required by the tests. The horse and rider should be in complete harmony throughout the performance, which should exude grace and elegance. At advanced levels, only the double bridle may be used, whereas the snaffle is used in all lower level tests with the option of either in the medium standards.

In the collective marks at the end of the test, a co-efficient is given effectively doubling the marks for the paces where freedom and regularity are of prime importance: impulsion – the desire to move freely forward, showing elasticity of the steps, suppleness of the back and engagement of the hindquarters; submission – obedience and confidence with lightness and ease of movements and true acceptance of the bridle; the rider's position together with correct and effective aids.

At the highest level, when the FEI tests are performed, these co-efficient marks are given for certain of the more advanced movements or the transitions into or from them. The Prix St George – Intermèdiaire I and II are the three lower international tests, with the Grand Prix and Grand Prix Special making up the top two tests. It is these latter two which are used for the Olympics and other major championships with the individual title being decided by the top twelve in the Grand Prix coming forward to perform the 'Special' test.

The freestyle or 'kur', now mostly performed to music, has become increasingly popular with riders and spectators alike, not to mention the horse which appears to show a particular awareness of the music and seems to enjoy this refreshing change to its standard training programme.

The standard of test influences the movements required for this, but it is the overall impression of the compulsory movements that the judges will be looking for and how these have been performed during your test. The artistic presentation marks are given for the composition of the test, choreography and the incorporation of the music – its choice and how it suits your horse. The tremendous impact made by this competition

Top: *Madame Dominique d'Esme from France shows relaxed suppleness on the circle at the European Dressage Championships. All international dressage is now ridden on sand.*

Above: *This young rider performing in the International Pony Dressage Competition shows promise, but is spoiling the overall picture by looking down rather than ahead. She is also using too strong a spur.*

may well lead to changes in the whole format of dressage judging in the future. Certainly, it has brought in the spectators and being judged on similar lines to figure skating it is much easier for the public to understand. The World Cup series started in 1986 and based mostly on winter indoor shows brought all the best dressage riders together for the finals staged at 's'-Hertogenbosch in Holland where Anne Grethe Jensen on Marzog was the first winner for Denmark.

Each country stages their own national championships at the various different levels and internationally there are the World Championships held in a four-year cycle, two years after the Olympics. There are also the European, Pan American and Asian Games and an international dressage competition for the so called 'under-developed' countries. The latter is divided into five regional groups. Group I includes Argentina, Brazil, Chile, Uruguay and South Africa. Group II consists of Colombia, Peru, Costa Rica and Mexico; Group III: Japan, New Zealand and Australia; Group IV: Korea, Taipei, Hong Kong, Philippines and Group V: India, Indonesia, Singapore and Malaysia. This has proved a popular competition and has greatly encouraged dressage riding within the member groups with the judges, mostly from Europe, taking courses and clinics during their visits.

SCORING

The scoring at dressage competitions is based on the total good marks attained, with each movement being marked out of ten.

The following scale is used at every level as follows: 10 – Excellent, 9 – Very Good, 8 – Good, 7 – Fairly Good, 6 – Satisfactory, 5 – Sufficient, 4 – Insufficient, 3 – Fairly Bad, 2 – Bad, 1 – Very Bad, 0 – Not performed.

The number of movements per test varies considerably, starting at the lower levels with around 12 fairly straightforward movements, up to the ultimate required for the Grand Prix test which currently consists of 37 movements.

Although many national tests may be 'commanded' up to a certain level, depending on local rules, the FEI tests must be performed from memory. Any errors are penalized with two marks for the first error, four for the second, eight for the third and elimination for a fourth mistake.

Judges normally need to be on a national judges list or on the FEI international judges list to be qualified to judge at international competitions. They may judge alone at the lower levels but as the standard rises, it is usual to have two or more judges. At the top level there are five judges placed at points E, B, H, C and M with all their marks counting towards the final score. This helps to give an accurate assessment of the horse's performance from the various angles around the arena which can look surprisingly different.

Right: *The FEI three-day event test is of medium standard and has been used for over ten years. Many riders feel that the FEI should change it every four years after the Olympics, or offer a choice of tests.*

The FEI Three-Day Event Dressage Test

		TEST	MAX. MARKS
1	A X	Enter at working canter Halt – Immobility – Salute Proceed at working trot.	10
2	C S EBE EV	Track to the left Medium trot Circle to the left 20 metre diameter Medium trot	10
3	V A L	Working trot Down centre line Circle to the left 10 metres diameter	10
4	LS	Half-pass [left]	10
5	C	Halt – Rein back 5 steps – Proceed at working trot without halting	10
6	R BEB BP	Medium trot Circle to the right 20 metres diameter Medium trot	10
7	P A L	Working trot Down centre line Circle to the right 10 metres diameter	10
8	LR	Half-pass [right]	10
9	C	Halt – Immobility 5 seconds – Proceed at working trot	10
10	HXF F	Change rein at extended trot [rising] Working trot	10
11	KXM M	Change rein at extended trot Working trot	10
12	C HSXPF F	Medium walk Change rein at extended walk Medium walk	10
13	A	Working canter – Circle to the right 10 metres diameter .. .. ,.	10
14	AC	Serpentine 3 loops, the first and the third true canter, the second counter canter	10
15	MXK K	Change rein at extended canter Working trot	10
16	A	Working Canter – Circle to the left 10 metres diameter	10
17	AC	Serpentine 3 loops, the first and the third true canter, the second counter canter	10
18	HXF F	Change rein at extended canter Working trot	10
19	A L	Down centre line Working canter to the right.	10
20	G	Halt – Immobility – Salute	10
	A	Leave arena on a long rein	
COLLECTIVE MARKS			
1		Paces [freedom and regularity].	10
2		Impulsion [desire to move forward, elasticity of the steps and engagement of the hind quarters]	10
3		Submission [attention and obedience, lightness and ease of movements, acceptance of the bit].	10
4		Position, seat of the rider, correct use of the aids	10
		MAXIMUM TOTAL MARKS	240

The Dressage Scene

CORRECT EQUIPMENT AND DRESS

The correct equipment and dress for dressage is usually laid down quite clearly in the rule book and it is always worth studying this carefully at the beginning of the season in case any slight changes have been made. At the basic novice levels, tweed coat, fawn breeches, boots, hat, collar and tie are quite acceptable. A blue or black coat and a hunting tie or stock may be required in any class above novice but are usually compulsory by medium standard, as are the wearing of gloves and spurs.

For advanced tests and all FEI tests, it is usual for top hat and tails to be worn except at junior or pony level.

For the horse, check that you have the correct bridle for the standard of test with none of the forbidden bits or nosebands. If in any doubt check with your steward before entering the arena, as it is a particularly maddening way to be disqualified. Also be sure that you are suitably dressed yourself. It is always correct to wear spurs but if you do not have them above a certain standard you may be in trouble – they are compulsory, along with gloves for all FEI tests.

Above: *Horse and rider look happy and all set to perform at novice level dressage. Tweed jackets and snaffle bridles are usual for this standard in Britain, but blue or black jackets are often worn elsewhere.*

Left: *Riding the test is a great art and requires a dedicated, single-minded approach. Each movement must be ridden accurately with horse and rider appearing in complete harmony throughout.*

A whip can usually be carried for national tests but may not in FEI tests. Remember to drop this before entering the arena if you wish to hold onto it until the last minute. Make quite sure you remove any boots or bandages before entering the arena.

RIDING THE TEST

This is the most important aspect of the whole day. After the work and preparation that goes into training the horse, it is pointless not to take the riding of the test very seriously indeed.

The way you present yourself to the judge will make an enormous difference to how he or she will mark you so always have this in the back of your mind. First impressions stick so be sure you give a good one on your entry. A straight entry and square halt must be the prime target to start with, so look carefully at the entrance to your arena as you warm up round the edge. Notice if there is any advantage or disadvantage to which way you approach A and give yourself adequate time to prepare your entry once you have heard the start signal.

Do not hurry your test. Keep your rhythm and pace the same as when training; it is a very common fault to over-ride your horse during competition. Sit up and hold your head up remembering to ride your horse forward and up in front of you.

Accuracy plays a big part in gaining good marks. Make sure the size of your circles is exact whether you are doing a novice test or competing at the top level. Ride your corners and turns accurately and especially have the

correct bend on any turn so that you come onto the centre line.

Above all make it look easy and enjoyable, even if you have had problems. Disguise this from the judge as best you can – it is part of the showmanship required to get those extra marks which can make all the difference to the result.

Warming Up

This is as important to the dressage horse as it is to a jet engine or athlete. The engine will not run smoothly until it is well warmed up; neither will the horse have the looseness or ability to perform at its best until it has warmed up well.

Let this be a gradual process so that you do not make the horse mentally agitated by being in a hurry. If you have your trainer with you, all well and good. Let him or her take you through a general routine which will bring your horse up to its peak in time for

Left: *Dressed in black jacket with hunting tie and the horse in a double bridle, this pair are now ready to perform at medium level. Dressage whips are allowed in most national tests but not for FEI tests.*

Above: *After a final warm-up with her trainer, gold medallist Reiner Klimke, this rider and her horse have their final tidy up before their test. Perfection in every aspect should be the aim.*

Below: *Margit Otto Crepin and Corlandus demonstrate the passage, requiring great collection and impulsion. French competition horses are home-bred and France has a fine equestrian record.*

your performance. With the young horse, you may need a few outings to be able to work this out, and even then as the horse's confidence builds up it may not present itself in the same way consistently for some time to come. It is usually best to give a little too much work in these early stages rather than let it get into a habit of being a little too exuberant or tense to give a good account of itself and so start off the wrong way.

However experienced a competitor you may be, it is extremely rare not to tense up a little in front of the judges, so do not think just because the horse is very relaxed outside that it will necessarily be the same once you have entered the arena. Take a deep breath yourself before you start and try to relax mentally and physically. This does make an enormous difference to how you actually perform. Be sure to remove boots, bandages and whip if necessary before entering the arena.

During your warm-up time, try and quietly practise the movements required once or twice so that they do not come as a surprise when asked for. This will help towards giving a consistent and smooth performance and will ensure that the horse's mind is on its work before entering the arena.

The Mental Approach

This is very important at this stage if you want to succeed and perform well. You must be well-prepared and confident about the test. Make sure you know it and have run through it not long before you start. Mentally let your mind centre on the job in hand, what you are aiming for and how you are to

Above: *Working the horse in well before doing a test is most important. This one is looking alert and happy in what it is being asked to do. Keeping calm at all times will help the horse to react in the same way.*

Below: *The practice ring is always much in demand and it is as well to use it early if you want to do some serious and undisturbed work. Boots or bandages worn all round are a sensible precaution against knocks.*

achieve it and get the best from your horse. Keep your mind on your horse and the test and what you are doing, blocking out all other distractions for the ten minutes or so before you go in. By doing this, you avoid the mistake, made by many, of losing concentration at the last minute, just when you really require the maximum amount. The single-minded approach is what brings success in the competition, and is the best way to help the horse achieve what is expected of it on the day.

After the Test

Study the score board and see how you have fared. Take notes on the type of tests that certain judges prefer, so that when you perform in front of them next time you can ride your horse a little more according to their preference. This can be quite helpful in gaining a few extra marks. Always try and find out what it is your particular judge likes to see. The serious-minded will always try and study some of the tests to see if the judge prefers a forward-going, positive test; collected and obedient; accurate but uninspiring or is concentrating more on the purity of the movements required. Some judges are quite difficult to analyse as to what they like, but then only the winner will ever be really satisfied!

It is never a bad thing to talk to more experienced riders or trainers to try and get an honest opinion from them. The only way to learn is by listening and watching and there is nearly always help at hand if you are prepared to accept and learn something from it.

Above: *Making the horse stand quietly and watch what is going on around should be a part of its early competitive education. Obedience, relaxation and willing forward movement are the essential requirements.*

Below: *So much of the fun of competing is in the talking about it afterwards! These riders are obviously discussing the ups and downs of their day as they prepare to put their horses away for the return journey.*

It is worth running through your performance straight away after the test, ideally with your trainer who can give advice whilst the experience is still fresh in your mind. If the horse has made any mistakes, now is the time to run through the movement again quietly to get it right. In this way the horse learns what is expected without feeling that you are angry with it. This would only build up tension for the next time and does no-one any good. Look at your dressage sheet when it is available and take note of what the judge has to say so that you can, if necessary, work towards what he or she wants to see before your next show. If you have another test to perform, well and good, but do not forget the horse will still require a period of warming up to do its best, however well it went in the first one.

The use of the video camera has been enormously helpful as a training aid and periodical use of this to assess progress is certainly very useful. What the judge sees and what you think you are presenting are, unfortunately, not always the same so study your test with your score sheet, look at where things could be improved and work on this for the next time. If it is possible to position the camera somewhere near where the judge is, it will give you a clearer idea of the judge's view. If taken from the other end it will seem quite different, with the judge's comments seeming totally irrelevant.

Problems

For the dressage horse, these nearly always consist of some sort of tension and this may either be caused by too little work or general nervousness over the sense of occasion. The more advanced the horse, the fitter it will be and those with a highly strung temperament may take some time to settle into their surroundings. Lunging is very good to help settle

Above: *The winning German team look more than a little happy as they pose with officials and grooms in front of Goodwood House following the European Championships held in 1987.*

Below: *Lunging is an excellent way of settling horses. Here, grooms are seen lunging their charges early in the morning, one using side reins and one without, at West Palm Beach.*

most horses. Take your time and keep the horse occupied with various changes of speed and pace, once it has settled, and be sure to lunge equally on both reins as the ground may not be ideal at your competition.

It is fatal to get after the horse too strongly, particularly away from home, however maddening it may be. Punishment, if necessary, must be immediate but never prolonged. It is nearly always better to change tactics and do something else and then come back to the movement you were having problems with rather than make an issue of something which is more than likely caused by tension on your part rather than the horse's.

If the horse gets very tense or excited at competitions, more work is required to settle it mentally and you may be better taking it on several outings without taking part. Work the horse quietly but hard. It is not unusual for this type to require at least two hours before they settle. Walk it around to look at the sights on a loose rein (if possible) and then work it again for a little while. Keep doing this until the horse is quite relaxed about starting to work again every time you collect it up. It should not be put away until this relaxation is achieved.

Care of the Horse

On the day, this very much depends on the climate and standard at which you are competing. At the lower levels, the horse will not be doing particularly strenuous work although it will probably have done quite a bit for its own level of training. The advanced horse, however, will have performed a very strenuous test and will need walking quietly to relax afterwards. It may be best to wash the horse well first if it has got very hot and sweaty, so that it can settle better afterwards. Be sure that there is enough water available for your horse and additional electrolytes may be wise if it is really hot weather.

Try and maintain a routine as much as possible and, if your horse is unsettled, let it have a short pick of grass or its haynet to keep it occupied and help it to relax.

Above: *This horse is being ridden strongly to ensure it does not lose impulsion and activity in its way of going. This is during the test at the Novice Dressage Championships at Stoneleigh, England.*

Below: *Washing down is a very refreshing pastime for horse and groom at the end of a hard day's competing. Horses in hot climates need this frequently to help them to remain cool.*

Far left: *This young rider, competing in a novice horse trial, has got a long way to go before she can drive her horse up off the forehand. This progress is crucial if she is to gain good marks.*

Left: *This horse is competing at the big three-day event in Stockholm. This will be the venue for the World Equestrian Festival in 1990 where all equestrian sport will be represented.*

The Show Jumping Scene

The show jumping world is very different from the quiet serenity of the dressage scene. The fact that jumping has immediacy means a very different atmosphere at the show. The competitive spirit is always very evident in show jumping regardless of the standard of competition.

Watching horses performing at the lower end of the scale, it is really quite amazing to see what they can achieve when jumping fences. The ladder to the top in any field is always a long one, but perhaps out of all the equestrian sports it is show jumping which offers the greatest chance of winning a prize. This may be because a certain element of luck on the day does appear to come into play. Some people seem to be able to rattle every pole without them falling, while others only touch the fence and it falls. The speed with which you can attack the jump-off course is all important in most cases and many people really rise to the challenge, as I believe do the horses. Many horses and riders appear fairly non-descript on the first round, but give them the competitive atmosphere of a jump-off and they become a real force to be reckoned with. The speed often gives the necessary extra 'ping' which a particular combination requires, serving to show previously unnoticed talent.

■ INTERNATIONAL COMPETITORS ■

The international flavour which is so evident in show jumping is perhaps due in part to the tremendous popularity of the sport, the fact that it is easy for the public to see and understand what is going on. Television has brought show jumping into millions of homes around the world where thrilling climaxes to many competitions have enthralled audiences. There is, however, no substitute for actually being at the scene of these events in person. The atmosphere is tremendous and to see the world's top riders taking part and watch the different riding styles is fascinating in itself. The tremendous discipline of the German horses and their sheer strength and power often contrasts quite sharply with the more happy-go-lucky British style which is nothing if not varied. The classical style of the American riders pays tribute to the training instilled for 25 years by Bert de Nemethy, as does Ireland's Eddie Macken and Paul Darragh, both protegés of that other great purist, Iris Kellet. France, Austria, Holland and Canada have also produced brilliant and consistent performances. In Australia many stars have appeared with Kevin Bacon, John Fahey and Vicky Roycroft keeping these 'kangaroo hoppers' well to the fore. In South Africa also the standard remains high despite the problems of quarantine regulations preventing free movement of horses.

Left: *The moment every rider dreads at the big Hickstead bank. A loss of balance and a slip on the descent from such a height makes the chances of survival quite slim, but Gerry Mullins sits tight and starts to give the horse a fuller rein to survive. The secret is to stay balanced and come down the bank absolutely straight.*

Top: *Canada's Ian Miller jumps confidently towards a sea of faces at the Olympic Games in Los Angeles. Sometimes the colour of the fences can dim into 'insignificance' against such a busy background, and this should always be borne in mind when competing where there are such large crowds.*

Above: *Germany's brilliant partnership of Paul Schockemöhle and the great Deister. They are seen here screwing slightly in the air as they jump this natural type fence of a stone wall with a rail over the top. Germany has an enviable record in the show jumping field at the highest competitive level exemplified by this superb combination.*

With such a wealth of talent spread around the world and with more and more international competitions being devised for every level in every continent, show jumping is in a very healthy situation.

THE CLASSES

The classes are designed to create a suitable training base at the lower levels to bring the horse on up through the various stages to the top level. Each country has its own individual way of doing this. In Germany the standards are divided into easy, medium and difficult courses under their L, M or S grading respectively. In Britain, much the same system is adopted with C, B and A grade governing the standard of the course. The amount of money won determines when you move up a grade. This system very much leaves the decision up to the rider on how much he or she jumps his or her horse – not necessarily a good thing. Some horses with talent tend to be jumped until they upgrade regardless of whether they have really had the necessary experience to be ready to do this.

The true professional and those dedicated to bringing on young horses have a much more long-term approach to competing. They plan out suitable programmes so that the horse is given the necessary time to mature and adapt to the greater demands being made on it.

In France the system is based more on the horse's age, which is fine if you find the horse at the right time but could perhaps be more flexible. The United States probably has one of the best systems, partly because at the lowest level there is no prize money given. This therefore allows the horse to jump just for the experience in the 'warm-up' and 'schooling' classes aimed at approximately 1.07 metres (3 feet 6 inches) in height. Competitors can then progress to Preliminary courses, which are between 1.22 and 1.40 metres (4 feet and 4 feet 6 inches) in height. Once the horse has won $2,500, it moves into the Intermediate section where courses of 1.4 to 1.5 metres (4 feet 6 inches to 5 feet) are met. Once it has won $5,000 at this level it becomes an Open jumper and is ready for the big time.

The phenomenal success of the Americans and their endless string of up-and-coming horses and riders does suggest that this steady preparation of the horse works. Certainly it seems to suit the higher quality or thoroughbred type of horse that the Americans generally favour.

Each nation has its own national competitions but, as with dressage and eventing, there are the World Championships held every four years in-between the Olympic Games. European, Pan American and other regional championships slot in between on two-year cycles. Championships for juniors, young riders and ponies are held annually and are becoming increasingly popular, also

Right: *Britain's Pam Carruthers has built courses throughout the world and is seen checking that everything is ready to start on time. She is the technical advisor for show jumping at the Seoul Olympics.*

providing an excellent grounding for those who wish to compete at the top when they reach the senior levels.

Various different types of competition are run to test different attributes of the horse such as speed, height and agility as well as the rider. There are classes for amateurs as well as professionals and individual and team championships. There are numerous classes for different standards of horse as well as the 'fun' classes such as relays, fancy dress, ride and drive etc. Special competitions such as Top Score, Power and Speed, Take Your Own Line, Fault and Out, Puissance, Six Bars and Knockouts all involve special rules relative to the particular event.

THE COURSE BUILDER

This is the person who governs how all these competitions are run and thus has a very important and responsible job. Most course designers have competed themselves, which is almost essential if they are to fully understand their job. The sport has changed considerably since the 'twice round the outside and once up the middle' type of course seen in the early days of show jumping.

Britain's Pam Carruthers, who has designed courses for the last 30 years all over the world and is Technical Advisor at the Seoul Olympics, 1988, believes that all courses up to medium standard should be straightforward and have good distances to build up the horse's confidence. She states that she is not frightened of using true verticals or square parallels at this level since the

Left: *America's outstanding Olympic champion, Conrad Homfeld on the grey stallion, Abdullah, at the Olympic Games. Their precision, style and sympathetic way of going made them a joy to watch.*

Left: *The victorious British team after competing at St Gallen. From the left, John Whitaker, Malcolm Pyrah, Ronnie Massarella – the Chef d'Equip, Nick Skelton and Michael Whitaker.*

Above: *The famous arena at Hickstead looks vast as the judges decide the final placings for one of the show classes. One of its key features is the large, natural obstacles which fill the arena.*

Below: *This design of the course and plan is filled in with colour to show the effect of the different fences. This is an international standard course design with several related distances.*

An International Standard Course Design and Plan

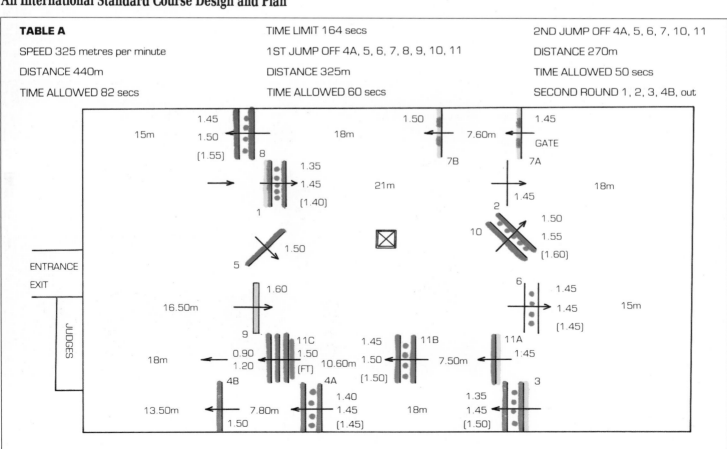

TABLE A		
SPEED 325 metres per minute	TIME LIMIT 164 secs	2ND JUMP OFF 4A, 5, 6, 7, 10, 11
DISTANCE 440m	1ST JUMP OFF 4A, 5, 6, 7, 8, 9, 10, 11	DISTANCE 270m
TIME ALLOWED 82 secs	DISTANCE 325m	TIME ALLOWED 50 secs
	TIME ALLOWED 60 secs	SECOND ROUND 1, 2, 3, 4B, out

The Show Jumping Scene

An Adult Open Course Plan

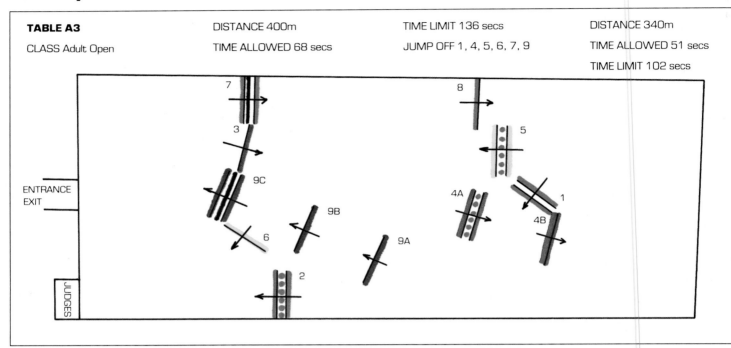

TABLE A3	DISTANCE 400m	TIME LIMIT 136 secs	DISTANCE 340m
CLASS Adult Open	TIME ALLOWED 68 secs	JUMP OFF 1, 4, 5, 6, 7, 9	TIME ALLOWED 51 secs
			TIME LIMIT 102 secs

Above: *A fairly straightforward adult open course finishing off with a one-stride treble and having two verticles and one double. At this level, the course must flow but also demand obedience.*

horse must be used to these before progressing. At the higher grades she uses slight distance problems, such as long strides to verticals, but does not agree with too long a stride to an oxer. She endeavours to build a course that will produce a good result without harm to horse or rider. 'I hate to see horse's struggling over something I've built' she says, and it is only when building for the very top that you start asking all the questions. It is important to get a balance of fences.

Courses should be built according to the types of horses competing. The start should be straightforward, increase the height and then introduce the problems. The use of colours against different backgrounds can make a big difference as to how horses see the fences.

In 1978 the FEI organized an International Course Designers Seminar chaired by the German, 'Mickey' Brenckmann, Pam Carruthers and the great Bertalan de Nemethy. Between them they put forward some good, positive ideas, which now dominate modern show jumping designs, and helped to create the more technical approach now seen in show jumping which tests the versatility of horse and rider.

Safety in the sport was underlined with guidelines being laid down on the type of poles, cups etc to be used, as well as stating that the classical traditions of riding should be encouraged. These included the well-trained horse; jumping ability; the galloping capacity and stamina of the horse; the fitness and general control of the rider. All these elements should be reflected in the course design.

The Course Designers Seminar in 1986 confirmed this general approach but underlined the correct measurement of the length and height of courses as well as the importance of speed as an integral part of jumping.

Some criticisms which have been made of modern course designing, according to Germany's Arno Gego, may be due to the over-emphasis of optical and distance problems and the playing down of the horse's galloping and jumping capabilities.

Television companies put pressure on course designers to ensure that there are not too many clear rounds and to generally try and ensure that the competitions are not too long and drawn out. While this approach might be popular with viewers, it is not necessarily to the horse's advantage.

WALKING THE COURSE

This is the most important part of the competition. It is the time when you have to decide quite quickly how you will tackle the problems set before you and which is the best strategy for your particular horse. Remember to take the going into account and think how this might affect your horse. Think what you are expecting from it, if it is young or inexperienced. If so, be sure to be positive

Above: *The American team walk the course and discuss tactics at Aachen. The fence is technically difficult with no ground line. This type of obstacle is often placed to demand control before another problem.*

Right: *The penalties for show jumping are the same worldwide, although some classes may have their own particular set of rules. Timings are varied according to the standard and type of class.*

and accurate in your approaches to give the horse the necessary confidence and impulsion to jump the fences with ease. Look carefully at your line into each fence and the turns and the corners before the fences. Know your start and finish line. Check that the colour of the fences does not blend or contrast starkly with the background, which could momentarily confuse the horse. Make quite certain in your own mind that you know every part of the course and exactly how you are going to jump it.

THE WARM-UP

Warming up in the practice ring is often where contests are won or lost. All too often at the lower levels one sees horses being jumped over fences that are far too big. Or the horse is not sufficiently warmed up on the flat and so is jumping stiffly and fast losing confidence in the atmosphere of the collecting ring, which is perhaps becoming sticky, if wet, or too hard to be pounding around on in the summer.

Just as at home, the horse requires a gradual build-up to loosen and warm up properly. There should be an upright and a spread in your practice area which must be jumped correctly in the proper direction leaving the red flags or uprights on your right-hand side. Try and stick to a routine so that the horse knows what to expect. This is sometimes extremely difficult with a mass of others all trying to jump, but try and warm up by jumping a few fences well rather than jumping for too long. Keep the horse fresh and do not let it fall asleep once you have warmed it up before starting the competition. Your aim with the young horse must be to enter the arena full of confidence and well-prepared for the occasion. With the experienced horse, you will have loosened it up and be concentrating on winning the

Below: *The US team at Aachen in 1987 prove that women are just as capable as men when it comes to most equestrian sports, and often the feminine touch has proved more successful with some difficult horses.*

Above: *The warm-up in the practice ring is where so many competitions are won or lost, especially with young horses. Try to stick to a set routine and be sure to jump with the red flag or colour on your right.*

competition. Watch to see if or where you might manage to save a few valuable seconds. If any fences are causing problems to other riders and horses, assess how or if these are likely to affect your horse. This is the crucial time in which to mentally prepare yourself to take any of the necessary precautions in the ring.

DRESS

Dress for show jumping is practically the same worldwide. Tweed coats may be used up to novice level and by children. At higher levels, blue or black coats are generally worn by women and red coats by men. National teams, however, may have their own colours such as green coats for the Irish, blue for the French, and red with blue collars for girls as well as men in the United States. Military uniform is worn wherever appropriate. The FEI are in the process of bringing in a rule about hats, where only approved skull caps with a harness may be used when jumping.

White hunting ties, white collar and tie or other acceptable white neckwear is now universal, except with a tweed coat when a plain tie or spotted stock and pin are generally used.

Breeches are normally beige or fawn with tweed, or white.

Boots, plain or with tops, complete the picture along with spurs, gloves and whips which should not exceed 76 centimetres (30 inches).

Always check your rule book to ensure you are correctly kitted out with clothes and equipment at the start of every season. National and FEI rules may have some subtle differences. If you require any additional or new equipment, it is as well to purchase it early in the season before the competitions start, to make sure that you have everything when and where you need it.

Table of Faults and Time Penalties

FAULTS AND TIME PENALTIES FEI TABLE 'A'	
First disobedience	3 Faults
Second disobedience	6 Faults
Third disobedience	Elimination
Faults for any disobedience are cumulative. This not only applies to disobedience faults at the same fence, but throughout the same round.	
Fence knocked down	4 Faults
One or more feet in the water	4 Faults
Landing on marking tape	4 Faults
Exceeding the Time Allowed	$\frac{1}{4}$ Fault/Sec
Fall of horse or rider, or both	8 Faults
The faults for the fall are additional to any other faults incurred at the same time.	
Exceeding the Time Limit (which is twice the Time Allowed)	Elimination

The Show Jumping Scene

SHOW JUMPING RULES

These are quite complicated, depending on the class and standard of your horse, and it is most important that you know them well as fines and suspensions are the general result for those who have contravened them. Keep a careful check on your horse's earnings, if these are likely to concern you – it may affect qualifications for different classes. Any abusive language or bad behaviour is being very firmly controlled. Contravention of any rules wittingly or unwittingly may result in a fine or suspension. Incorrect passports or vaccination certificates and irregularities in registrations, etc of horse owner or rider may result in disciplinary action. The sport is now so big worldwide that it has to be tough and run professionally to maintain its high standing, so it is as well to make quite sure you know everything all that is necessary when competing.

LIFE ON THE SHOW CIRCUIT

The show jumper can spend long spells away from home, so these trips require careful planning. At the lower levels, day trips to various shows to gain experience are relatively easy to cope with, since it does not take too long to get into the routine of packing up the necessary equipment required.

As you reach the higher rungs of the ladder, you may set off to do several shows up and down the country. This will involve arrangements for stabling, fodder and accommodation for you and your team – although more and more people now tend to use their horseboxes as mobile homes for their trips. It is not too unlike a mobile road show, but to be successful and to keep the horses fresh and competing at their best every aspect needs to be worked out and catered for to make it all worthwhile. The groom plays an extremely important part and shoulders great responsibility on these trips. Obviously even more is involved if trips abroad are envisaged, with all the extra paperwork and equipment necessary for such travels.

Show jumping horses are usually the best behaved of all competitive equines since they probably travel and compete more than any other, due to the nature of the sport. Nonetheless, there are always precautions that need to be taken to ensure their safety and security on such trips; many shows erect temporary stabling, which is not always as robust as it might be. Many of the European horses in particular are stallions and this may occasionally cause problems if you find there is only a flimsy barrier between your stallion and the next competitor's interesting looking mare! The stable managers are normally very helpful over taking steps to resolve problems of this kind.

Facilities at shows may vary tremendously, so it is always best to ensure you have everything, plus spares, to cope with all eventualities. The difficult feeder can be a problem on long trips away from home, but generally most horses will eat better at night when it is quieter. So try and offer them more food in the evening and again before you retire for the night.

Shoeing needs to be done a few days before you leave on a long trip and, if possible, take a few spare sets with you so that your horse does not have to be shod by a strange farrier and have strange shoes as well. There are very different methods and types of shoe used in various countries which could cause problems. It can be an expensive trip if your horse goes lame because of an unfamiliar type of shoe.

Fodder may also be quite different in other countries and, while the show jumper becomes very versatile, changes of food are never a good thing if they can be avoided or at least be introduced gradually along with some of the horse's usual diet.

Remember that in colder climates temporary stabling can be draughty, so extra rugs or blankets may be necessary and, if the boxes are small or a bit rough, bandages as protection may be a wise precaution at night.

COPING WITH PROBLEMS

Problems can occur at any time when competing, especially with the younger horses. If something goes wrong in the ring, the sooner you can put it right the better.

If it is a matter of the horse being overfaced, then you have to restore confidence by working at home and competing over easier courses until you are quite sure the horse is happy to continue. Sometimes the ground conditions can unnerve the horse. Check that you have appropriate studs and that the horse is not slipping. If the ground is very hard the horse may be feeling this and not enjoy jumping in such conditions. The horse may be 'jarred up', so check it over for any physical signs as well as checking its shoes.

Problems with jumping a clear round may be caused by rider error, lack of agility through stiffness, insufficient training and many other reasons. Try and analyse why you cannot establish a consistent record and set about putting it right. Careful warming up is very important, especially after long journeys.

Left: *The grooms have a hard time on the show circuit, trying to keep their horses looking clean and tidy as well as happy in their work, especially when they are often travelling to and from competitions for weeks at a time.*

Right: *A good groom is invaluable and it certainly helps if they are good at giving a leg up. Here, Sue Pountain is being given a leg up by her groom onto an immaculately turned out horse at the Royal International Horse of the Year Show.*

Below: *Preparations and conversations for those that wait patiently at Hickstead for the jump-off. There are often long waits in the big classes for those lucky enough to get there, but few complain about such an achievement.*

Are you under sufficient control and is your bit effective and exerting the right influence on your horse? Are you riding with sufficient impulsion for the size or siting of the fences? Try and work out why things are not successful – then you can sort out the problem.

Remember the horse is not a machine. There are many factors governing how often your horse can compete and every horse will be different, requiring carefully devised programmes depending on its experience, physique, necessity to qualify for a certain competition and so on. What may suit one horse could be disastrous for another, so treat each horse as an individual.

Keep the horse warm at all times to prevent stiffness but particularly so when waiting for the jump-offs. Keep it walking around rather than standing for too long when it gets near the time for it to compete, and for a while until it stops blowing after its round.

If the horse is mentally and physically contented and in good shape, has been well prepared and trained for what you expect of it and has what it takes to be a 'star', you will have few problems to cope with anyway.

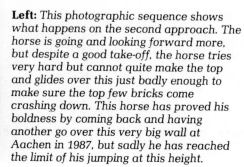

Left: *The Puissance is a class for the high jump specialist. The imposing wall requires a horse with this particular ability, but things have not gone quite right for this Swiss horse and rider. The horse has gone into the fence with inadequate impulsion and is backing off before deciding that the jump was not for him. Having stopped once, it is quite a daunting prospect to have to go back for a second attempt at jumping such an uncomprising a fence that is well over 6ft 6in (1.9m) in height.*

Left: *This photographic sequence shows what happens on the second approach. The horse is going and looking forward more, but despite a good take-off, the horse tries very hard but cannot quite make the top and glides over this just badly enough to make sure the top few bricks come crashing down. This horse has proved his boldness by coming back and having another go over this very big wall at Aachen in 1987, but sadly he has reached the limit of his jumping at this height.*

The Eventing Scene

This is much the most complex of the three sports by its very nature; it requires more space, a lot more people to organize it and generally a longer build-up of horse and rider in preparation for the sport in its three different phases. There is also a limit as to how often the event horse can compete because of the amount and type of work necessary to prepare and train for eventing.

With dressage and show jumping in particular, there are numerous shows to choose from and you may decide to do two or three in one week and then have a break before the next stint. You cannot do this with the eventer if you want to keep the horse sound – it is expecting too much of it physically. At novice level it may be acceptable to do a 2.4 kilometre (1½ mile) course for three weekends running, if the ground is good, and then have a fortnight off before doing another batch. But as you get to the more advanced courses, this amount of competition work undoubtedly leads to trouble with most horses. Competing once a fortnight is ample and if you are aiming for a three-day event at the end, you must be careful not to overdo these twice-weekly outings, so that your horse is overworked in its build-up for the major event. If you are not aiming for a three-day event, then it is quite possible to plan on doing a greater number of one-day events.

ONE-DAY EVENTS

In one-day events, the classes are divided into three different grades in most countries with novice, intermediate and advanced being a fairly self explanatory way of dividing them into the different groups. In the

Left: *An impressive jump takes this horse and rider over the big log-pile uphill at Gatcombe's British Championships. The grease on the horse's legs protects them if caught or entangled in a fence.*

Above: *This photograph captures an inspired moment as this horse makes a lovely jump over a parallel at the Wylye Horse Trials – a jump which would be the envy of any rider.*

Below: *The popularity of horse trials is clear to see as the crowds gather at Gatcombe Park to watch horses and riders through the water complex at the British Open Championships.*

United States, 'training' levels, and more recently in Britain pre-novice classes, prove valuable as an introduction to the sport over slightly lower and generally straightforward courses before competitors start in earnest.

The novice, or preliminary courses in the United States, should give the horse the grounding to progress to the next stage and should include as many different types of fences as possible in a fairly simple form. Cross-country is generally up to 2.4 kilometres (1½ miles) long and fences are mostly up to 1.07 metres (3 feet 6 inches) at this level, with fences of around 1.10 metres (3 feet 7 inches) for the show or stadium jumping. The dressage tests are simple and straightforward with the emphasis placed on a smooth, obedient and forward-going performance.

At intermediate standard, 1.15 metres (3 feet 9 inches) is the general height for the cross-country and jumping phases with an intermediate or elementary standard dressage test. The latter demands a more col-

Below: *Dual Badminton winner, Ian Stark, is trying desperately hard to achieve a clear round at the Los Angeles Olympics. A very close finish resulted in a Gold for the US team with Great Britain taking the Silver.*

Above: *Many things have to be learnt to be able to reach the top levels and to ride safely, you must learn to cope with spray at water obstacles. Excessive speed creates too much, making vision difficult.*

Left: *A lovely active trot showing a good bend on the turn. Dressage in horse trials is of medium standard for the top level and horses must be active, obedient and supple but ready to cope with the cross-country.*

lected performance, some elementary lateral work and counter canter.

The cross-country will be more demanding with more combination and 'problem' fences than at novice level and the courses should be aimed at training the horse to cope with these higher and more complicated fences in preparation for the next level.

At advanced level the horse is expected to perform a good, medium level dressage test showing collection and extensions, lateral work and a generally pleasing performance throughout, demonstrating a well-trained and prepared horse.

The cross-country at this level may be around 4 kilometres (2½ miles) long with fences up to 1.19 metres (3 feet 11 inches) in height. The course will expect the horse to have been trained to cope with sophisticated jumps, often involving several elements and imposing water obstacles. The jumping test will also be at 1.19 metres (3 feet 11 inches) and many include trebles and a water jump.

The above are the requirements for a one-day event which really serves as the training ground for the three-day event, giving the horse the necessary experience without too much stress in comparison to a full, three-day event.

TWO-DAY EVENTS

Some countries run two-day events to enable competitors to get used to the roads and

Minimum and Maximum Speeds, Times and Distances for Three-day Events

COMPETITION	PHASES A & C ROAD & TRACKS			PHASE B STEEPLECHASE			PHASE D CROSS-COUNTRY		
	Speed [m/m]	Time [mins]	Distance [m]	Speed [m/m]	Time [mins]	Distance [m]	Speed [m/m]	Time [mins]	Distance [m]
CCI*	220	45–73	9900–16060	640–690	4	2560–2760	520–570	10–11	5200–6270
CCI**	220	45–73	9900–16060	660–690	4–4½	2640–3105	550–570	11–12	6050–6840
CCI***	220	45–73	9900–16060	690	4½–5	3105–3450	570	12–13	6840–7410
CCIO	220	73–90	16060–19800	690	4½ or 5	3105–3450	570	13–14	7410–7980
CCA	220	45–73	9900–16060	640–670	4 or 4½	2560–3015	520–550	10–13	5200–7150
Championships for Ponies	200	15–20	3000–4000	NOT APPLICABLE			400—500	5—6	2000–3000
Championships for Juniors	220	36–45	7920–9900	640	3½	2240	520	6½–9½	3380–4940
Championships for Young Riders	220	45–63	9900–13860	660	4	2640	550	10	5500

Above: *The FEI requirements for the different standards of event. The chart shows times and distances for the three phases relevant to the speed and endurance sections of the three-day event.*

Right: *A good impression in the dressage is most important if good marks are to be achieved. A consistent, smooth and accurate performance is required, with calmness maintained throughout the test.*

tracks and steeplechase phases. These events normally take the form of the dressage and jumping on day one with the speed and endurance, as it is known when all phases are included, taking place on the second day.

The classes may be aimed at any standard but will usually have certain provisos and qualifications to ensure that both horse and rider have had some basic experience and have proved themselves in a number of one-day events.

Below: *This type of information is usually found in the programme. Always check with your official time sheet before working out proper times in case adjustments have been made since the programme was printed.*

□ THREE-DAY EVENTS □

The three-day event is really what the sport is all about. Often, with so many wanting to compete, two days of dressage are necessary and, as the event is always preceded by a compulsory veterinary inspection which generally takes place the day before it starts, you may well find that it turns into a five-day event! This is generally the case at the big international three-day events.

The first of three veterinary inspections takes place before the competition can commence, and any horse failing this will not be allowed to start. The dressage test is set to reflect the standard of the horse competing. If there are two days of this you do have a day's break in-between, which may or may not be a good thing for those worried about the cross-country!

The speed and endurance day starts with **Phase A**, the first warm-up phase of roads

and tracks, the length of which varies according to the standard but may be up to 6 kilometres (3.7 miles). **Phase B,** the steeplechase, follows on over a course of six to ten fences. These may be on a round or figure of eight course, and on completion you are already on **Phase C,** the second or recovery phase of the roads and tracks. These are generally somewhere between 6 to 10 kilometres (3.7 to 6.2 miles). The longer this Phase C is in duration, the better since your horse has more time to recover after the steeplechase, contrary to what some uneducated people seem to think.

At the end of Phase C you enter 'the box' area where the second compulsory veterinary inspection takes place during your ten-minute break. This is a brief but important check by the veterinarians to ensure your horse is fit enough to continue. If they are worried about your horse at this stage, they may ask to see it again in a few minutes or can eliminate it at this stage. This is only done on rare occasions and is in the horse's

A Typical Example of Distances, Speeds and Times

PHASE	NATURE	DISTANCE		SPEED	OPTIMUM TIME		
		Km	M	M/min	Hr	Mins	Secs
A	Roads and Tracks	5	500	220		25	00
B	Steeplechase	3	105	690		4	30
C	Roads and Tracks	7	260	220		33	00
	Veterinary Inspection					10	00
D	Cross-country	6	900	570		12	06
	TOTAL	22	765		1	24	36

The Eventing Scene

interests if things are not right for one reason or another, however disappointing it may seem at the time. Better a grateful horse than no horse at all.

Phase D, the all important cross-country phase, consists of a course of solid obstacles ranging from about 20 to 35 in number, which may include any of the typical cross-country fences in any form and often a few surprise fences dreamed up by an imaginative course designer!

The speeds and distances for these vary according to the standard of the event being run, but the chart on page 165 serves as a general guide.

On the third day there is the third compulsory veterinary inspection which must be passed before you can tackle the final show jumping or stadium phase.

This single round in the stadium is designed to show that your horse is still in good shape after the rigours of the previous day and ready to carry on in work. This is the real test of horsemastership and the moment when you can be proud or disappointed in your efforts at producing your horse fit and well-prepared to cope with the demands of eventing.

The course is generally fairly straightforward and may include a water jump, but for the horse that has been galloping fast over big, solid fences, the relative ease with which a show jump falls is quite a test on its training and fitness at this stage of the proceedings. Because it is so challenging for the horse, many a medal has been lost in this important last phase.

The following chart has been taken from the official FEI rules as a general guide but national rules, regulations, distances and times may vary from time to time. Therefore, remember to check carefully with your latest up-to-date rule book.

Below: *The roads and tracks phases are normally carried out at a steady trot or a relaxed canter. On phase A, it is worth having a short pipe-opener on a suitable piece of ground before the steeplechase.*

A Typical Example of Three-day Event Penalties

FAULTS AT OBSTACLES	
Competitors are only penalised if faults occur within an area surrounding each obstacle known as the Penalty Zone, as follows:	
Entering, then leaving, Penalty Zone without having addressed the obstacle to be negotiated [Note: This does not count as a refusal, etc.]	20 penalties
First Refusal, run-out, circle of horse at obstacle	20 penalties
Second Refusal, run-out, circle of horse at same obstacle	40 penalties
Third Refusal, run-out, circle of horse at same obstacle	Elimination
Fall of horse and/or rider	60 penalties
Second fall of horse and/or rider during the Steeplechase Phase	Elimination
Third fall of horse and/or rider during the Cross Country Phase	Elimination
Omission of obstacle or Red or White flag	Elimination
Retaking an obstacle already jumped	Elimination
Jumping obstacles in wrong order	Elimination

Note: These penalties are cumulative

TIME PENALTIES	
PHASE A AND C	A competitor is penalised one point for each second in excess of the Optimum Time up to the Time Limit, after which he is eliminated.
PHASE B	A competitor is penalised 0.8 of a point for each second in excess of the Optimum Time up to the time Limit, after which he is eliminated.
PHASE D	A competitor is penalised 0.4 of a point for each second in excess of the Optimum Time up to the Time Limit, after which he is eliminated.

VETERINARY INSPECTION

Between Phases C and D there will be a break of 10 minutes in the timetable for each horse. During this interval a Committee composed of a veterinary surgeon and one or two judges will examine each horse in order to decide whether it is fit enough to continue. Should they decide that any horse is unfit, they are responsible for ordering its immediate withdrawal.

JUDGING AND SCORING

The judges for eventing are numerous. There are the dressage judges – three for national championships and all international events but probably only one or two for one-day classes; a judge for the show jumping phase plus a fence judge for every obstacle on the course, which adds up to quite a collection. All their score sheets have to be collected up and taken to the scorers who add up and check through every score of every competitor to ensure the correct result is obtained. Under FEI rules, this is not as simple as it may sound as various calculations have to be made to the dressage scores to ensure that the correct relative value of the three phases (3.12.1) is maintained; the dressage scores are multiplied by a factor of 0.6.

There is also the multiplying factor decided by the Technical Deligate at a three-day event, and this is used to determine the relative influence of the dressage scores on the results of the whole event. It may vary, between 0.5 and 1.5. The FEI states that if the endurance competition is estimated to be a relatively easy test for the standard of horses and competitors entered, the scores in the endurance competition can therefore be expected to be low and consequently the influence of the dressage scores should be reduced by applying a multiplying factor of less than one. If the endurance competition is estimated to be relatively severe for the standard of competitors, the multiplying factor should be more than one.

PLANNING THE DAY FOR A ONE-DAY EVENT

This is vital preparation if all is to go well. Once you know your starting times for the three phases you can then work everything out, but unfortunately it is rare to know these until the day before the competition starts. If you have a long distance to travel, it is always best to travel down the day before so that you are nearby and can walk your course and give your horse a chance to see the sights as well.

If you are going to do the whole thing in one day, you must be fully prepared and organized, allowing time for problems so that you arrive in plenty of time to do everything necessary once there. This all very much depends on whether your times allow you the chance to walk your course **after** the dressage, which is really ideal as you can concentrate on it more then and it will be fresh in your mind. On the minus side, there is so much going on during the competition that it may be difficult to concentrate properly and anyway you will probably only have time for one walk instead of two.

Be sure you decide how much work you want to give the horse before the dressage, since this is usually the factor governing arrival time. Collect numbers, remembering to take vaccination certificates with you if you are likely to be checked, and see if there are any important notices posted at the secretaries' tent relevant to you or your horse.

Arrange with your groom or helpers when you want the horse ready or whether you want it lunged. Be sure to specify meeting places, type of tack, studs etc and when you want anything ready.

Try to get a chance to walk the show jumping course, before it starts if possible since, although there are usually breaks during the day, these may not run to time and you may be busy elsewhere when the course is clear. Take the time to watch a few competitors jumping the course to see if anything in particular is causing a problem and try and assess why so that you can hopefully avoid making a mistake as well.

Look around on arrival to see exactly where everything is. Sometimes dressage or cross-country starts may be some way away, which could make a difference as to when you need to set off to get there on time. Or if you need your groom there, he or she will need to know where to meet you.

Check which is your dressage arena and find your dressage steward and ascertain

Above: *Waiting for the final results can be frustrating and nerve-racking, but the fairly complicated scores take time to add up and double check with all the different phases to be worked out.*

Below: *The weather conditions can make a tremendous difference to the going, which will suit some horses better than others. The event horse must be taught to cope with all types of ground, both hard and soft.*

Left: *The complete range of penalties on the different phases, both for faults at the obstacles and for time. Dressage and show jumping scores are added to give the final penalty points; the lowest is the winner.*

Above: *The show jumping phase comes on the last day in a three-day event but in many countries, this takes place before the cross-country in one-day events so that more riders are accommodated.*

who you follow and if there have been any last minute withdrawals which might affect your starting time. You are perfectly entitled to wait for your proper time if things are running early, but it is maddening for judges having too many gaps so they may be more amenable if you go in a fraction early, especially if you are last to go!

Make sure you have someone at hand to remove boots, bandages, the whip or whatever. This is usually best done at least a few minutes before you go in, since a last-minute rush may undo all the quietening work you have given your horse beforehand. Ask your groom to be quick but quiet and avoid any unnecessary fussing at this crucial time. Just keep working the horse quietly with frequent changes of direction to keep it occupied.

Some countries show jump before the cross-country at one-day event level because it enables more riders to compete, whereas after the cross-country the horses require a longer break to recover. If riding in a different country, do check the format.

Walk the cross-country course preferably either alone or with your trainer so that you can concentrate on what you have to do. Too often one sees competitors walking with far too many people when it becomes quite impossible to make decisions and remember the course properly. At least one walk round

Below: *At one-day events, there are often two or three different standards of cross-country courses going on during the day. They should be clearly marked and obvious, but do not be caught out when walking them.*

Above: *Anne-Marie Taylor looks very thoughtful as she contemplates her course at a novice horse trial. In FEI competitions, courses may only be walked fully dressed for competing with hats on.*

Right: *The box is always busy during the competition with horses starting or coming back from or in the middle of the ten-minute halt. Relaxation with the minimum of fuss and calm handling make a great difference.*

A One-day Event Course Map

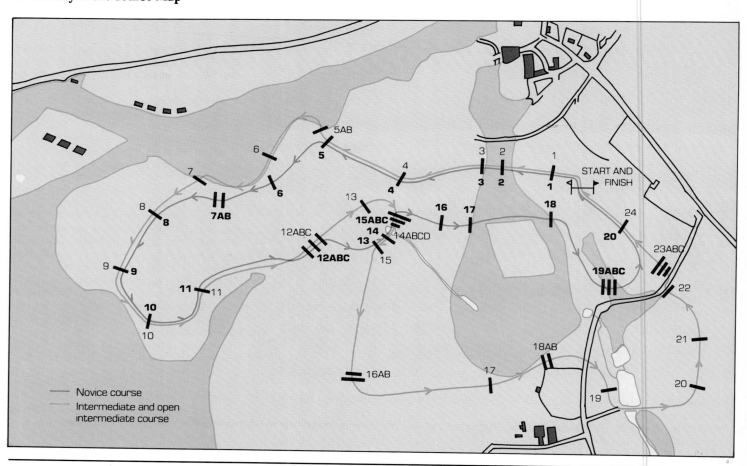

the course should be made just on your own or with your trainer.

Study the start and how far you have to get your horse going before the first fence. Make sure you count the numbers of each fence as you go round the course to ensure you have not missed any out.

Look at each fence in relation to the rest of the course and the ground also. Sometimes it will be necessary to take the first part of the course a little steady if you are to cope with a difficult or tiring bit near the end. The going can make an enormous difference to a course. A well-prepared horse may make nothing of going to time in good ground, whereas that would be over stressing it if the going was very deep and sticky. In very hard ground horses will tend to shorten their stride. Whatever the conditions the speed will often very much depend on the course itself: whether this is routed through trees or up and down hills; whether it is designed to suit bold, onward jumping or is the awkward, trappy course requiring quite a lot of control. This latter type is time consuming and may well involve losing several more seconds than the course where you can get going into a rhythm and stick to it.

Study each fence carefully and look back along your route to ensure you have chosen the quickest and safest line. There will

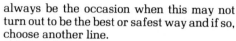

Above: *During the ten-minute halt, the vet will examine the horses to ensure that they are fit and well to continue onto the cross-country. It is the rider's responsibility not to over-tax the horse and ride it according to its state of fitness.*

always be the occasion when this may not turn out to be the best or safest way and if so, choose another line.

At combination fences look at all the options before deciding where you are going to tackle it, but have a second option ready in your mind in case it appears that way is causing problems or the ground there is deteriorating. Look also at each element and be sure you know what to do and where to jump if you are unlucky enough to have a refusal anywhere at the fence. It is so important to be able to react quickly on such occasions so that you do not waste even more valuable seconds through your indecision. Check that you have gone through all the right elements between the red and white flags – it can sometimes be a bit complicated in the heat of the moment.

Make quite sure you know where any compulsory flags are situated on the course and be sure to go round them leaving the red flag on your right or the white on your left. These may have been added since the course plan in the programme was printed, so always check the official course plan before you start your walk round. Direction markers are not compulsory and may be passed on either side.

On completing your round be sure to pass through the finish. This can sometimes look quite confusing, especially if it is adjacent to the start. So when you are walking the course, study your approach to this carefully and look again at it if possible before you start.

At the end of your walk round it is worthwhile mentally riding your course to be sure you can remember it. If you have walked it on the previous day, do try and get round it again on the actual day so that it is all fresh in your memory and you can note any

Left: *Positive and bold riding, giving the horse all the assistance it needs, is the most important aspect of good cross-country riding. Uphill fences require plenty of impulsion to make up for loss of momentum. Balance must be maintained throughout.*

Left: A good attitude from both horse and rider is captured in this photograph, as they clear a typical cross-country fence in fine style. Cross-country fences should be ridden at boldly, maintaining a steady, strong pace throughout.

changes in the going if there has been over-night rain etc.

In a three-day event it is compulsory to weigh out and in again before the cross-country, so allow time to do this when planning your day. The minimum weight is 75 kilogrammes (11 stone 11 pounds or 165 pounds). This may include your tack but not bridle or whip although the bridle may be claimed if you are under the weight when weighing in at the end. Under penalty of elimination, it is essential that only the official weigher has access to you and the horse until you have weighed in at the end of your round.

CARE OF THE HORSE AT THE ONE-DAY EVENT

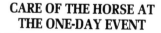

This is obviously very important if the horse is to be able to perform well. Rest and relaxation are particularly important for the

event horse, which needs to conserve its energy for the three phases. Feeding and watering needs careful thought and generally hay is best avoided until after the cross-country. However, if this is very late in the day, the horse will certainly require either a very small net early on or a feed up to four hours before galloping. Many people have different ideas on what to do with their horses during their day at an event but the principle must be not to gallop within four to six hours of feeding but also to ensure the horse has some food during a long and busy day. Water is essential, especially in hot weather, and short drinks of up to a third of a bucket should be offered regularly until two hours before galloping. As soon as the horse has stopped blowing after its cross-country, again offer it short drinks every ten minutes until it is satisfied.

It is very important that the horse does not get too hot or dehydrated during the day in

Above: *The finish of phase D and nearly the end of months of hard work, training and preparation. Depending on the standard, it is many people's ambition to complete a three-day event. Others look on it as a qualification or stepping stone to a big two or three-star event.*

Right: *It is most important to weigh in at the end of the three day event, even if you are over the 165lb (75kg) minimum weight. This must also be done before you start phase A, so always allow enough time to tack up afterwards and have some spare lead handy in case you are a bit light.*

Left: *Bruce Davidson prepares to sit up quickly on landing before tackling this impressive slide downhill. The event horse must be able to go up or down steep slopes with ease; the sooner they learn, the better they will be.*

hot weather and every form of ventilation to encourage a free flow of air should be used. Open all windows and ramps if it is very hot and remove rugs or sheets and if possible park in a shady area.

In cold weather keep the horse warm at all times and be very careful not to let it get chilled, especially when you first get out of the horsebox. Always keep a rug over it to prevent its muscles going into spasm due to sudden changes of temperature.

Leg protection is sensible at all times. After all the work that has gone into getting to an event it is worth preventing a silly knock on the day, especially as your horse may be prone to all sorts of excitable bucks and kicks on a cold day at the beginning of the season.

After the cross-country make sure your horse is walked around until it stops blowing. This is important since it allows the lactic acid that builds up in the muscles during

Left: *This interesting sequence shows how horse and rider have successfully negotiated the road crossing at Gatcombe with one stride being taken on the road and one after the jump-up before the rail. The horse is having to stretch a bit on the road, indicating that some more impulsion could have been mustered before the jump. The rider has been tipped forward and has rather an insecure leg position over the rails. Riding a couple of holes shorter on the cross-country helps security.*

exertion to be reabsorbed, and your horse will be far less stiff the next day if it has had this gentle 'winding down' period. It also helps to mentally relax the horse so that it settles well afterwards.

Washing down should be done quickly so that the horse is not made to stand for too long before being walked, and in cold weather keep this to a minimum over the back and loins. In hot weather frequent washing and scraping will help cool the horse and allow for natural evaporation.

Check the horse over thoroughly for any knocks or cuts and treat as necessary and bandage well for the journey home. Remember to remove studs and pick out the feet before putting it away.

Once the day is over and your horse is settled and happily eating its hay, having had a small feed if this is practical, the sooner you can get it home or into your stabling to relax the better. Encourage it to stale and keep it warm; rub its ears well if they are cold or in a 'cold sweat' and try and leave it to rest and get over its day as soon as possible.

CARE OF THE HORSE AT THE THREE-DAY EVENT

This requires much more of a long-term plan and very much depends on how your horse copes away from home. Most horses are remarkably good, but there are always the odd few who get themselves in quite a state, go off their feed, sweat up and generally become wound up!

Try and keep as near to your normal routine as possible. If practical, lead the horse out to graze once or twice a day but do not do this if the grass is very different; just lead it out for a nice walk. If the horse goes off its feed, give half the quantity, or even miss out the lunch feed if this is given and give more in the evening when the horse is more likely to eat up. Sometimes it is best to miss out a feed altogether, let the horse get a little hungry and then introduce more later.

Exercising must be carefully worked out to fit around your times and walking of the course. Try and take your horse on a good

wander round to see the sights on arrival to help it to relax and settle. If it is really fresh to start with, then work it hard and wander about at the end to cool it off. Try and get into the collecting ring and familiarize the horse with its surroundings as often as possible.

Make quite sure you have studied where you are allowed to exercise before setting out, since it would be more than frustrating to discover you were eliminated before the event started because you were riding, albeit unwittingly, on part of the course.

Do not take any risks; always have proper leg protection whenever out on your horse and be sure that you ride only in permitted dressage tack until after you have done your test, regardless of whether you are jumping or not.

PLANNING THE DAY FOR A THREE-DAY EVENT

The competitors' briefing usually takes place the day before the competition starts and it is as well to take a notepad and pen to jot down any relevant points about the com-

Above: *The grooms have a busy week at the three-day event and riders should always ensure that they have adequate facilities to look after themselves and their charges, and given free time whenever possible.*

Right: *Getting ready to start phase A, this rider has her team of helpers, all busy at something. One to hold the horse and two to do the necessary is about right, but make sure they all know what you expect of them.*

Right: *The overall layout map of the three-day event showing the roads and tracks of phases A and C, as well as the steeplechase and cross-country courses. As you walk round the courses, make sure you carefully check the flags, as marked on the map, and the check points.*

Below: *That great feeling when it is all over at the end of the cross-country and horse and rider are safely back. At this point you can start to relax a bit, but there is another day to go and your horse will be tired and may be stiff and sore.*

petition and those you should tell your groom. You will normally be given a map of the course, numbers and any other relevant information at this time.

This is then followed by the official tour of the roads and tracks and steeplechase. If you have not got your own four-wheel drive vehicle, get a place quickly in someone else's with a front seat so that you can study the route and take notes.

Look at the ground and terrain and notice where the kilometre markers are situated and whether there are checkpoint flags to go through and how many. On Phase A, see if there is a stretch of good ground to give your horse a short, sharp pipe-opener in preparation for the steeplechase; it need only be a few hundred metres or yards. Notice if there are any bad or slow areas that will require extra time and where you can make up time, especially on Phase C.

The steeplechase is usually walked on foot and becomes rather a nightmare on this first official walk as there are too many people and everyone is chatting. Have a quick look but come back later and walk it thoroughly, looking back to work out your fastest route in-between fences and check if there are any patches of ground; what is the best approach to any of the fences and the location of the start and finish. Also know where the official stop-point is at the end so that if you need assistance such as a blacksmith this can be attended to.

A Three-day Event Course Map

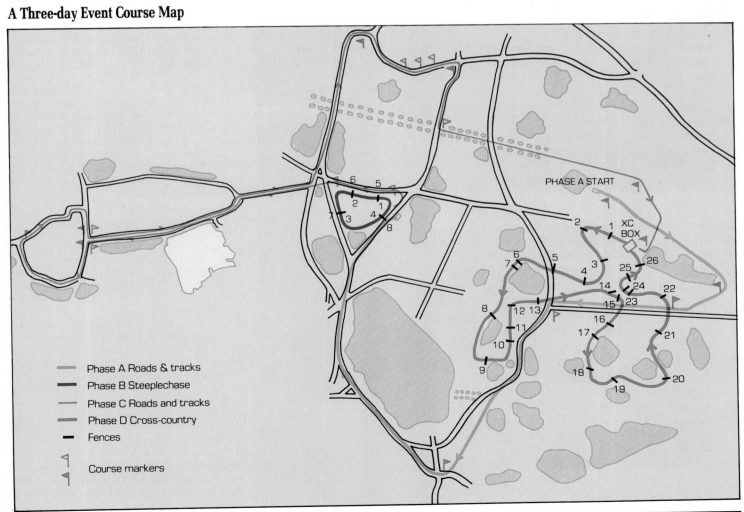

Phase A Roads & tracks
Phase B Steeplechase
Phase C Roads and tracks
Phase D Cross-country
Fences

Course markers

'The box' is the area in which the ten-minute halt takes place and the horses are prepared for the cross-country, so it is here that all your kit is brought. Study the box carefully so that you know what it consists of and especially check to see if it has water so that you do not have to bring your water container to the area.

You need washing-down kit; spare boots or bandages and over-reach boots; studs; rugs; sweat sheet or cooler; iced water if very hot; towels; grease for legs; spare tack and any different bridle required; dry gloves, a drink and coat, if cold for the rider, and any other particular bits and pieces to refresh both horse and rider during this important ten-minute period.

Walking the Cross-country Course

Walking the cross country course for a three-day event is much the same as for a one-day event except longer, but there are two points that you must remember to bear in mind. The first is the fact that the horse

Below: *Careful walking of the course is by far the most important aspect of successful cross-country riding. Check distances and the most suitable line into each fence, and know your alternatives in case of problems.*

will have done two lots of roads and tracks and a steeplechase course before it embarks on this crucial part of the course; the second is the existence of penalty zones.

Penalty zones are the set area around both steeplechase and cross-country fences, inside which you will incur penalties for a fall, refusals or run out as well as entering and leaving it before jumping the fence. Anything that happens outside this area, whether or not it is connected with the fence, does not count.

Study your penalty zones carefully when walking the course to be certain you do not enter then leave the penalty zone on your approach to the fence. This may sound rather strange but it can quite easily be done at some fences.

Do not take risks at the end of the course, so study each fence carefully to be able to give your horse the best possible and safest line through. Always be quite sure you know your plan of action through combinations, especially since you have the added complication of penalty zones to cope with.

Bottom: *The ten-minute halt inspection is very important to ensure the horse is in good shape to continue. Britain's Col Peter Hodgson and top show jumping trainer, Dick Stillwell, check the horses at Windsor.*

Veterinary Inspections

These take place at the beginning of the event and before the show jumping on the last day and they are the times when your horse should be proudly shown-off, looking immaculate. Have your horse plaited and looking its best. Keep the horse walking and if it is cold be particularly careful that it does not get a chill, so have it well rugged up. The inspections usually go in numerical order and can take a considerable time, but whatever you do be sure to be there as you may be eliminated if not. Remember that you will probably not know how many drop-outs there have been and it is not unusual to find a dozen or so have not appeared in front of you. Have a hoof pick with you and pick out the feet just before you run the horse up to be certain there are no stones or whatever. Lead your horse straight and do not pull its head round. This will inevitably make it put more weight on the one leg and the inspection panel will start nodding their heads. Turn the horse away from you slowly and get it straight before breaking into a trot leaving its head as free as possible.

The Show Jumping Phase

Before the final show jumping phase, your horse will already have had the initial stiffness taken out of it as you will have loosened it up before the veterinary inspection. However, it will not feel as free as it did in a one-day event, and having galloped fast the day before it may have become a little careless. You must loosen the horse up without over-tiring it and give it a few jumps to get its mind thinking of the precision required for this phase.

Find out whether you are to salute the judges, royal box etc before your round. Very often there is still a parade of competitors in the competition before the show jumping, and usually all competitors who compete on all three days come in for the final prize-giving, which is the climax to your equestrian dreams – even better if you are the one at the top of the line!

Speed and Endurance Times

Working out your times for the speed and endurance can be done as soon as you receive the official starting times which will show the times you need to be at the start and finish of each phase if you are not to incur any time penalties.

You can either work out where you should be at each kilometre mark according to your actual time, or set your times from 12 o'clock whatever time you actually go. At two minutes before you set off you set your own watch to two minutes to twelve, and two minutes later away you go, having also started your stop watch as you pass the start. The advantage of this method is that it is easier to see exactly what time you are doing; if there has been a hold-up at any stage; your real times will have become distorted and it will be more difficult to see when you should be at a given point. I have found using my watch from 12 o'clock so

Competitors' Times Using a 12 O'clock Start

START A	START B	FINISH B	FINISH C	10 MINS	START D
12.00	12.24	12.28	1.02		1.12

Kilometres and Times

START PHASE	A — 12.00	START PHASE	C — 12.28
	K1 — 12.04		K1 — 12.32
	K2 — 12.08		K2 — 12.37
	K3 — 12.12		K3 — 12.41
	K4 — 12.16		K4 — 12.45
	K5 — 12.20		K5 — 12.49
	FINISH A — 12.22		K6 — 12.53
			K7 — 12.57
START PHASE	B — 12.24	FINISH C	1.00
	half-way — 12.26		
	FINISH B — 12.28	START PHASE	D — 1.12

Top: *Many riders find it easier to start on a 12 o'clock time so that it corresponds to a stopwatch. Five minutes before starting, set your watch at five to twelve and stick to that time throughout your round.*

Above: *A typical rundown of kilometres and other times using a 12 o'clock start. Note K2 has allowed extra time so that the horse can slow up after the steeplechase. Four minutes is usual per kilometre otherwise.*

Above: *The loneliness of the roads and tracks is captured here as John Thelwell checks his watch to ensure he is on time so that he does not have to hurry the horse before phase D, the cross-country.*

much easier since you view it like a stop watch and know exactly where you are time-wise. Do not forget, however, to make sure you have wound it up properly, or checked the battery, before you start!

The Ten-minute Halt

Care of the horse in 'the box' during the ten-minute halt can win or lose a competition. The crucial point to remember is that this period is designed to refresh and relax your horse before setting off round the course.

After you have been released by the veterinary panel your 'team' of helpers should set to work refreshing your horse. Some people just loosen the girths, others like to remove the saddle altogether. What you do will rather depend on the weather, your experience and the temperament of the horse. If it is very hot, it is best to remove the saddle and wash the horse down thoroughly, washing and scraping. Place a cold towel round the head and iced packs to the throat, jugular area and up between the hind legs where the prominent femoral arteries can be seen. This will all help considerably to reduce the temperature in very hot conditions. In more temperate weather, a good wash down should suffice but in cold weather great care must be taken to ensure the horse does not get cold and washing down, especially over the back and loin area should be done in moderation in case you cause muscle spasm after the horse has been sweating a lot. Sponging out the mouth with a saturated sponge is very refreshing but some horses will not stand for this sort of interference. The important aim must be to refresh the horse in a calm manner without fuss.

Check that all your shoes and studs are in place; if you have a problem here the farrier

Above: *Checking that all is well before starting off is very important. Attention to detail can make all the difference in something as vital as the three-day event. Never leave anything to chance.*

Right: *Having freshened up the horse in the ten-minute halt, keep it moving quietly to prevent it stiffening up. It is a matter of preference as to whether the saddle is removed during this time or not.*

must be summoned immediately and will be at his designated post inside the box, hopefully! You can carry on sponging your horse whilst he is at work, but if cold keep a good cover over the horse to keep it warm.

At the five-minute call by the steward, you should put the saddle on again remembering to pull the weight cloth, if used, well up into the front arch of the saddle as you tighten the girths in case it presses down onto the withers.

Make sure your reins are dry and that you have your whip and gloves and have secured your hat before mounting by the time the two-minute call is made. You will not have much room, but wake your horse up well and if possible trot it on for a few strides after its break, before getting into the start box for Phase D about five to ten seconds before you are due to set off.

Some people grease their horses' legs down the front of both front and hind legs. This is to help reduce the risk of injury should the horse straddle a fence or make a mistake anywhere, and a thick layer of grease should be run from the stifle or forearm down over the hock and knee joints to below the fetlock joints. Do this last of all, preferably after the rider has mounted as it is terribly important that the grease does not get on the reins or anywhere else vital to control as the two are not altogether compatible!

The rider should make the best possible use of the ten-minute halt hopefully finding out from his or her team how the course is

Above: *At the bigger events you will have to perform in front of quite big crowds, so do not get distracted but concentrate on the job in hand. Put your whole mind and body into doing your very best on the day.*

Below: *A lovely shot of Lucinda Green and her great horse, Regal Realm, as they jump a fence in perfect balance on the cross-country course in Los Angeles during the Olympic Games in 1984.*

riding and whether any fences are causing problems. Sometimes there is a video available but do not let watching a video make you waver from what you think is right for your horse. Make sure when you mentally run through your course that you are thinking positively about your approach to each fence.

Facilities for nature's call should be provided but do not let rider's nerves overtake you and make sure one of your team is aware of where you are so that they can come and whisk you out if you fail to appear!

USEFUL REMINDERS

Nerves are all part of the competitive scene and are partly why we engage in these various sports, but it is important to keep them under control so that you do not let this natural phenomenon take over and cloud your judgement and cause you to lose your drive. For those aiming for the top and into teams, this is one very important aspect that the selectors will be watching. However brilliant the combination of horse and rider, all will be lost if competition nerves are allowed to take over just when the horse and rider should be putting everything they have got into riding at their very best round the course. The best advice is to keep occupied and not to think about it too much!

Looking after your horse and giving it the very best chance to do its utmost for you is

really common sense. There will be numerous tips that you pick up from other competitors along the way which perhaps you may find better than your methods. Other methods may surprise you, but always think what is practical for you and your horse and act on the tips that suit you. Nearly all the top competitors have learnt new techniques etc along the way from watching other riders and learning as they go.

Dedication to what you are doing and a well-informed and thoroughly reliable back-up team will really be the vital elements of success if you have a good horse that is well-prepared and trained to do all that you are asking.

Two World Championships for America's Bruce Davidson; six incredible Badminton wins for Lucinda Green, three Olympic gold medals for Richard Meade and the amazingly consistent performances of Virginia Leng, all three from Britain; as well as New Zealander Mark Todd's performances ranging from Olympic gold to Badminton and Burghley wins on many different horses – all were achieved through sheer hard work, dedication to what they were doing and careful planning from the start with their back-up teams right through to the climax of each big event in the calendar.

POST-COMPETITION

Once the season is over or your horse has done its three-day event, a rest period is essential to give the horse time to unwind mentally and physically and rest its legs, quite apart from the fact that any horse needs a respite from the hard slog of fitness and training.

Let the horse down gradually over a period of ten days to a fortnight. If there is any heat in the legs, a few days out for a good walk may be better than turning it out when it could gallop around and do something silly. Gradually decrease the corn rations and introduce more bulk and fattening foods into the diet. You can allow the horse to have more hay and generally encourage it to get a little 'fat and happy', although with some horses you must be careful not to overdo the former part.

How long a rest is always difficult to determine but at the end of a busy season a couple of months is usual, with the horse being turned out completely or out by day and in at night; or rested but just kept ticking over by being quietly ridden once or twice a week. There are arguments for and against all of these methods, but everyone agrees that some form of good break is essential at the end of the season and certainly after a big three-day event.

In the middle of the year or at the end of the spring season, there is not time to give the horse too long off but you should allow for a month if you are to keep your horse sound.

It is worth checking your horse over after a three-day event or at the end of the season, especially if there is any suspicion of heat in the legs. Get your veterinarian's advice in case it would be wise to give any specific treatment at this time. Although the horse may be perfectly sound, if there is any prob-

Above: *The price of fame – former British Olympic rider, Hugh Thomas, interviews Lucinda Green following an outstanding ride at Burghley, which she has won twice as well having a record-breaking six wins at Badminton to her credit.*

Left: *'Shucks to you, I'm having a good time!' At the end of a busy season, most eventers need a couple of months' rest and relaxation. Mentally and physically they deserve a break from competitive life.*

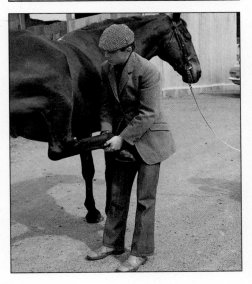

Above: *At the end of the season or at any time when you might be worried, your horse should have a thorough check by your vet for any niggling problems which might need treating before the rest period.*

lem, however slight, now is the time to be quite sure it is treated properly and given adequate time to settle down before thinking of doing any more work with the horse. A daily check of the event horse's legs and immediate action, if necessary, is the secret of keeping your horse competing in the long run. There is nearly always a little bit of heat somewhere a few days before a bigger strain or problem. If you can notice and act at this stage rather than let it get worse you will often find that only a week's 'easy' or less is required; ignoring the problem can mean a month or longer which could put you out for the season.

Even though the horse is out, make sure its feet are regularly trimmed, that it is wormed on schedule and its teeth attended to as necessary. Make sure it looks well, especially at the end of the year when it is most likely to be turned out, since there is seldom very much goodness left in the grass at that time of year. Therefore, extra feeding will more than likely be necessary in this case, especially if the horse has been competing in a long, hard season.

Tips For Success

You will learn useful tips for competition all the time, and inevitably it is a combination of these which goes towards making a successful partnership, whatever the sport. Attention to detail and the importance of producing the horse at its best – fit, confident and ready both mentally and physically to perform as required – will not happen without a great deal of preparation, as has been discussed throughout this book.

Right from the beginning train your horse in such a way that it will be a pleasure to have around wherever you go. The horse must be easy to transport to shows in the box, to be tied up inside or out and stand quietly, so that even if you are by yourself you can cope without any hassle. If the horse is young, take it around to as many outings as possible until it settles and is quite used to the competitive atmosphere. It is often good to go along to shows and just ride the horse quietly without competing on it so that it takes everything in its stride without getting mentally worked up over the big occasion.

Neat and Tidy Turnout

This should always be aimed for and gives the air of professionalism which is always a bonus, especially when trying to impress dressage judges. A clean and spotless rider

Left: On top of the world, Olympic champions Mark Todd from New Zealand wins the Gold, Karen Stives, the USA, the Silver and Virginia Holgate (Leng) the Bronze for Britain. The picture says it all.

Above: The British team proudly line up for the national anthem behind Chef d'Equip, Lord Patrick Beresford. Rachel Hunt, Lucinda Green, Ginny Leng and Jon Evans after their exertions at Stockholm.

Below: Safely over the last show jump, it is a great relief to finish well in a three-day event. The US riders are usually to the fore and both horses and riders are always well turned out during the event.

Tips For Success

with immaculate boots and spurs and a well-plaited and beautifully groomed horse with oiled feet will always help to give a good impression. It is not just the judges, however, but also the spectators who appreciate good turn-out of horse and rider.

Warming-up

Making the most of your warming-up is so very important, particularly following a long journey. Loosen up first then work your horse until it is going at its best and as you feel is right for the occasion. Needless to say, at the competition the same degree of perfection is rarely achieved as was felt at home, especially with a young horse. However, work with patience and allow plenty of time for the horse to settle and find out over a period of time the most successful way of getting the best from your horse. One will need hours of work while another only a short time. Some will be best worked in canter to start with after the initial loosening up period, while another will be better worked in trot. Others may be better starting on the lunge. Work it all out and act on what is best for that particular horse.

Good Manners

Being polite and friendly, especially to organizers, secretaries and officials, should not need any mention but unfortunately a few people spoil the scene for others by being demanding, unsportsmanlike and very occasionally rude and abusive. There will always be times when things do not go according to plan, either for you or the orga-

Right: *Warm-up areas and practice arenas are well laid out at top level competitions but this is rarely the case at small shows, which are usually desperately short of space. Car parks are often the answer.*

Below: *Making the effort to talk to and thank organizers, officials etc is always appreciated. Most competitions are run on a lot of goodwill and voluntary help, however big they are, so your thanks will be very welcome.*

Bottom: *An impressive line-up of show jumping stars headed by the smallest of the lot, resplendent in his winner's wreath. A moment to savour and remember the rewards of reaching the top.*

nizers. It is a fact of life that has to be accepted and your understanding in such situations and taking it all in your stride as just the luck of the day will make life easier for everyone, however maddening the situation may be at the time.

If the show is badly run you need not go back there, but nowadays shows and events have to be successful to survive. It will often be appreciated if you make constructive suggestions that would improve facilities for another time, but be careful not to make your comments sound too critical especially when the organizers and secretaries are frantically trying to get numbers out or attend to the million and one things that have to be done.

Polite thanks for the day never goes amiss and may well ensure that you do not get balloted out another year. It certainly helps to have the reputation of being a 'good competitor' when balloting is a likelihood. Many is the time I have heard an organizer say 'we will not have him (or her) again' if someone has been difficult or rude, and some organizers keep a notebook to record names. Who can blame them when the majority of competitors are easy-going, sporting and a pleasure to have around. After all, it is for the competitors that shows are run so it is up to you to make sure organizers are made to feel it is worth their while!

Security at Competitions

This cannot be too strongly stressed. It is a sad reflection on the times but you are asking for trouble if you do not take reasonable precautions to safeguard your horses and equipment.

The saying 'out of sight out of mind' is as good a guide as any. Do not leave your best equipment on obvious view, do not leave the box open for all to see what you have inside and do not leave anything lying around which could easily be picked up.

Marked tack is definitely a deterrent and more and more people are now having their tack security marked, but even this does not stop the tack thieves who steal literally thousands of pounds of equipment weekly. If possible, keep everything under observation and do not leave the box unattended. If you do, make sure you shut everything out of sight, or at the very least cover it up from view, and lock away if possible.

Above: *Security is a growing problem worldwide and equestrian events are no exception. Take all reasonable precautions and avoid leaving tack and equipment lying about. Be vigilant at all times.*

Below: *The well-loved face of a great horse, Ryan's Son; he dominated numerous competitions with John Whitaker for a decade. A great character, Ryan's Son attracted a massive fan club.*

It is not unheard of for horses to be stolen and certainly horseboxes, cars and trailers have all done the disappearing act before now. The attitude of 'it won't happen to us' is sadly unrealistic – it can happen to anyone. Freezemarking and brands, where they still exist, are a definite deterrent to the horse thief and many horses thus marked have been saved from the abbatoir, thanks to being more easily traceable through these methods.

Your vehicles are safer with distinctive characteristics, such as logos or other prominently displayed characters, and engraving windows with your registration number is another worthwhile precaution. The latter is a cheap and easy method which you can do yourself with a hand engraver. Thieves may change a number plate but it is much more difficult and hardly worth the effort to change all the windows.

If the stabling area is not behind a security fence it may be worth considering whether to lock your horse in its stable. The pros of this must be weighed against the problems involved should there be a fire, but certainly tack boxes should be kept locked if they are unattended.

Knowing Your Rules

This is vital if you are not to unknowingly break them. Although already discussed throughout the book, it is so important to be sure that you are competing within the rules of the competition. The stewards cannot check up on everyone but it is to no-one's advantage to find out too late that you have contravened certain rules. Quite apart from being rather embarrassing, it is always the

Tips For Success

competitor's responsibility to ensure that he or she competes within them.

It is worth studying the rules carefully at the beginning of each season to take note of any new ones which will affect you. Always have your rule book with you so that you can check up on anything. Pay particular attention to regulations on tack and equipment. The use of fences in the warm-up area tends to change quite frequently, so read this section carefully. Speeds and distances, heights of fences etc are all occasionally slightly modified so they should be checked. This is especially important if you are moving into a new grade as some of these factors will definitely affect you.

Above: *The rules change regularly but be sure to check them each year to see what is permissible, especially in the collecting ring over the practice fence, and what tack is or is not allowed in the competition.*

Below: *This picturesque scene hardly seems to be real, but it can be clearly seen that this is not a small fence being jumped on snow. Ground conditions must always be carefully considered.*

Taking the Going into Account

This is essential if you are to compete successfully in different ground conditions and you must be able to adjust your riding to suit the conditions on the day.

It is no good trying to ride dressage in a bog! Luckily, only the lower levels may find themselves having to cope with wet grass arenas since most of the advanced dressage is performed on sand or other suitable surfaces nowadays. However, there are exceptions and in wet and holding ground the horse will require a little more freedom and impulsion to be able to cope in such conditions. On very hard ground it will tend to shorten its stride and lose a little of the free forward movement, so again you will have to ride it accordingly.

With the jumper it is very important to be able to assess the ground and how to ride in the different conditions and it is worth bearing the following points in mind:

☐ Generally a horse will lengthen its stride slightly in open areas and in a large arena, whereas it will shorten the stride slightly in a small arena or if indoors.

☐ Going downhill it will take longer strides unless the hill is very steep, whereas going uphill it will tend to take shorter strides.

☐ Deep going will shorten the horse's stride, as will very hard ground, but good going will tend to lengthen the stride.

The rider should always have these points in the back of his or her mind and ride accordingly. An experienced course builder will also have taken the ground into account and may or may not have eased the distances a little as a result.

The eventer will need to remember this and also assess how the ground will affect the cross-country course as the same considerations will apply there. But mistakes cannot be made with solid, cross-country fences so the right degree of impulsion and control must be achieved to make up for the ground conditions. In the wet, hold on to the horse's head a little more and ride forward positively sitting just a fraction more upright to keep the weight off the forehand.

Falling Off

This is an occupational hazard that happens to everyone at some time or other, but the effect can be reduced considerably if you can organize yourself to fall correctly and roll away from your horse.

The secret is relaxation – it is easy to say, but not always easy to do in the situations generally encountered. Having tried to stay on for as long as possible, the moment of no return approaches fast and it is very important to try to relax as you hit the ground then, if possible, roll away from the horse. This rolling process tends to absorb some of the pain, acting as a kind of shock absorber. It is also helpful to take a deep breath as soon as you can as some tumbles really do knock the breath out of you. Get up as soon as you can, all being well – your body will hurt far less if you get moving than lying there thinking about it! If possible, keep hold of the horse. This is not always practical but should always be in the back of your mind.

If your horse has fallen, give it a quick check over before remounting, but so long as

Above: *The landing appears quite deep for this young horse which is still a little on its forehand. The rider's upright position is helpful and his legs are already driving it forward to the next fence.*

Below: *The sand arena is used for all top level dressage nowadays, being considered the most uniformly even surface. This picture clearly demonstrates the isolation experienced by many riders in the arena.*

all is well the sooner you get back on and jump another fence, the better for both of you. There is no doubt that a fall at a fence can shake your confidence, and equally there is little doubt that the sooner you can restore this the better. For the sake of both horse and rider, if it is possible to jump even another couple of fences and then pull up only if necessary it would help enormously.

With some falls you may not be so lucky and you may occasionally require the first aid teams. If this is the case, preservation of your riding clothes must be first priority after you have been picked up! First aiders love getting their scissors out and, before you know it, will have snipped your best coat, breeches and, even worse, boots in their efforts to examine the damage. If they must cut your clothes implore them to cut down seams which can be more easily repaired. A scalpel cuts down the seams of boots very effectively so that they can then be repaired, whereas indiscriminate cutting wrecks them completely.

Collar bones, ankles and head injuries are the commonest riding injuries with the latter emphasizing the necessity of wearing a properly-secured hat. Afterwards is too late, so make sure you are well protected at all times. Do not take silly risks and do not rush the vital preparation of your horse which will help make it safer to ride.

Conserving Your Energy

Keeping back energy so that you can put your all into the big moment can be quite difficult where there is so much to do on the day. Try to think things through so that you do not expend too much energy unnecessarily. Check times, arenas, classes etc on your trip to collect numbers from the secretary's tent. When doing this, look to see where everything is so that you can set off in the right direction for whatever is required.

While dressage and show jumping require maximum effort for a short time, eventing involves a series of medium efforts during the day. Therefore, try and sit quietly for half an hour relaxing before the important part of the day – the cross-country. A little relaxation at this time can work wonders, both

Top: *The moment every competitor dreads – a fall on the take-off side of a fence. This obstacle at the Burghley Horse Trials required bold, accurate riding to encourage a neat jump into the Trout Hatchery, but it did not materialize for this combination.*

Above: *The horse has refused at the second element of this bounce downhill, catapulting the rider right out of the saddle to a very painful fall. The speed and correct degree of impulsion are vital at this type of fence so that it is met at the best possible pace for that particular horse.*

Left: *This horse appears remarkably unconcerned as it jumps the fence, with its rider well out of the saddle. Falls do happen and will continue to do so, but if the rider is well protected, the chance of injury can be kept to the very minimum.*

mentally and physically, if you can make yourself 'switch off', meditate or whatever suits you at the time.

Eating sensibly during a competition day will help you to stay in good shape. The body will last on the adrenalin produced at the sense of occasion but cannot really keep going on nothing all day. Many riders tend to say they cannot eat until 'it's all over', but this is not the right attitude. After all the work that goes into preparing the horse, it is only fair that you make the effort to produce yourself in top shape to last the long and strenuous day out.

Do not, however, fill yourself too full just before you expect to do a dressage test involving long periods of sitting trot, or have a large curry just before jumping a course of show jumps. Obtain some reasonable sustenance to keep you going, especially sweet or high-energy foods.

In the hot weather, be careful not to get dehydrated. It is just as important that you do not suffer from this as it is your horse. Drink small amounts frequently but avoid alcohol of any kind until after you have competed at the show or event.

Keep cool if it is very hot and always have an appropriate change of clothes in such weather. Likewise, be prepared for all types of weather depending on where you are. You will use up a lot of energy through trying to keep warm, getting too hot or generally running about too much. Conserve your strength so that you really can put everything into the competition.

Coping with Nerves

This is sometimes quite a problem depending on your temperament. Some people thrive on the competitive atmosphere doing their very best on the day, being rather unimpressive at home. Others who have great ability let it all fall apart on the big day through being unable to cope with the tension. Many people just become generally nervous. If you are the first type, well and good, but for those that get in a state at the competition, the following may be useful hints.

Always have a little something to eat before you start the day – black coffee is not enough. A few calories are necessary so that at least your poor stomach has something to do rather than coping with your own butterflies!

Keep occupied without dashing madly about. Go and watch the show jumping if that is your scene and try and learn something instead of thinking just of yourself. Watch how the riders turn into their fences, how many strides they take, time them, look at their style, what tack is being used. There is so much to get absorbed in if you set your mind to it.

With dressage, watch the warming-up area and study the different methods used and see if you can pick up useful ideas. Look at the riders as if you were the judge and see if anything comes from that which you do not like and ask yourself if this fact also relates to you. Study how the horses are turned out – is there anything that could be improved upon? All these thoughts and many more can

Above: *How it should be done and making it all seem so easy. The horse looks happy and confident as it jumps boldly into the water at Gatcombe during the British Open Championships in 1987.*

Below: *Almost showing off, both horse and rider are immaculately turned out and are giving a thoroughly professional and confident performance, which is the secret when riding a dressage test in the arena.*

absorb your mind so that you no longer get into a nervous state.

With eventing, when perhaps you are worried about a particular fence, go and see it jumped. Inevitably, the majority of competitors will sail over it without mishap. Look at it constructively, however, so that if a rider does have a problem you will not let this put you off more. Think carefully why that particular rider got it wrong and then you can avoid making the same mistake. Watch another competitor over the fence so that you leave it knowing that it is quite jumpable but with the correct method of approach clearly in your mind.

Keeping yourself occupied is the best answer and there are dozens of things that can be done in-between competing. It is a wonderful opportunity to clean out parts of the horsebox or your car, although make sure you have got something suitable to wear otherwise you will get yourself in a state worrying about the mess you have got into!

Writing letters, reading a book, studying the rules are all useful nerve-calmers and it is always worth taking something along with you to do during the day as so often there are long periods of time when nothing much is happening.

However, one of the most important things, if you do suffer from competition nerves, is to keep them under control and put mind over matter. It is ridiculous to let them take over and cloud your performance, so really take yourself in hand, keep mentally occupied until the big moment arrives and then concentrate only on your job.

Coping with the Nervous Horse

This can be very similar to coping with a pent-up rider. Some horses get themselves in a tremendous state as soon as you start washing manes or tails, bandaging them or plaiting them up etc. Trembling, sweating, breaking out and going off their food are all

typical signs and sometimes present quite a problem.

Obviously the aim must be to minimize the amount of stress the horse is under since by getting itself into a state, it is going to use up a lot of energy, especially one getting ready for a three-day event where the mental stress time is so long. By the time the horse gets to the crucial speed and endurance day, it will have half worn itself out by worrying.

Ideally, this sort of problem should have been overcome with early training and really should not arise if the horse has been quietly and carefully brought on so that any form of outing is a relaxed and pleasurable experience. Unfortunately, however, most people acquire their horses after the damage has been done and it may take months to encourage your horse to relax once it has learnt to get itself worked up.

Try to do as little as possible to the horse that is different from its ordinary daily routine. Avoid the big 'day before' syndrome

Below: *An anxious moment for this rider who took off too far away making an already wide fence almost unjumpable. She struggles to keep her balance and give the horse sufficient rein to get over.*

Below: *This combination have met the same fence off a much better stride and are well clear, giving it plenty of room. Watching other competitors is very interesting and can be helpful in planning your round.*

Right: *Reacting in the right way to a nervous horse can make all the difference. It can be seen quite clearly how this horse looks apprehensive about what is going on. Always be quiet and sympathetic.*

when trimming up, mane and tail washing etc generally tend to take place. A good grooming should suffice in most cases, if the horse is kept properly in the first place.

Let the horse eat its breakfast before going in to fuss it and if you have several going to the show get the others ready first. Avoid a lot of dashing about. An organized stable should have everything prepared in advance so that there is no necessity to create an atmosphere of tension before leaving. Keep everything as near to normal as possible. Once you have loaded your worked-up horse, it is usually better to get moving straight away so that it does not start banging in the box. A haynet may help to settle it once it is on its way. Even those who do not normally like their horses to travel with hay may find that it works wonders for this type of horse and a small haynet will not upset the horse's performance unless it has to gallop within two to three hours of arriving at the competition site.

Above: *Two top riders over the same fence. The upper one has taken off to far from the fence and so has difficulty in making the spread. The one below has a better take-off spot and so clears it with ease.*

Below: *The back-up team at work, removing bandages and giving a final check-over before the rider goes in for the test. Calmness at all times will help to keep nerves at bay whilst waiting to compete.*

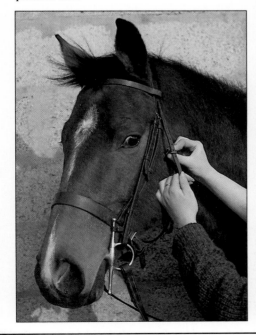

These horses tend to sweat up a lot so an anti-sweat sheet may be good for travelling. Little else is needed depending on the weather, but be sure the horse does not get chilled along its back.

Once you have arrived, try and avoid the 'instant action' effect. Let the horses stand and settle for five minutes before opening up and then work quietly. Even lead the horse out for a short graze if this might be to its benefit. Allow yourself plenty of time so that there is no sense of rush which will immediately communicate itself to the horse.

Lunging has a soporific effect and is often better than riding to start with, if the horse is the sort that is very silly when ridden as well. Most horses, however, settle very quickly once ridden. Some may be better wandered round quietly to see the sights and then worked; other may be best reversing this. If your horse gets silly the moment you stop working, remove boots or bandages in plenty of time before doing a dressage test and keep it working quietly.

After everything is over, some horses settle down, cool off and know the excitement is over. Others, however, seem quite unable to relax and carry on competing mentally for hours or even days afterwards, breaking out in cold sweats, trembling and only eating sporadically.

The usual treatment for cooling off and rubbing their ears and towel drying may all help but probably one of the best ways is to turn them out, preferably with a very quiet pony which will act as a stabilizing influence. Some people even turn them out the night before leaving for a show.

There is no doubt that the person who looks after the horse can have a great influence on the horse. A placid, quiet person will be far better caring for this type of horse than the

very active, busy sort of person. Keep everything very low key, take the horse around in the box as much as possible and persevere with patience and understanding and with luck your horse will gradually learn to relax and settle and take less out of itself.

Assessing the Opposition

This is very useful at times, although not always essential, but in everything tactics play quite an important part if you really want to do well.

It is not always that easy to see what you are up against, but with dressage it may well be possible to work out what sort of tests the judges are favouring. Watch the other riders working and then try and make an impact

Above: *Keeping the competition horse relaxed and happy is vital if it is to perform at its best. Turning out can make a tremendous difference, but care needs to be taken to protect the legs of the type of horse which might gallop about.*

Right: *Assessing the opposition is always an interesting pastime. If you know what the judges are looking for in the dressage arena and can ride your horse in that way, you should be able to earn better marks.*

Right: *Madeleine Winter on Chagall go all out across the arena in extended trot at Goodwood. The rhythm must be retained at all times and the horse must lengthen the stride to its utmost for this movement.*

Left: *A nice medium trot. It is important that the judge is left in no doubt as to what pace and movement you are displaying. The overall picture is rather spoilt by the rider's hat being tipped too far back.*

Below: *Jeannie Sinclair on Diorella Power across the arena in extended trot, as they warm up for their big moment in the arena. The horse looks attentive, obedient, calm and all set to perform at its best.*

with your own performance. To be just another quite good test along with many others is probably going to merit only quite good marks. If you have seen one really outstanding performance which got very good marks, try and produce the same sort of test. Was it very accurate? Did it show more collection, a greater difference of pace? Was it more free going or more precise? If there was no particularly good performance before you, them make up your mind you are going to be the one that makes the judges sit up and think 'Ah, this is a bit different' to earn some higher marks. It is nearly always the test that is just that little bit more interesting which will get the top marks, and presentation is really what it is all about. It is not so much what you do but how you do it that will win on the day.

The same very much applies to show jumping, where innumerable different styles of riding and types of horses are to be seen. Jumping a clear round is the first important point, but how you do this in the jump-off is really what matters. You hope, in this case, that you are drawn last so that you can watch the others make the mistakes from which you might benefit. But if you find you are first to go, you have to decide whether to go for a safe clear or stir the rest of the opposition by putting up a really cracking round which they will really have to try hard to beat. The elusive clear round may be quite hard to achieve, both for you and those who follow, but at least you will have given them all something to go for.

Unfortunately, the eventer often has little chance of knowing what the rest of the opposition is up to because of the rather more complicated scoring system, but a consistent, all-round performance with clear rounds in both show jumping and cross-country plus a fast time will help to get you in the ribbons. A good test is essential to start you off, although an outstanding cross-country performance within the time may move you up several places – even today when the overall standard has risen so much.

Most eventers are under no illusions that all will not be trying hard since there are relatively few events compared to dressage and show jumping classes. It is, therefore, very competitive anyway but the same principles apply with the different phases. Watch the opposition, assess how best to beat it or at least equal it and then have a real crack at the cross-country to achieve a safe and fast clear round, if conditions and your horse's ability merit this.

Above: *Eventing is extremely competitive and every rider, if still in with a chance after the first two phases, sets off to compete in the cross-country. Bold riding and accurate jumping is required.*

Right: *The two riders have just returned from yet another fitness session of slow work to harden leg muscles and tendons before the competitive season gets under way and more serious training commences.*

Left: *A fascinating sequence of horse and rider jumping on and off this imposing bank and rail. Each stage demonstrates the way the horse uses itself during every split second of the jump. Notice the strain on landing as a quick turn is made.*

Below: *Farrier tools are always useful to have with you in case a clench comes up, or some other emergency arises. Most shows have a farrier on site to cope with any urgent re-shoeing jobs.*

USEFUL COMPETITION EQUIPMENT

Such a list could fill pages but the following are the items I have found to be the most useful to have on hand.

Leather punch A must for you and others who are almost certain to come and ask if you have one at some stage during the season. They are so useful if tack breaks or you need an extra hole anywhere.

Farrier kit This may be required at any time, and although most events have a farrier laid on there is always the odd occasion when he or she is not to be found and your horse has a clench up or shoe half off. At least if you have the kit yourself you can do something to prevent the horse damaging itself. You will require a hammer, pincers, rasp, buffer and paring knife, and it is always wise to have a spare set of shoes which have been recently measured for your horse. Ask your farrier

for some nails, then if there just happens to be a farrier around without a kit he or she may be able to do a quick repair job. Many Australians and New Zealanders do their own shoeing so you could be lucky if there are any around at your competition!

A variety of nosebands These may well come in useful. It is worth having a grackle (figure of eight), flash or drop which you can use if a little more control is required or your horse decides to open its mouth and become resistant in all the excitement.

A collection of bits Advisable for added control, especially if you are not sure how your horse is going to react. A gag, roller, snaffle, French bridoon and hackamore – so long as your horse has been ridden in one before – constitute quite a useful collection. A double bridle may be worth putting in for jumping or dressage in case the horse gets too strong before its test. It is such a versatile

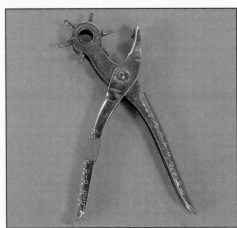

Above: *The leather punch is a most useful tool to have with you for a variety of purposes. It will probably be borrowed by everybody, so keep a careful check on it or make sure it is well marked.*

Above: *The double bridle correctly fitted with curb chain, allowing the curb bit to lie at a 45 degree-angle. Make sure the browband does not pinch behind the ears and that the noseband is the right size.*

Above: *The bitless bridle or hackamore is often useful on horses with difficult mouths. The noseband must be well padded all round to ensure no rubbing or pinching occurs. It must not be too low on the nose.*

Below: *Some useful bits to have with you in case extra brakes are required: a French bridoon, rubber gag and copper roller. It makes sense to try them out at home first so that you know they work.*

bridle that it is a shame more people do not use it in preference to some of the amazing gadgets seen around.

A spare hoofpick It is highly likely that this will do the disappearing act at some stage so a spare is always handy.

A small stool Makes unplaiting a lot easier, but a sturdy bucket or feedbin may act just as well as one of these.

Some small change, notebook and pen These should be kept in the cab for use in emergency if you should break down. If you have a puncture there are numerous tyre replacement specialists in the telephone book. Usually if you say you have horses on board they will come as quickly as they can. If you belong to a breakdown service make sure you have your number with you or written in the cab.

Spare water Save any in the water container in case the horsebox boils, but wait until it cools down before putting the water in or you could crack the engine block. The horses might also be grateful for a drink if they have to hang around for long.

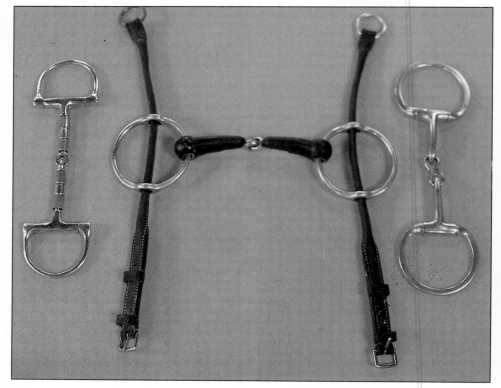

A spare set of keys This gives you more flexibility and means both you and your groom can have a set, making it easier to lock up if you need to and ensuring a little more security. Check that they are always returned to their correct place at the end of the competition.

For the Rider

A change of clothes and footwear makes the journey home much more comfortable. A spare tie or stock and pin will always be useful. Spare gloves and breeches as well as handkerchieves will all be needed at some stage.

Some food and drink to eat while travelling is always welcome so prepare a large thermos flask appropriately filled and a basket of goodies. Some people really go to town and celebrate their day in style, so if you are going to do this remember the bottle opener, glasses of some sort, a knife to spread anything and, if necessary, a tin opener. Then you can settle into enjoying the celebrations. One of the most useful items is a good pen knife which includes a bottle opener, several blades and numerous other gadgets. These will all come in handy at many different stages during the competition.

COMPETITION DO'S AND DON'TS

The do's and don'ts at a competition very much depend on the type of class as well as the show. Most riders do not need reminders, but the newcomer may benefit from reading some of the accepted, unwritten rules.

You should remember that we are all ambassadors for our chosen sport and as such have a responsibility not to let the side down and to behave in a sportsmanlike way throughout. It is important to make sure you set a good example at all times to the public and young up-and-coming riders.

Do's

Do prepare your horse in plenty of time so that it will do its best.

Do be ready to enter the arena or start box when called.

Do remember to thank organizers and secretaries at the end of the day – you will always be welcomed back.

Do leave your stabling clean and tidy – ask the stable manager how the bedding should be left.

Do prepare your horse and self to perform at the very best on the day.

Do remember to look after your helpers or hard-working groom; he or she will more than likely have been up hours before you.

Do sign autographs for children – it is the price of success and a small penalty to pay and they love it even though they probably have not a clue who you are!

Do reward your horse by looking after it well and attending to its every need.

Above: *For the spectators it seems that life is one long picnic and sometimes they do not seem particularly interested in the horses. But without the paying public, many events or shows could not survive.*

Below: *Two expectant horses look contentedly out over their stable doors, probably wondering more about their next meal-time than competing. But their generosity gives us hours of pleasure.*

Above: *World Champion and former European gold medalist, Lucinda Green, sets off over the first fence at the Burghley Horse Trials on her ex-Australian stock horse, Regal Realm. Many top event horses have come from unusual backgrounds.*

Right: *The most enjoyable feeling of cantering around the arena after a well-deserved win makes all the time and effort seem more than worthwhile. The rapport between horse and rider is a prime factor in the success of a partnership.*

Below: *Winning is the ultimate aim of all competitors but this can only be achieved through dedication, hard work, a good horse and that bit of luck which ensures that all goes well on the day. A perfect setting for a win – Blenheim Palace.*

Do enjoy yourself because that is what competitive sports are all about and it is the very reason why so many thousands of riders in all parts of the world get together and compete at a show or event.

Don'ts

Don't be late for your class or start time.

Don't break any rules – know what you can and cannot do and check if you are unsure.

Don't take any risks with your horse – it is simply not worth it.

Don't be a litter lout. Take all your litter home. Only tip out any manure if there is a good hedgerow nearby or if the field is obviously going to be well-harrowed afterwards.

Don't ever be seen to lose your temper. The frustrations often get to boiling point but keep cool at all times. Otherwise you will only regret your actions afterwards.

Don't argue with any show official, however maddening the situation may be – it will do you no good and the sport even less.

Don't forget to collect score sheets, passports or other documents if applicable – cups and prize money if you have had a good day.

THE REWARDS

There will be successes and failures, good times and bad times – this is what competitive riding is all about. But the satisfaction of producing a horse for a competition, having trained it and gone through all the weeks, months or maybe even years to achieve your goal at whatever level, makes it all worthwhile.

Talk to your horse so that it can get to know you and your voice – it is so important to build up the rapport between you and your horse if you really wish to succeed. Never take anything for granted; it is just as important that your horse is mentally happy and contented in its work as its preparation to peak physical fitness. If you have not created the right attitude you have failed. Variation in the horse's work, periods of relaxation and playtime must be slotted into the fitness and schooling necessary to keep your top competition horse happy and contented – it will reward you with a good performance.

In conclusion, I can only wish all those who compete in any of the three sports covered as much pleasure, fun, heartache and thrill as I have had during many years of riding. There is no substitute for success. However, it is not so much the winning but the taking part which draws the thousands of riders into the competitive world of equestrian sport.

Right: *Nick Skelton and Raffles Apollo stand and salute during the playing of the national anthem at the European Championships. Every rider tends to find such a moment more than a little moving when they remember and reflect on all the people that have contributed towards this very special moment of glory.*

Riders and Horses

Above: *Probably the greatest event rider of all time, Lucinda Green has won the three-day event at Badminton an incredible six times, twice been European Champion on Regal Realm, pictured here, and World Champion at Luhmühlen in 1982.*

Below: *Paul Schockemöhle has won no less than three great European show jumping championships for Germany as well as numerous other Grand Prixs. Seen here with the brilliant Deister, on whom so many of his successes have been achieved.*

Below: *Jeff McVean talks to fellow Australian, Susanne Bond Leone. Both rode in the Nation's Cup at Hickstead. Australian riders have been very successful over the years despite the limits placed on their horses by quarantine regulations.*

Above: *A strong British contingent contemplate a large fence at Dinard. On the left, Nick Skelton discusses tactics with team trainer, Peter Robeson who won so much for Britain in the 60's. John Whitaker, the backbone of many great team wins, stands beside the Chef d'Equip, Ronnie Massarella, who has steered his teams to win many great victories over the years. Pre-planning and good gamesmanship are vital.*

Right: *Australia's Vicki Roycroft talks to Armand Leone of Austria at Aachen whilst walking the course. International events such as these bring top sportsmen and women together, making for really top-class and nail-biting competitions.*

Above: *Diana 'Tiny' Clapham has been one of the mainstays of several successful teams eventing for Britain. Coming from a large riding family, Tiny has ridden at most of the major three-day events on the calendar with Windjammer, now retired, as her best.*

Above: *New Zealander, Mark Todd, has won not only Badminton and Burghley three-day events but, with the diminutive Charisma, won the most sought after title of all, the Olympic Gold Medal in Los Angeles. Mark is now based in Britain.*

Above: *Priceless, the outstanding partner to Ginny Leng and winner of the European Championship at Burghley and the World Championship in 1986. He holds the amazing record of never having refused a fence throughout his competitive career.*

Below right: *Tigre, ridden by Caroline Bradley, owned by Mr D R Bannocks. He went from total novice to grade A in six months. Winner of two French Grand Prixs, the Canadian Grand Prix and top British horse, World Championship, Aachen, 1978.*

Below: *Granat, perhaps the most majestic dressage champion of all time. He and his tiny rider, Christine Stuckelberger, won the Olympic Gold for Switzerland in Montreal in 1976 and the World Championships at Goodwood in 1978.*

Left: *Philco, ridden by David Broome. He has won over £180,000 in show jumping. His many wins include the King's Cup and the Victor Ladorum in 1973. He represented Great Britain in Vienna in 1977 and won the Calgary Grand Prix in 1982.*

Above: *Dutch Courage, winner of Britain's first ever dressaage medal with Jennie Loriston-Clarke. He won the Bronze Medal at Goodwood in 1978 and was National Champion on six occasions. A highly successful sire of competition horses.*

Above: *Jet Run, ridden by Michael Matz, has won numerous championships for the USA including the World Cup final in 1981. A brilliant jumper who always tries his hardest, he has captured the hearts of millions throughout the world.*

Left: *Ahlerich, ridden by Germany's Reiner Klimke. Montreal Olympic Bronze Medallist in 1976, he became the outstanding Olympic champion in 1984 in Los Angeles following their World Championship victory over Granat in 1982 in Lausanne.*

Below: *Charisma. This diminutive horse was New Zealand's national champion. He went on to win Badminton and became the Olympic Gold Medallist in Los Angeles. He was narrowly beaten at Burghley '87 and is Mark Todd's ride in the Seoul Olympics.*

Appendix

FURTHER READING

The Complete Guide to Dressage, Jennie Loriston-Clarke, Stanley-Paul

Guide to Dressage, Louise Mills Wilde, Breakthrough

This is Riding, Gunnar Hedland, George Harrap and Co Ltd

The Art of Horsemanship, Xenophon, J A Allen and Co Ltd

Horse and Stable Management, Jeremy Houghton-Brown and Vincent Powell-Smith, Granada Publishing

Thinking Riding, Molly Sivewright, J A Allen

Advanced Techniques of Riding, The Official Instruction Handbook of the German National Equestrian Federation, Threshold Books

L'Annee Hippique – The International Equestrian Year, Henk Brüger

The British Horse Society Equitation Book, Hamlyn Publishing Group Ltd

Course Design and Construction for Horse Trials, Mary Gordon-Watson, Threshold Books

The Horse in Sport, Steinkraus and Stoneridge, Stewart Tabori and Chang New York and Macdonald Orbis and Co London

The Event Rider's Notebook, Mary Rose, George Harrap and Co Ltd

Getting Horses Fit, Sally Pilliner, Collins Publishers

The Riding Instructor's Handbook, Monty Mortimer, David and Charles

Practical Eventing, Sally 'O' Connor, Press of Whittlet and Sheppeson

Training Show Jumpers, Anthony Paulmen, J A Allen and Co Ltd

The de Nemethy Method, Bertalan de Nemethy, Doubleday

NATIONAL FEDERATIONS AFFILIATED TO THE FEI

Argentina ARG
Federacion Ecuestre Argentina
Gorostiaga 2287
Casilla de Correo 59 – Sucursal 26 B
1426 Buenos Aires

Australia AUS
Equestrian Federation of Australia Inc
Federal Secretariat, 2nd Floor
77 King William Road
North Adelaide
South Australia 5006

Austria AUT
Bundesfachverband fur Reiten und Fahren in Oesterreich
Prinz-Eugen-Strasse 14/6a
A-1040 Wien

Belgium BEL
Federation Royale Belge des Sports Equestres
Avenue Hamoir 38
B-1180 Bruxelles

Brazil BRA
Confederacao Brasileira de Hipismo
81 rua Sete de Setembro 81-3 andar
Rio de Janeiro
Brazil 20050

Canada Can
Canadian Equestrian Federation
333 Riber Road
Ottawa
Ontario KIL 8H9

Chile CHI
Federation Ecuestre de Chile
Vicuna Mackenna no 40
Santiago de Chile

Denmark DEN
Dansk Ride Forbund
ldraettems Hus
DK-2605 Brondby

Arab Republic of Egypt EGY
Federation Equestre Egyptienne
13 rue-Kasr-Elnil
Le Caire
Egypte

Spain ESP
Federacion Hipica Espanola
Calle Monte Esquinza 8
E-28010 Madrid

Finland FIN
Suomen Ratsastajainliitto
Radiokatu 12
SF-00240 Helsinki 24

France FRA
Federation Equestre Francaise
164 rue du Faulbourg St Honore
F-75008 Paris

Germany Federal Republic FRG
Deutsche Reiterliche Vereinigung e.V.
Freiherr-von-Langen Strasse 13
D-4410 Warendorf 1

Great Britain GBR
British Equestrian Federation
British Equestrian Centre
Kenilworth
Warwickshire CV8 2LR

Germany Democratic Republic GDR
Dentscher Pferdesport-Verband der
Deutschen Demokratischen Republik
Storokower Strasse 118
DDR-10055 Berlin

Greece GRE
Association Hellenique d'Athletisme
Amateur (SEGAS)
Avenue Syngrou 137 Nea Smyrni
Athenes
Grece

Holland HOL
Stichting Nederlandsche Hippische Sportbond
Amsterdamsestraatweg 57
NL-3744 MA Baarn

Ireland IRL
Equestrian Federation of Ireland
Irish Farm Centre
Bluebell
Dublin 12

Italy ITA
Federazione Italiana Sport Equestri
Palazzo delle Federazioni
Viale Tiziano 70
1-00196 Roma

Jamaica JAM
Jamaica Horse Association
10 LongLane
P O Box 100
Kingston 8

Korea KOR
Korean Equestrian Federation
K A S A Bldg – Room 607
19, Mukyo-Dong Chung-ku
Seoul
Korea 100-00

Mexico MEX
Federacion Ecuestre Mexicana A C
Cda. de Agustin Ahumada No 31
Col. Lomas de Chapultepec C P.11000
A P No 41-951
Mexico D F

New Zealand NZL
New Zealand Horse Society Inc
P O Box 1046
Hastings
Hawke's Bay
New Zealand

Poland POL
Federation Equestre Polonaise
ul. Sienkiewicza 12
00-010 Warszawa
Pologne

Portugal POR
Federacao Equestre Portuguesa
Rua do Arco do Cego 90 5°
p-1096 Lisboa Codex

Switzerland SUI
Association Suisse d'Equitation et d'Attelge
Postfach 45
Blankweg 70
CH-3072 Ostermundigen

Sweden SWE
Svenska Ridsportens Centralforbund
Luntmakargatan 13
S-111 37 Stockholm

USSR URS
Federation Equestre de l'URSS
Luzhnetskaya b 8
119270 Moscou
URSS

United States of America USA
American Horse Shows Association Inc
220 East 42nd Street
Fourth Floor
New York NY 10017 - 5806

Zambia ZAM
Zambia Horse Society
P O Box 31049
Lusaka

Index

Index

Credits

Author's Acknowledgments
The author would like to thank the following for their help, both past and present, without which this book could not have been written: Gunnar Anderson; Ernst Bachinger; Helena Charlesworth; Pat Burgess; Paul Fielder; John Hall; Bertie Hill; Iris Kellet; Pat Manning; Bert de Nemethy; Greta Phillips; Franz Rochowanski; Lady Hugh Russell; Bill Steinkraus; Dick Stillwell; Frank Weldon; Pam Carruthers; the British Horse Society and the FEI. I would also like to thank all my family who have encouraged and helped me over the years particularly my sister and brother, Jennie Loriston-Clarke and Michael Bullen. My grateful thanks also go to Helen Sainsbury who patiently struggled through and typed the manuscript from my hand written notes; all the other people who have helped me in many ways; to Bob Langrish for all his photographs.

Editor's Acknowledgments
I would like to thank Jackie Peace for checking the galleys, Terry Doyle for checking page proofs and Helen Baz for compiling the index.

Picture Credits
Ronald Sheridan, The Ancient Art and Architecture Collection pages 14, 15; Mary Evans Picture Library pages 16 (top), 17 (bottom), 18–19 (bottom); Allsport/ Trevor Jones pages 6–7, 132, 155 (top), 156 (top), 164 (bottom), 176 (bottom), 178; Kit Houghton pages 64, 129 (bottom); Spanish Riding School of Vienna page 97; Sandra Langrish pages 8, 118–9, 127 (top sequence), 182 (bottom). All other photography, Bob Langrish.